Indigenous and Ethnic Empowerment

T0361917

Indigenous, ethnic and rural peoples throughout the world struggle to effectively deal with the challenges triggered by outside economic and social intervention. This book presents business methods in a manner that reflects the needs, desires and priorities of indigenous peoples and provides the tools communities need to envision and deal with the full impact of social and economic intervention. In particular, the book helps local leaders and their advocates to better understand the full implications of the choices before them and develop skills to articulate and deal with local goals, needs, and priorities.

The book is distinctive because it helps people embrace opportunities and change on their own terms. As a result, leaders and their advocates will be better able to evaluate and respond to opportunities in an informed and systematic manner. Various business disciplines (such as accounting, finance, human resource management, organizational theory, and marketing) are discussed in ways that help the reader to envision both mainstream perspectives and the distinctive issues faced by ethnic enclaves.

Alf Walle is a specialist in indigenous economic development and is a former professor of tribal management who worked with Alaska Natives above the Arctic Circle. In addition, he has extensive experience in Central America and in Asia. He is currently providing consulting services. His website is alfhwalle.com.

Indigenous and Ethnic Empowerment

Parity, Equity and Strategy

Alf Walle

Routledge
Taylor & Francis Group

LONDON AND NEW YORK

First published 2019
by Routledge
2 Park Square, Milton Park, Abingdon, Oxon OX14 4RN

and by Routledge
605 Third Avenue, New York, NY 10017

First issued in paperback 2020

Routledge is an imprint of the Taylor & Francis Group, an informa business

British Library Cataloguing-in-Publication Data
A catalogue record for this book is available from the British Library

Library of Congress Cataloging-in-Publication Data
Names: Walle, Alf H., author.
Title: Indigenous and ethnic empowerment : parity, equity and strategy / Alf Walle.
Description: Abingdon, Oxon ; New York, NY : Routledge, 2019.
| Includes index.
Identifiers: LCCN 2018029464 | ISBN 9781138350854 (hbk)
Subjects: LCSH: Indigenous peoples--Economic conditions. | Indigenous peoples--Social conditions. | Minorities--Economic conditions. | Minorities--Social conditions. | Equality.
Classification: LCC GN380 .W34 2019 | DDC 305.8--dc23
LC record available at https://lccn.loc.gov/2018029464

ISBN 13: 978-0-367-73278-3 (pbk)
ISBN 13: 978-1-138-35085-4 (hbk)

Typeset in Bembo
by Wearset Ltd, Boldon, Tyne and Wear

Throughout the world, indigenous people, ethnic groups, and traditional people are struggling to forge social and economic relationships that are empowering and reflect self-determinism. This book is dedicated to their efforts and their achievements.

Contents

PART III
Providing service   169

Figures

Tables

Foreword and summary

Today, many regions of the world are experiencing unprecedented levels of economic development, outside intervention, and change. Although these impacts are largely positive, hurtful side effects often occur as people struggle to cope and adjust. Negative potentials need to be anticipated and addressed, ideally in a preemptive manner.

The goal of this book is to provide a useful orientation regarding the full implications of social and economic development that effects indigenous people, rural enclaves, and ethnic minorities. The goal is to make these discussions relevant to individuals and communities (as well as their advocates) in ways that lead to understanding, empowerment, and self-determinism. Although well-known business practices are introduced, the fact that they might conflict with the needs, wants, and desires of various peoples, communities, and populations is also emphasized. Under such circumstances, the quest for "universal best practices" typically emerges as an unrealistic goal. By accepting this reality, a broader and more culturally appropriate range of goals, methods, and standards of evaluation can be envisioned and employed.

Thus, if generic guidelines based upon Western and industrialized experiences dominate, even highly trained and well-meaning professionals might fail to treat specific peoples in an appropriate and insightful manner. By embracing culturally sensitive perspectives, in contrast, more equitable and tailored options can be envisioned and implemented.

Even the best and most equitable social and economic development plans, however, inevitably cause changes (many of which have the potential to be hurtful, painful, and disruptive). In today's world of globalization, not only are increased social contacts and economic interrelationships commonplace, they potentially inflict harm by, among other possibilities, undercutting local empowerment, priorities, and parity.

Thus, at least two key issues need to be simultaneously addressed: (1) promoting plans of social and economic development that help people and (2) prevention or mitigation of the possible negative ramifications. This book focuses thought and action in both directions using cultural sensitivity as a key asset and tactic.

Providing a brief overview of the material to be covered in this book can be useful to the reader. As a result, an abstract of where we will be going is provided below.

Chapter 1 "Culture, development and economics" lays a foundation by discussing a range of economic paradigms that influence the way people think, feel, and act. The discussion begins with a review of neo-classical economics that currently dominates in the realms of business and economic development.

Neo-classicism assumes that economic responses are rational and universal. According to this orientation, best practices exist that can be applied to all people in any situation. Increasingly, however, the dominance of the neo-classical model is weakening. Behavioral Economics, for example, expands economic thought by recognizing the importance of irrational psychological influences. Substantive economic anthropology, furthermore, focuses upon the specific culture and how its beliefs, standards, and modes of interaction impact economic decisions and activities. As a result of these non-rational and non-universal influences, a range of economic paradigms and strategies are emerging. The impact of specific cultures, not economic or psychological universals, furthermore, exerts a great influence that will be addressed throughout this book.

Having recognized that a variety of perspectives exist for analyzing and evaluating economic behavior, issues regarding negotiation, conflict, and how to deal with them are considered. This topic is especially important because many non-mainstream peoples might be ill-equipped to understand and adequately respond to conventions that are commonly employed within the mainstream world. These considerations are analyzed within a three-chapter section that deals specifically with negotiation and the resolution of conflicts.

Chapter 2: "Negotiating with the mainstream world" discusses typical processes of negotiation in business and economic development. These approaches, unfortunately, are often at odds with the techniques and processes employed by local people when making decisions and forging agreements. This background provides actionable and useable advice regarding the mainstream processes of negotiation and how they tend to operate. Much of what is presented is common knowledge, although the discussion is slanted towards the needs of indigenous, ethnic, and rural enclaves.

In addition to mainstream techniques of negotiation and decision making, alternative methods (such as mediation, arbitration, and litigation) are analyzed in Chapter 3: "Remedies for conflict." In addition, this chapter deals with the fact that the option of "indigenous conflict resolution" that reflects a people's unique culture and traditions might play a valuable role. By introducing and comparing this wide variety of options, potentially useful methods for insuring equity, parity, and self-determinism are introduced within a useful context.

Many indigenous, ethnic, and rural peoples struggle for empowerment. In recent years, techniques such as Community-based Research Management have arisen in which governments share the decision-making process with local people. When this strategy is used, governments seek the cooperation of local people by giving them a degree of control and an ability to benefit from local resources. Although this method often provides a win–win situation for all relevant stakeholders, on other occasions, local people choose to fight for rights by opposing the government. In a number of circumstances, doing so has been fruitful, although there are significant risks and costs involved when following this path. Such issues are addressed in Chapter 4: "Creating an atmosphere of empowerment."

Together this cluster of chapters introduces a wide variety of invaluable techniques that indigenous, ethnic, and rural people can use in attempts to control their destinies.

Having considered various modes of the decision-making process within a variety of contexts, an array of commonly used business and management tools are introduced in the next four chapters. The goal is to present a range of prevailing and dominant techniques along with discussions regarding how specific people might seek to adjust them in ways that are appropriate to their circumstances, priorities, vulnerabilities, and so forth.

Chapter 5: "Strategic thought" deals with decisions and their implications. Two significant strategic activities involve deciding "what business the organization is in" and determining the degree to which outsiders will control, direct, and dictate important decisions. With these perspectives in mind, a representative sample of classic strategic orientations is discussed including (1) The Diffusion of Innovations Model, (2) The BCG Growth Market Share Grid, (3) The McKinsey Matrix, and (4) SWOT Analysis. These non-exhaustive overviews of popular techniques are used to address issues regarding appropriate strategic choices for specific peoples. On many occasions, local communities might seek strategies that are distinctive and at variance with conventional rules of thumb. When this is true, these people and their advocates can better equip themselves by understanding the way in which their counterparts think. By developing this sort of insight, distinctive people and their advocates can best present their positions. Thus, this chapter both introduces useful concepts and provides insights for those who might want to expand beyond mainstream thinking and conventional solutions.

In addition to providing a strategic orientation, the tools of management are also concerned with developing and applying methods of organization that are most appropriate to the local community. A sampling of useful and well-known techniques is discussed in Chapter 6: "Organizational concerns." In this analysis, different orientations are compared and juxtaposed. Beginning with a retrospective discussion of nineteenth century views of organization and their implications, later developments update these pioneering thoughts. An analysis of formal vs. informal theories of bureaucracies and organization follows although an overview of the evolution of American culture and business methods is provided as useful background material. Nonetheless, the needs of indigenous, ethnic, and rural peoples are emphasized.

Although broad organizational issues are vital to success, motivating specific people is also a vital concern. Chapter 7: "Motivation" deals with motivation and its implications. When employing mainstream models of motivation, it is useful to remember that most of these tools have been strongly influenced by research conducted in the West and with reference to industrialized societies. Nevertheless, helpful techniques exist. The dichotomy of Theory "X" vs. Theory "Y" emphasizes that some managers dismiss workers are lazy and untrustworthy while others believe that workers are potentially loyal, ambitious and, dedicated if they are treated in a sensitive and appropriate manner.

Theory Z expands the discussion by emphasizing the impact of culture upon motivation. The work of David McClelland further advances the perspective that cultural considerations are of importance when seeking to motivate specific individuals and members of particular cultures and/or communities. This selective and non-exhaustive discussion of motivation is presented in order to address the needs of indigenous, ethnic, and rural peoples.

In addition to dealing with people and communities, business leaders are also interested in measuring and insuring success. The field of accounting is a key resource in this regard and it is discussed in Chapter 8: "Accounting and other tools of evaluation." Most commonly, accounting involves record keeping expressed in monetary terms. Financial accounting evaluates the health and performance of the organization, while managerial accounting manipulates financial information in ways that provide information of value to the decision-making process.

Other, more robust forms of evaluation, however, also exist that typically expand from a purely monetary focus in order to consider additional issues of importance. The "Triple Bottom Line" mode of appraisal popularized by John Elkington, for example, considers social and ecological issues as well as financial information and profits. Some sort of broader perspective is often useful when evaluating economic development projects involving indigenous, ethnic, and rural peoples. To make these tools most effective, evaluations might need to be tailored to the specific community and its circumstances.

Economic and development strategies inevitably seek ways to provide service. But service to who? Customers or clients of the community need to be served as well as the community and its members. Both of these targets for service are significant and they are discussed in separate chapters. Of course, an ideal strategy is able to simultaneously serve both clients and the community, and do so in equitable ways.

Chapter 9: "Internal service" deals with the needs and wants of individuals and the local community. These considerations can be very different from the desires and agendas of outsiders and the demands of partners who focus upon the profits that derive from serving others. People and communities (especially when they are atypical) need to remember who they are, as well as how their goals and hopes can best be achieved. These considerations should not be overlooked in the frenzy to profit by pleasing others. This is an issue that mainstream economic development specialists and business partners can easily overlook.

Chapter 10: "External service" deals with the other side of the coin. In order for economic development schemes to be successful and, thereby, help communities achieve their goals, outsiders such as customers and clients need to be effectively served. In business, these concerns are typically addressed by the discipline of marketing that focuses upon the needs of customers while centering relatively little attention upon the priorities of those who are providing services. Indeed, "the marketing concept" (the lodestar of the discipline) proclaims that the only justification for an organization to exist is to provide service to others.

Individuals and communities need to walk a fine line in order to address both of these issues in meaningful and equitable ways. Serving others is a significant tactic for those who seek to prosper. But in doing so, local and individual needs, goals, and vulnerabilities should not be forgotten.

Chapter 11: "Vulnerabilities and responses" provides a culmination of what has been discussed by focusing upon the vulnerabilities that people potentially face as well as the type of responses that individuals and communities might make when confronted by change.

The traumatic nature of change and the need for its mitigation are addressed. Hurtful potentials are analyzed with reference to the concept of "anomie" in which socially acceptable goals can no longer be achieved in socially acceptable ways. Specific responses to anomie are explored.

In addition, the "tyranny of the majority" in which people's needs are denied after being outvoted is considered. Strategies such as recognizing the rights of the "concurrent majority" (a distinctive minority with its own traditions and claims to self-determinism) demonstrate how minorities can protect themselves from inequitable outside domination. By using insights from Chapter 11 when applying the suggestions made in earlier chapters, indigenous, ethnic, and rural leaders and their advocates can more effectively navigate the complexities of negotiation, economic development, and empowerment.

Acknowledgments

Melding strategic thinking with the theoretical social sciences is a tricky course of action, but potentially very productive and much needed. Doing so has strong roots in applied anthropology, especially the work of Ruth Benedict and Margaret Mead who brought practitioner significance to the work of legendary anthropologist Franz Boas. From business thinking, I have been inspired by the field of macromarketing and its emphasis on the full impacts upon all relevant stakeholders, evaluated from a systems theory perspective. I acknowledge these influences and hope to expand beyond them.

Chapter 1

Culture, development and economics

Learning objectives

The long dominant neoclassical paradigm views economic behavior as universal and largely rational; exceptions and variations are treated as random and irrelevant. Behavioral economics expands economic thought by recognizing the importance of irrational psychological influences, moderating neoclassicism accordingly. Substantive alternatives, in contrast to both, view economic behavior from a social and cultural perspective. Thus, a range of economic paradigms exist. Specific learning objectives of this chapter include:

1 Understanding neoclassicism as a rational and universal model.
2 Envisioning behavioral economics as an acknowledgement of irrational forces.
3 Viewing substantive economics as a way of dealing with cultural influences.
4 Appreciating the theoretic contributions made by each of these tools.
5 Considering appropriate applications for each paradigm.

Introduction

A basic focus of this book is that those from the urban, "developed," and cash/wage economies tend to view the world in distinctive ways. As a result of their backgrounds, "mainstream" people might fail to understand the subtle strategies that other people employ. When this is true, consultants and advisors potentially provide poor advice to people who follow a different way of life. This problem can continue to be true even in an era where greater cultural understanding is replacing the chauvinism and prejudice of the "modern" world.

One way to explore this problem is by comparing the universal and rational paradigm of neoclassical economics that dominates business theory and practice with alternative methods that are more psychologically or culturally centered. This first chapter explores these differences and their implications.

Neoclassicism, long a dominant paradigm, envisions economic choices as rational and universal in nature (not emotional and culturally specific). In recent decades, a broader perspective has been advanced by behavioral economists who acknowledge the influence of non-rational psychological factors. Substantive economic anthropology, expanding beyond both, is more socially and culturally oriented. Thus, a wide array of economic paradigms exist. Nevertheless, neoclassicism continues as a powerful force.

After providing an overview of neoclassical economics, a specific application of this paradigm (modern marketing management) is presented. Doing so sets the stage to analyze the contributions of behavioral economics, an emerging sub-discipline that uses psychology to transcend rationality. This expansion and revision of economic theory parallels developments in consumer behavior within marketing that embrace psychological theory as a means of catapulting business thinking beyond rational explanations.

Both neoclassicism and behavioral economics, however, tend to ignore or deemphasize cultural factors. Substantive economic anthropology, in contrast, focuses upon such social variables. Although the substantive position is clearly relevant when dealing with many ethnic groups, mainstream decision makers might hesitate to embrace yet another model (1) that is not universal and (2) largely ignores rational choice and decision making. In spite of this possibility, the culturally focused substantive paradigm is useful under many circumstances, especially when dealing with the small-scale, face-to-face cultures/communities of many indigenous, ethnic, and rural peoples.

Neoclassicism: rational, universal, acultural

Neoclassicism is the mainstream economic paradigm that dominates the West and the developed regions of the world. Certainly, internal disagreements exist, but most neoclassical economists agree on the basic premises, paradigms, and conceptual perspectives of the neoclassical model.

Neoclassicists use rational and universal models when describing how scarce resources are allocated. A representative and non-exhaustive listing of assumptions held by neoclassicism includes:

> Economic decisions are essentially rational in nature.
> People have access to perfect information.
> Individuals/consumers seek utility, organizations seek profits.

These premises are discussed below.

Economic Man Model: Neoclassicalism assumes that people act in rational ways to achieve perceived goals that are designed to maximize benefits and/or minimize costs. In this manner, people are viewed as (1) seeking specific and predetermined goals (2) while hoping to gain these benefits at the lowest possible cost (in whatever way costs and benefits are defined). These assumptions, of course, do not imply that people's choices are inevitably wise, intelligent, or truly in their self-interest, but merely that economic actors are using some sort of calculated rational thought in an (overt or covert) attempt to maximize benefits and/or minimize costs.

Perfect Information Model: Neoclassicists often assume that economic actors have access to perfect information when evaluating their choices and that a condition of perfect competition exists. In other words, all participants in an economic sphere are treated as if they possess all the information they need (regarding costs, product quality, and so forth) to make optimum decisions. While common sense tells us this is seldom completely true, the model has proved useful in many contexts.

Utility/Profit Motives: Although customers and consumers seek to gain the most for the least, firms attempt to maximize profits. Thus, buyers seek benefits at the lowest price while organizations pursue a strategic advantage over competitors in order to maximize profits by (among other tactics) earning the patronage of desired target markets.

To be fair to neoclassicists, it should be added that all students of economics (except the most naïve undergraduates) acknowledge that economic decisions are complicated and result from many causes. Few economists, for example, would deny the obvious fact that emotions often impact decisions (although the degree to which it does so is a matter of debate). And certainly, all economists recognize that not everybody has access to perfect information. Nonetheless, neoclassicists insist that accepting these assumptions allows economic behavior to be modeled in a useful and eloquent manner that is capable of generating actionable insights (see Table 1.1).

Table 1.1 Relevant neoclassical premises

Issue	Analysis
Economic Man Model	People act in rational ways to achieve perceived goals. Strategies involve gaining maximum benefits and/or doing so at the lowest price.
Perfect Information	Economic actors have access to all of the information they need to make optimum decisions. A state of perfect competition exists.
Utility/Profit Motives	Economic organizations seek maximum profits. They pursue the patronage of desired clients/customers in a rational manner when doing so.

DISCUSSION
The neoclassical model assumes that economic responses are rational and that both organizations and their customers/clients have the tools and information needed to make informed and rational decisions.

In summary, the neoclassical model simplifies the analysis of economic behavior by making certain assumptions that are obviously not totally accurate. Although neoclassicists realize their assumptions do not perfectly reflect reality, the model is viewed as accurate enough to usefully portray and predict economic responses.

Critics, however, maintain that the neoclassical model distorts reality to such a degree that it often fails to accurately reflect how people actually think and react. Nevertheless, the neoclassical model has withstood the test of time, dominates the analytic and decision-making processes of many leaders, and has served well in a wide variety of circumstances.

Marketing management and neoclassical thought

Contemporary marketing theory is an example of neoclassical thinking. Its pivotal premise is the "marketing concept" that argues that the only reason for organizations to exist is catering to the needs their customers/clients perceive in order to earn a profit. The typical process by which this is accomplished involves understanding what a specific target market demands and serving it better than other competitors. In short, organizations are viewed as rationally providing customers with what they rationally desire.

Today, this approach to marketing is generally known as *"4 Ps" marketing management* since each of the controllable variables the organization manipulates to please a target market (**P**roduct, **P**rice, **P**lace, and **P**romotion) starts with "P." The approach, stemming from E. Jerome McCarthy's seminal text (1960) has become almost universal. Although many marketing texts are available today, they all tend to be organized according to the McCarthy schema. Graphically, this arrangement can be portrayed as is in Table 1.2.

Focusing (1) upon the needs of a target market and (2) adjusting the organization's controllable variables in order to satisfy these potential customers or clients fits in well with and reflects the neoclassical model (and its rational and universal perspectives).

Thus, neoclassical economics asserts that its methods and models can be applied universally and cross-culturally both within developed, industrial regions and among small scale societies (such as small indigenous, ethnic, and rural communities). This position is maintained even though a wide range of scarce resources (that may run the gambit from wealth, to security, to spare time, to respect, to attractive members of the opposite sex, and so on) may be the focus of exchange. Neoclassicists believe that once these scarce and desirable items (whatever they are) are identified, rational and universal neoclassical principles can be used to an advantage.

In summary, the 4 Ps Marketing Management seeks to identify the products, benefits and "utilities" that people rationally seek. After doing so, the firm's controllable variables are manipulated in order to help them to systematically and consciously achieve their goals.

Table 1.2 Marketing management: an overview

Variable	Characteristics	Impacts	Implications
Product	The actual good or service being sold to the target market.	To be successful, the product must respond to the demands, expectations, etc. of an adequate target market.	The product or service can take advantage of consumer demands that are typically perceived or felt.
Price	The price which the organization charges for its goods and services.	The price can influence the size of the market and determine when people will buy the product.	Price can be quickly adjusted as a short-term tactic or changed as part of an evolving long-term strategy.
Place	The distribution network and where the product will be made available.	Where the product is and who sells it may influence the level of sales and who buys the product.	Getting the product to where it can be reached and purchased by an appropriate target market.
Promotion	The communication between the organization and its relevant stakeholders that facilitates the marketing effort and/or the general health of the organization.	In order to most effectively sell a product, the organization must communicate effectively with relevant stakeholders.	Communication should (1) reinforce the other marketing variables and (2) address specific stakeholders on their own terms.
Marketing management	Rationally coordinating all of the controllable variables so the benefits of synergism make the organization's products more marketable.	By consciously interlacing the various controllable variables, the organization is able to more efficiently and effectively market the product.	By rationally combining the controllable variables into a synergistic campaign, the organization more effectively markets its products.

DISCUSSION

Mainstream 4 Ps marketing reflects neoclassical perspectives. Customers/clients are assumed to (1) basically understand what they want and (2) search the marketplace for the item that best suits their conscious needs. Organizations seek to understand customers/clients in order to rationally provide them with precisely what they want. Thus, (1) customers seek maximum utility as (2) organizations pursue maximum profits (or whatever yardstick of evaluation is used to measure success).

As marketing has become more sophisticated, however, a greater complexity has been recognized. In particular, scholars and practitioners have noted a wide range of responses and influences that do not reflect neoclassical predictions. The struggle to explain these deviant cases led to the development of a sub-discipline of marketing (some would argue that it is a separate discipline), known as "consumer research," that employs psychological and social theories in order to address the limitations and blind-spots of neoclassical theory. These efforts mirror movements in economic thought that will be discussed below.

Behavioral economic alternatives

As previously indicated, neoclassical economists are aware that their approach simplifies reality, but they defend their methods as accurate enough to use-fully model economic life and facilitate effective decision making. Critics of neoclassicism, in contrast, argue that the inaccuracies that advocates downplay as trivial and insignificant are actually so great that they need to be factored into economic analysis. Behavioral economics has arisen as a means of sys-tematically dealing with psychological influences that neoclassicists trivialize.

Contradicting the neoclassical paradigm, psychologists emphasize that people make decisions in a wide variety of ways. On the one hand, rational responses clearly exist, requiring reasoning, logic, and the use of overt or overt "algorithms" (which are methods of analysis and calculation). Neoclas-sical economics, however, focuses upon different sorts of responses in ways that add complexity to economic interpretations.

A psychologist friend of mine explained this from an evolutionary point of view. Certainly, he acknowledged, rational thought provides people with a competitive advantage that increases their chances of survival. As a result, the process of evolution has genetically honed these skills. But, my friend con-tinued, other situations exist that require an ability to quickly make decisions using techniques that are not based upon such complicated and sophisticated thought. The development of these abilities and the potential of using them has also been a part of the evolutionary process. Because alternative means of decision making exists, neoclassicism's tendency to focus upon rationality has resulted in an inadequate acknowledgement of other important decision-making processes that need to be recognized.

Nobel Prize winner Herbert Simon (1991), for example, uses the term "bounded rationality" to underscore that focusing upon the ability of people to rationally make decisions has its limits. In that regard, Kanherman (2003) points out that in many situations people make decisions without reference to rational analysis. One implication of such observations is that people com-monly make irrational decisions and do so in ways that contradict the neo-classical economic model.

One example of this tendency is "heuristics," a term from psychology that refers to the process of making decisions with reference to some formula or rule of thumb in ways that do not rely upon rational thought or some kind of logical calculation.

"Affect heuristics," for example, involves a decision-making shortcut in which emotions play an important role in drawing conclusions and choosing a course of action (Finucane et al. 2000). As a result of relying upon this process, the time and effort needed to make a decision is reduced. Finucane et al. (2000) furthermore, find that when attitudes towards something are positive, people are more likely to discount the risks and focus upon the benefits. When their feelings towards something are negative, in contrast, they are more likely to anticipate high risks and low benefits and act accordingly.

Relating this to economic decision making, it appears that these patterns of response have the potential to trigger decisions that are not optimum because the decision-making process might be influenced by emotional factors that are not rational and are not based upon an impartial analysis of the facts. When rationality is not in effect, of course, the neoclassical model is compromised.

In addition, people might make decisions that do not reflect the neoclassical model due to what is known as the "availability heuristic" which involves decision making that is based upon whatever facts and information are available and/or readily come to mind. In other words, whatever evidence, opinions, and so forth can be immediately retrieved by a decision maker tend to exert a strong role in the decision-making process (Schwarz et al. 1991). This tendency, of course, conflicts with the neoclassical model that assumes that economic actors have access to and correctly process perfect information.

Marketers and consumer behavior specialists have long employed an intuitive and independently invented form of the availability heuristic known as the "evoked set." This long-established concept predicts that when people buy products they tend to search their minds for possible brands or options; after this intuitive and non-exhaustive search, they begin their search process in earnest typically using the list provided by the evoked set as a starting point. As a result, marketers go to great lengths to ensure that their product will be part of the evoked set among their target market.

Once again, a moment's reflection will demonstrate that this tendency contradicts the neoclassical model that emphasizes that people are rational and have access to perfect information. The concept of the evoked set, in contrast to neoclassical principles, recognizes that people often lack perfect information and, as a result, firms must fight for space in the consumer's mind in an attempt to defeat (or augment) rational analysis and evaluation.

In addition to heuristics, a concept called "framing" is commonly used to deal with the fact that the manner in which an option is presented can impact people's responses in non-rational ways. In summary, framing refers to the way in which a fact is articulated or phrased and the impact that specific presentations have upon decision making. In some situations, for example, the same fact can be presented in two distinct ways. In one example, "This product has a 95% success rate" can also be presented as "This product has a 5% failure rate." Although these statements are rationally the same, a greater tendency for the product to be deemed acceptable exists when it is associated with the 95% success statement and is more likely to be viewed as unacceptable when the 5% failure rate is emphasized (Linville et al. 1992). In economics and finance, this type of framing is also known as "prospect theory" because it focuses upon the prospects of loss or gain.

It is understandable that consumers, who often make uninformed decisions for emotional reasons, would be likely to violate neoclassical principles. The investment and financial industry, in contrast, is made up of informed professionals overtly attempting to use rational thought to make optimum decisions. Intuitively, it appears that the behavior of these professionals would reflect the neoclassical model. Even here, however, emotions seemingly play a bigger role in decision making than is commonly recognized.

One of the classic books about investing is Burton Malkiel's *A Random Walk Down Wall Street* (1973). The basic point of this blockbuster is that the mutual funds of the era (that were administered by high paid managers and their staffs acting rationally on their client's behalf) were typically unable to do better than the stock market indices. He affirms "What we need is a ... mutual fund that simply buy the hundreds of stocks ... and does no trading from security to security in order to catch the winners" (1973: 226–227). By doing so, the investment would earn a rate of return that mirrors the market indices and, in the process, providing better results than those offered by thoughtful and rational investment managers.

In other words, rational thought in the investment industry typically accomplishes nothing and may even be counterproductive. Due to this revelation, a new financial product (the "index fund") came into existence. Instead of hiring geniuses and their staffs to make rational neoclassical-styled decisions, a portfolio is purchased that mirrors the stock market (or some segment of it). Doing so eliminates rational thought from the investment process. The results of this strategy tend to be competitive and managerial fees are reduced because high paid analysts are eliminated. These examples can be portrayed in Table 1.3.

As indicated above, sophisticated advocates of the neoclassical model are willing to admit that (1) some economic responses are not rational, (2) that perfect information might not be available, and so forth. Advocates of neoclassicism, however, assert that in spite of relatively minor problems, the neoclassical model provides a useful reflection of reality. The work of behavioral economics, in contrast, suggests that the importance of other issues needs to be recognized.

Above, we saw how mainstream marketing management can be viewed as an example of the applications of neoclassical principles. Eventually the field of consumer research began to temper these neoclassical notions by initially

Table 1.3 Examples of behavioral economics

Example	Description	Analysis
Heuristics	The process of making decisions with reference to some formula or rule of thumb. Decisions do not result from rational thought or logical calculation.	People often rely upon mental shortcuts and make decisions that are not rational and calculating. This common style of decision making transcends the neoclassical model.
Framing	The same rational thought can often be presented in different ways. The way the idea is presented can impact how people respond.	In addition to rational thought, rhetorical style can impact decision making in ways that transcend rationality. When this occurs, the neoclassical model breaks down.
Prospect theory	An application of framing to the professional financial and investment decision makers.	Irrational thought is sometimes involved when professionals analyze financial options involving potential profit and loss.
Behavioral finance	Behavioral economic principles can be applied to the financial and investment industries in ways that question their rational nature.	Investment professionals are expected to make rational decisions. Nonetheless, their behavior also appears to respond to emotions and operate in ways that transcend neoclassicism.

DISCUSSION

Behavioral economics is an emerging sub-discipline that uses psychological theories in order to demonstrate that economic behavior is often influenced by irrational forces. The findings of this field challenge the neoclassical model and look for wider explanations for economic responses.

pointing to psychological impacts that are not inherently rational nor based upon perfect information. Thus, this first phase of consumer research reflects and mirrors behavioral economics. As time has gone on, consumer researchers have increasingly looked at unique cultural, not universal, psychological responses. This trend sets the stage for considering economic models that are specific and cultural, not universal and psychological.

Behavioral economics, is in its infancy but it is making a significant contribution to economic thought by expanding beyond the neoclassical framework. It does so by employing psychological theories that acknowledge that the human mind is more than a rational calculating machine. Although this focus is useful, is not designed to provide a robust analysis of cultural, social, and ethnic variables. These issues can be addressed using substantive economic theory.

The substantive alternative

As was discussed above, the business disciplines and many economists tend to embrace the neoclassical paradigm. Behavioral economists, however, temper this rational and universal model by acknowledging irrational psychological responses and their significance. Because behavioral economics focuses upon the universal mind, however, it tends to underemphasize specific cultural factors.

In many circumstances, more culturally sensitive models need to be employed when economic behavior is examined, analyzed, and modeled. This reality creates a need for anthropological and sociological alternatives to neoclassical and behavioral economic models. Substantive economic anthropology can well serve in such a capacity.

The classic statement of the substantive position, of course, is found in Karl Polanyi's *The Great Transformation* which argues that a great divide in humanity is marked by the transition from small-scale societies (in which people interact in intimate ways involving face-to-face contact) to the environment spawned by the industrial revolution (that is typified by wage labor, increasingly impersonal relationships, and an economy based on money). Polanyi argues that the transformations triggered by industrialization led to patterns of life and human interaction that are profoundly different from what had been experienced in earlier times and still exists in small-scale societies (Polanyi 1968).

Polanyi and those who embrace his perspectives (who are known as substantive economic anthropologists) believe that the modern industrial world is a specific realm where rational actions and strategic decisions (largely reflective of the neoclassical model) dominate. People in such a system are assumed to be striving to advance their individual situation in overt, rational, and calculated ways that might reflect the neoclassical model. These substantivists, however, insist that that rational and universal patterns of response are not universal and that the neoclassical framework is an artifact of the industrial age, not a reflection of human economic response, in general.

The substantive paradigm can be juxtaposed with the work of "formalist" economic anthropologists, such as Raymond Firth, who adopted a neoclassical style of analysis and applied it to indigenous people as he did to the Maori of New Zealand (see Firth's 1929, 1967, 2000 [1939]). Harold K. Schneider is another prominent anthropologist who embraced formalist perspectives to good advantage. Although the formalist approach has made contributions, as time went on many anthropologists turned to the Polanyi model in order to nest economic behavior within a unique cultural or social setting, instead of dealing with it as a universal and rational response.

The substantivist approach, in contrast to neoclassical and formalist alternatives, argues that within many small-scale societies, economic activity is not
a separate and distinct realm of strategic behavior; instead, it is subtly intertwined within the entire culture (including kinship patterns, mores, religion/
ceremony, etc.). When social, cultural, and economic pressures and responses
become enmeshed in such a manner, one-dimensional neoclassical analysis is
not robust enough to adequately portray economic behavior.

Polanyi made significant use of two terms, "redistribution" and "reciprocity." Reciprocity involves a long-term pattern of mutually exchanging goods
and/or services, typically among those who are perceived to be equals. Interacting in this way emerges as part of the fabric of life and not as payment,
charity, or a calculated "quid pro quo." Redistribution, in contrast, takes
place when a strong leader, political force, or so forth gathers resources that
are then doled out in accordance with some culturally established formula.
Scarce and desirable goods are dispersed even though the rational and formal
marketplace (that is modeled by neoclassical theory) is not the mechanism
that does so.

Polanyi and the substantivists use the term "embedded" to indicate how
this process actually works. Instead of economic activity being viewed as a
distinct and discrete part of life and culture, distribution and allocation is
nested within the entire cultural and social framework. Thus, economic life is
not totally dictated by rational and universal responses that take place in relative isolation. For a fuller discussion see Granovetter (1985).

Many examples of such non-neoclassical behavior have been documented.
I, personally, have participated in the redistribution that takes place among
the Inupiaq of the North Slope of Alaska when a whale is caught. The
majority of the meat is shared with the community, given away in a traditional fashion. The home of the successful whaling boat captain is opened to
the public for a feast and everybody goes home with a sack of whale blubber
and meat. At various other times in the year (such as Thanksgiving) additional
redistributions take place. This culturally regulated distribution of valuable
resources remains a significant part of life on the North Slope, even if it is but
a pale reflection of the subsistence economy that long dominated there.

Certainly, neoclassical economists can portray the acts of these donors as
merely capturing respect (a scarce and desired commodity) through the redistribution of commodities (in a manner reminiscent of philanthropists in the
developed world who seek prestige and notoriety through charity). Nonetheless, the whole process is much more complex and it is intimately connected
to the cultural heritage of the people. The behaviors are structured in accordance with long-standing tradition. Adherence to these cultural dictates is not
viewed as optional or strategic; this pattern of sharing is part of the Inupiaq's
established patterns of behavior. Under such circumstances, economic activities and other aspects of life are seamlessly intertwined with one another in
ways that make conformity to them a natural and intuitive response. Thus,

substantivist economic anthropologists view the various institutions of the culture (family, social structure, religion, mores, and so forth) as creating the frame within which specific economic responses take place. This provides a much richer and robust understanding than neoclassical analysis.

In traditional and small-scale societies, a subsistence way of life often continues to prevail even if a market/cash economy exists side by side with it. These substantivist responses tend to benefit the entire community, not specific segments that are working to achieve their own partisan goals.

When specific indigenous, ethnic, and rural people are considering their options, they can often benefit by thinking beyond the neoclassical model. In short, neoclassical thinking can be envisioned as an artifact of the industrial world and the modern global economy; substantivism, in contrast, emerges as a way to understand cultural distinctiveness in ways that downplay rational thought and economic universals.

As with any other paradigm, the substantive model is not immune to criticisms. Thus, Prattis (1982) reminds us that the distinction between primitive and modern economies is largely arbitrary even though Polanyi seemingly argued in black and white terms. My rebuttal of this critique is that Polanyi was merely using the dialectical form of argumentation to demonstrate the benefits of his approach. I'm sure Polanyi recognized the obvious: many different variants exists in economic life (as well as in all other phases of human life and culture).

A further critique of the substantivist model comes from members of a splinter group often called the culturalists, such as Steven Gudeman (1986). Even more culturally focused than the substantivists, the culturalists prefer analyzing economic activities with reference to the perceptions of actual social and economic actors. Rejecting universal views deriving from the experiences of the developed world, the culturalists insist that local, culturally derived viewpoints should dominate the way economic activity is envisioned, modeled, and studied. Gudeman, for example, uses the phrase "people's own economic construction" (1986: 1) when doing so.

I believe that although the culturalists make some good points, their work is merely a useful and clarifying refinement of the substantivist approach, not a new school functioning in contrast to it.

In summary, the substantivist position augments the neoclassical model and the psychological revisions provided by the behavioral economists. It does so by focusing upon the cultural context of economic behavior and choice. As a result, a more varied picture of economic response results. Doing so however, tends to go against the grain in some ways because business strategists and leaders prefer universal models, theories, and tactics that can be applied in innumerable situations and by rote. The substantive model moves in the other direction and emphasizes the development of models and strategies with reference to the unique situation in which economic behavior occurs.

Discussion

The economic models that negotiators and leaders embrace have a profound impact upon the decisions they make. For many years, neoclassical theory depicted economic behavior as universal and rational. Although behavioral economics points to the role of a wide range of psychological responses upon economic choices, the impact of culture and society upon economic behavior was not adequately addressed.

When economic choices are evaluated outside of an adequate cultural or social context, the potential for hurtful error can creep in. This is especially true when the people being examined are distinctive, as is the case with many indigenous, ethnic, and rural communities (see Table 1.4).

Fortunately, a variety of paradigms that expand beyond and temper neo-classicism exist. They include behavioral economics and substantive economic anthropology. These alternatives can be compared in Table 1.4.

When analyzing the economic responses of cultural distinct social groups, the assumptions of neoclassical economics should not be covertly embraced.

Table 1.4 Range of options

Paradigm	Analysis	Importance
Neoclassical	Economic behavior is viewed as resulting from a rational analysis of relevant and perfect information.	Economic behavior involves the allocation of scarce resources. This is often accomplished in a rational manner. Neoclassicism deals with these processes.
Behavioral	Psychology includes analyzing non-rational responses. Economic behavior is often triggered by non-rational thought and action.	An overreliance upon rational thought and calculation in economic decision making ignores other significant influences. Psychological alternatives exist.
Substantive	Economic behavior takes place within a cultural context. As a result, universal models often need to give way to specific social perspectives.	Besides psychological alternatives to the neoclassical model, cultural factors also possess a specific role in impacting the way economics factors function within society.

DISCUSSION
Long the dominant paradigm, neoclassical economic thought is being revised with reference to both psychological and social analysis. Doing so provides a richer and more robust understanding of economic response.

The approach offered here acknowledges the insights of behavioral economics while embracing the methods and perspectives of substantive economic anthropology (and allied chains of thought related to it) in order to provide a more complex and nuanced view of economic response.

This chapter has observed that neoclassical theory, that presupposes rationality and universality, dominates the academic and practitioner realms of business. This paradigm, useful though it is, possesses profound blind spots that need to be addressed. Behavior economics points to ways in which psychology can help overcome the biases and limitations of the neoclassical model. Substantive economic anthropology adds a relevant cultural focus.

Relevant terms

4 Ps marketing: The process manipulating the controllable variables of product, price, place, and promotion in synergistic ways to please customers.

Bounded rationality: The premise that rational thought has its limits. Inspired by Nobel Prize winner Herbert Simon.

Behavioral economics: The premise that some economic behavior is irrational (in contrast to neoclassical perspectives.

Behavior finance: The application of behavioral economic principles to finance and investing.

Culturalists: Substantive economic anthropologists who emphasize cultural influences on economic behavior.

Economic Man Model: The belief that economic choices are rationally made with an eye to maximizing benefits.

Embedded: Economic responses that are based upon the culture and not inherent.

Formalist economic anthropology: Economic anthropology that embraces neoclassical principles. Raymond Firth is a key member of this school.

Heuristics: Using irrational rules of thumb to facilitate decision making.

Marketing management: Strategically orchestrating the 4 Ps in order to achieve goals.

Neoclassicism: An economic paradigm that assumes people are rational, possess perfect information, and so forth. Long the dominant economic model.

Perfect information: The neoclassical assumption that customers have perfect information regarding the products they want to buy.

Place: The location or distribution of a product. One of the 4 Ps.

Polanyi, Karl: A leader of substantive economic anthropology.

Price: The price charged for a product. One of the 4 Ps.

Product: The actual item or service sold. One of the 4 Ps.

Prospect theory: Behavioral economic applied to professional investors and their irrational responses.

Promotion: Strategically communicating about a good or service. One of the 4Ps.

Redistribution: The process of a centralized authority gathering assets and giving them out according to some formula.

Substantive theory: The belief that economic activity is based on specific cultural phenomena and not universal responses (as the neoclassical model asserts).

Utility/profit motive: People make economic decisions in order to consciously benefit themselves.

Discussion questions

1   Describe the basic neoclassical model. Where does it work? Where is it inappropriate? What limitations exist in its use? What tradeoffs must be accepted when using it?
2   What is behavioral economics? How does it temper neoclassicism? How relevant do you feel neoclassicism is when dealing with indigenous, ethnic, and rural peoples?
3   How does substantive economic anthropology supplement neoclassicism? How does substantive economic anthropology supplement behavioral economics? Why (or why not) is this important?
4   Point to the benefits of neoclassicism, behavioral economic, and substantive economic anthropology. What benefits and tradeoffs should be considered?
5   Using an example of your own choice, discuss all three models in relation to each other.

References

Finucane, M. L., Alhakami, A., Slovic, P. and Johnson, S. M. (January 2000). "The Affect Heuristic in Judgment of Risks and Benefits." *Journal of Behavioral Decision Making*, 13(1), 1–17.

Firth, Raymond W. (1929). *The Primitive Economics of the New Zealand Maori* (London: George Routledge and Sons).

Firth, Raymond W. (1967). "Themes in Economic Anthropology: A General Comment" in Firth, Raymond W (Ed.). *Themes in Economic Anthropology* (London: Tavistock).

Firth, Raymond W. (2004 [1939]). *Primitive Polynesian Economy* (London: Routledge).

Granovetter, M. (1985). "Economic Action and Social Structure: The Problem of Embeddedness." *The American Journal of Sociology*, 91(3), 481–510.

Gudeman, S. (1986). *Economics as Culture: Models and Metaphors of Livelihood* (London: Routledge).

Kanherman, Daniel (2003). "A Perspective on Judgment and Choice." *American Psychologist*, 58, 697–720.

Linville, P. W., Fischer, G. W. and Fischoff, B. (1992). "AIDS Risk Protection and Decision Biases." *The Social Psychology of HIV Infection* (Hillsdale, NJ: Erlbalm).

Malkiel, Burton (1973). *A Random Walk Down Wall Street* (New York: Norton).

McCarthy, E. Jerome (1960). *Basic Marketing: A Managerial Approach* (Homewood IL: Irwin).

Polanyi, K (1944). *The Great Transformation* (Boston: Beacon Press).

Polanyi, K. (1968). "The Economy as Instituted Process" in LeClair, E. and Schneider, H. (Eds.). *Economic Anthropology* (New York: Holt, Rinehart and Winston).

Prattis, J. I. (1982). "Synthesis, or a New Problematic in Economic Anthropology." *Theory and Society*, 11(2), 205–228.

Schwarz, N., Bless, H., Strack, F., Klumpp, G., Rittenauer-Schatka, H. and Simons, A. (1991). "Ease of Retrieval as Information: Another Look at the Availability Heuristic." *Journal of Personality and Social Psychology*, 61(2), 195–202.

Simon, Herbert (1991). "Bounded Rationality and Organizational Learning." *Organization Science*, 2(1), 125–134.

Negotiating and resolving conflict

Part I

Negotiating and resolving
conflict

Chapter 2

Negotiating with the mainstream world

Learning objectives

Indigenous and rural populations often negotiate with members of the mainstream world. The views, goals, and perspectives of these outsiders, however, often clash with those of local people. When this occurs, misunderstanding, miscommunication, and conflict can emerge. In order to receive a fair hearing, distinct groups need to communicate in ways that their mainstream counterparts can understand and appreciate. Having read this chapter, the reader will:

1 Understand the concept of "informed self-determinism" and its importance to communities.
2 Address the perspectives of mainstream decision makers.
3 Be able to distinguish between mainstream and local priorities.
4 Develop an awareness of the sub-disciplines of business and their distinctiveness.
5 Recognize the typical planning continuum of business and its implications.

Local goals and their advocates

In Chapter 1, the case was made that conventional, mainstream goals tend to reflect the quest for short-term profits as pursued through the use of rational and universal neoclassical economic methods. Many indigenous, ethnic, and rural people from small-scale communities, in contrast, are more likely to view economic behavior from (1) a more intimate substantive perspective, and (2) using a longer-term perspective. As a result of these differences, misunderstanding, miscommunication, and conflict can easily develop.

To effectively present their community's needs, goals, and vulnerabilities in ways that others appreciate, appropriate strategies and tactics of communication must be embraced. In this chapter, advice is given regarding how the mainstream negotiation process tends to operate and how local people can present their views and demands using these conventions of thought and presentation. By understanding these procedures and how to use them, local people can more effectively negotiate with mainstream outsiders.

Small-scale communities that are typical of indigenous peoples, ethnic subgroups, and rural enclaves are often motivated by distinctive goals that extend beyond short-term profits. On many occasions, however, outsiders with a generic business background fail to understand the distinctive points of view and their legitimacy. As a result, local sentiments are often written off as fuzzy minded and amateurish.

Many people (although perhaps worldly and sophisticated) are also members of indigenous and rural communities that are characterized by unique cultures and ways of life. These people often possess traditions and a heritage that they seek to nurture, protect, and preserve when pitted against relentless change.

When such people consider their options and negotiate with outsiders, anticipating and recognizing the (often hidden) impacts of the choices offered is essential. As a result, advocates of self-determinism need to emphasize **informed self-determinism** that involves people being aware of the full and long-term implications of their choices and actions.

Cultures and their members have a right to preserve, cherish, and follow their way of life. To do so, they need to foresee the probable impacts of the choices before them as well as considering how to deal with the hurtful change triggered by particular options.

With these realities in mind, Chapter 3 presents an overview of how plans and decisions tend to be made and the types of people involved in this process. This discussion is followed by a complementary chapter on alternative methods of dispute resolution, and indigenous conflict resolution.

Priorities of mainstream decision makers

Small, rural ethnic groups are often primarily concerned with their cultures and the local environment that makes their way of life possible. This orientation can easily collide with the views and priorities of outsiders whose goals are likely to be based upon a quest for short-term profits viewed with reference to the neoclassical economic model as discussed in Chapter 1.

When host cultures harbor distinct views, mainstream decision makers can easily write them off as thoughtless, irresponsible, and uninformed. Many mainstream decision makers, furthermore, embrace a fatalism regarding the future of the cultures and regions they seek to influence, assuming the host culture and its heritage are ultimately doomed to extinction due to the onslaught of the global age.

In reality, this extinction theory is merely a self-fulfilling prophecy: the ways of life that people embrace are not inevitably condemned to extermination unless unenlightened views push them past the breaking point. Thus, local people often seek to preserve their way of life while mainstream decision makers might write them off as vestigial remains that will fade in the wake of progress and cultural convergence. If the outsiders are ethical and compassionate, they may seek to cushion the pain of outside intervention, but if they believe the culture is inevitably doomed little effort will be made to preserve and nurture what is potentially being lost. Decisions and strategies are often made from that perspective. Table 2.1 provides a comparison of these two clusters of beliefs.

This comparison portrays profound differences. Local communities need to skillfully articulate their distinctive desires and points of view. Otherwise outsiders will gain the upper hand in negotiations and dominate (either covertly or overtly).

The art of negotiation

Indigenous, ethnic, and rural ethnic peoples often find that their views conflict with the orientations of outsiders. The goal of this chapter is to provide practical suggestions regarding how local communities can present ideas in ways that members of the business community will understand and respect.

Table 2.1 Local vs. mainstream outsiders

Orientation	Local community	Mainstream outsiders
Focus	Host culture, community, and their needs.	Some sort of concession that provides access to an opportunity.
View of culture	Host culture is viewed as distinctive and exerting a unique, positive influence.	Host cultures tends to be viewed as old fashioned and as a vestigial remain.
Value of host culture	Host cultures have a profound value that needs to be nurtured and preserved.	Host cultures have value if they can be used to achieve ad hoc goals.
Fate of host culture	The fate of the host culture depends upon decisions that are made and the opportunities that are available.	In our modern world, it is only a matter of time until distinctive peoples are absorbed into the mainstream world.

DISCUSSION
The views of mainstream people and the host community are very different. Outsiders tend to apply universal models, often reflective of neoclassical views. Members of small scale, rural communities, in contrast, tend to focus upon their distinctiveness, more substantive relationships, and the preservation of their heritage.

In order to do so, it is important to understand how the goals and points of view of various business disciplines are distinctive. Although when viewed from a distance, business leaders might appear to be interchangeable, in reality significant differences exist. What concerns the members of one business discipline, for example, might not greatly influence another. Understanding how to communicate with specific kinds of business people is invaluable.

Planning, furthermore, is a distinct and multi-step process that needs to be understood. Ranging all the way from seeking new ideas to refining what already exists, tactics that are effective at one phase of planning will be inappropriate in other contexts. When local leaders work within the world of mainstream business, they need to know how to respond during different phases of the planning process. Today, a largely systematized planning method has become almost universal within mainstream business; working within this structure is a vital part of effective communication and negotiation.

This chapter, therefore, provides a primer on the art of negotiation within the world of business. It is presented in order to enhance the abilities of indigenous, ethnic, and rural communities as they navigate through the negotiation process.

The variety of decision makers

A first step in learning how to effectively negotiate is to consider the variety of those who are typically involved in the planning process. Active participants usually include those from the various functional areas of business such as "Management," "Marketing," "Finance," and "Accounting"; each is an established business discipline that has its own special universe of discourse.

Management is the traditional business discipline and it continues to assert a primary role. Just as philosophers continue to view their discipline as the "mother" of all scholarship (and therefore entitled to a seat at the head of the table) management, points to its historic role, and asserts dominance accordingly.

Management, like philosophy, however, has had to give ground to other disciplines. As a result, management has increasingly concentrated in two areas. One is usually called "human relations management" which has emerged as the applied psychological/social scientific discipline that deals with and motivates employees. The second area concentrates on the forging of strategic plans. As other disciplines have gained parity, however, decision making has increasingly become a collective process that is conducted by various disciplines working together in an often-contentious manner.

Marketing, for example, started out as a subordinate discipline that dealt with specialized and ad hoc issues involving distribution. Eventually, however, marketers insisted that organizations exist to serve customers and that marketers understand customers better than anyone else in the organization. As a result, marketing has emerged as a premier strategic discipline that often dominates the decision-making process. In response, management thought has, in recent years, come to embrace the essence of the marketing concept: the notion that organizations exist merely to serve customers. One example of this tendency is the vogue of what is called "total quality management," a model that, like the marketing concept, is customer oriented and urges everyone in the organization to give customers and other stakeholders what they want. Thus, both management and marketing have converged upon service.

Finance is the business discipline that deals with raising money and how to strategically deal with and manage debt. As in the case of marketing, finance was once viewed as subordinate to management; the complexity of financial methods and the increased scarcity of money, however, have given the field significant independence, clout, and prestige.

Accounting started out as the discipline that kept the financial history of the organization. As tax laws and public disclosure requirements have become more complex, accounting has become increasingly intricate and important. Record-keeping activities are called financial accounting and they focus upon legal requirements as well as internal checks and balances. Such tasks are not directly concerned with organizational strategy and planning activities.

A strategic sub-discipline known as "managerial accounting," however, gathers and processes large amounts of data involving financial facts and transactions. By examining this information and extrapolating information from it, managerial accountants tease out important clues that may prove useful to the strategic planning process. In a simple example, accounting records can easily be used to determine which customers have paid their bills on time and which customers tend to pay late. This information may be useful in providing incentives and rewards to good customers as well as devising ways to deal with those who are likely to be delinquent.

Accountants typically possess a great deal of propriety information that can be reworked in useful and strategic ways. If gathered and properly processed, this data can provide insights that create a unique competitive edge. One of the current buzzwords of business is "data mining" that refers to the process of taking vast amounts of data and culling useful information from it. Managerial accountants are excellent data miners.

These business disciplines are routinely involved in the planning process. Their input is recognized as legitimate and the mission and role of each discipline is generally understood. Local leaders are not a part of this group. And being outsiders, their input is likely to be under-appreciated and not adequately considered when strategies and tactics are forged. Being in such a subordinate role, local leaders are apt to be viewed as adversaries that are brought in to be convinced after decisions have been made. Unless these local leaders are equal partners throughout the planning process, they and the perspectives they represent will contribute little as plans and strategies are developed.

There are, however, at least two ways in which local leaders can emerge equal partners in the planning process. The first is for their input to be mandated. In many projects involving economic development, such as those involving World Bank money, the use of social and environmental impact assessment professionals is required if the project is to receive funding. The work mandated by this requirement typically includes conducting relevant research and reporting the findings to the ultimate decision makers. Where requirements such as this exist, local leaders or their advocates will have an entree into the decision making process.

Decision making

Some organizations, in addition, may understand the importance of local cultures and seek strategies, tactics, and policies that address their needs, desires, and vulnerabilities. When this occurs, local priorities will be recognized when plans are forged.

In any event, a key point to remember is that strategic plans and organizational tactics tend to be developed and accepted long before they take effect. Once plans are established, however, it becomes more difficult to alter them or to act contrary to their guidelines. As a result, local communities need to be actively involved in the initial planning processes and throughout the entire process of strategy development. If not, the future of the community might be excessively dictated by outsiders.

The traditional business disciplines are usually represented when plans are forged. Since local leaders and their advocates are typically viewed as outside of this group, they must aggressively fight for a significant role in the decision-making process. Although the participation of local people might be mandated in some cases, actually gaining respect and power within the decision-making process can be an entirely different matter. The local community and its advocates need to influence the decision-making process in forceful and meaningful ways. Graphically, the cast of characters involved in the planning process can be depicted as is in Table 2.2.

At first glance, an organization might appear to an outsider as a homogeneous cadre of likeminded individuals. In reality, the members of different business disciplines have distinct goals, perspectives, and even personalities. During the planning process, each of these professions tends to bring their unique vision to the project. As a result, when negotiating with a planning committee, developing specific tactics for influencing particular segments of the negotiating team may be more effective than relying upon one overarching strategy that is designed to influence the group as a whole. In addition, gaining membership in the planning committee and using this position effectively is vital. Otherwise, communities will be forced to deal with and adapt to plans and strategies that were established by others with minimal local input.

Table 2.2 A range of decision makers

Profession	Description	Authority	Strengths	Weaknesses
Management	Original strategic discipline.	Human resources and strategy development.	The long-standing strategic science.	Fragmented and diverse. Losing ground.
Marketing	Centers upon customers and clients.	Developing ways to attract and serve customers.	In close touch with and understand customer/client base	Focusing upon customers/clients can ignore other variables.
Finance	Determines the most effective way to raise money and pay bills.	Attracting capital and developing strategies to meet obligations.	Meshing funding issues with goals of the organization.	Does not deal with the actual business, merely finances it.
Accounting	Keeping financial records. Using accounting data strategically.	Record keeping. Using accounting data to prompt decisions.	Generating strategic information from accounting data.	Deals with financial data, other variables ignored.
Others	Stakeholders that are required or included.	Whatever is mandated or granted by the organization.	Whatever specific authority emerges.	A limited role? May not be taken seriously by others.

DISCUSSION

During the planning process, a wide variety of professionals with different backgrounds and priorities collaborate. Local leaders and their advocates might be (overtly or covertly) excluded from this group. Gaining a seat at the table and gaining respect once granted that recognition is vital if communities are to have a role in forging their destiny and not merely react to the decisions of others after they have been established.

The planning continuum: an overview

The planning process presents an opportunity for all stakeholders to influence projects and their impacts. As a result, the significance of the planning phase cannot be overstated. By understanding mainstream planning methods as they have evolved, local leaders will be better able to negotiate in ways that truly reflect community needs and wants.

To facilitate a better understanding of how various types of planning occur, a brief overview of planning, as a strategic function, is presented. As usually envisioned and discussed, three distinct although interconnected types of planning exist. They are typically known, as "Strategic," "Long Range," and "Operational" planning. Various writers, of course, place their own labels on these activities. Thus, Henry Sisk (1969: 88) refers to them as "Policies," "Procedures," and "Methods," respectively. Even when the terminology varies, the planning process is almost always broken down into distinct and identifiable categories such as these.

Strategic planning seeks to establish major policies. It deals with a longer time frame and asks the most basic questions. The goal of strategic planning is to develop a framework for decision-making within which other policies and tactics are nested and conceptualized.

Because of its importance, strategic planning typically attracts the attention and the participation of the highest-ranking individuals in the organization. This is also a time when consultants and other outsiders provide contributions. As a result of strategic planning, organizational negotiators and their community counterparts often devise or revise what are usually called "mission statements" that codify guidelines for the future. As a result of their long-term implications, mission statements are very important.

Using established mission statements as a guide, long-range planning devises broad methods or tactics for achieving these goals. Doing so typically includes both specific goals and targeted time frames for achieving them. The performance of the organization, furthermore, is periodically reviewed (formally and at specified times which are known in advance as well as during a crisis) with reference to the mission statement and directives stemming from it. Long range planning is the pragmatic link between strategic planning and the day-to-day operation of the organization.

Operational planning provides guidelines for short-term decision making. Although they should be established with strategic and long-range objectives in mind, operational plans are primarily ad hoc and pragmatic in nature and subordinates typically forge them and implement them. In addition, operational plans can be quickly adjusted even after they are put into effect.

Graphically, these three levels of the planning process can be portrayed as in Table 2.3

By understanding the multiple components of the planning process, as it exists in business and policy science, local leaders will be better able to predict how and when decisions will be made. In addition, who will establish policies

Table 2.3 Planning phases

Issue	Strategic	Long range	Operational
Time frame	Longest	Midrange	Shortest
Role	Establishing mission statement, general guidelines.	Formulating specific ways to achieve the organizational mission.	Short-term operational procedures.
Established by	Upper management, consultants, and others as required.	Division heads, and others using the mission statement as a guide.	Subordinates pursuing as hoc goals with long-term priorities in mind.

DISCUSSION

A variety of plans exist, ranging from long-term strategic to ad hoc operations. Each has its own role and each attracts the participation of a certain type of decision maker. In order to effectively impact these planning processes, being aware of the type of planning that is being developed and focusing on the characteristics and priorities of the primary decision maker influencing these plans is vital.

and tactics becomes easier to understand. These assessments are useful as communities attempt to develop and influence strategies in order to protect and reflect their priorities and interests.

Significantly, local leaders (and everyone else) experience different opportunities and constraints when various types of plans are established and operationalized. In order to better perceive the resulting framework and its implications, a brief discussion of each phase is useful.

Influencing strategic planning

As indicated above, mission statements and the strategic planning that derives from them define the essence of organizations, projects, and their goals. As a result, local communities can profoundly advance their goals by being actively involved when strategic plans involving them are being forged.

Local perspectives have a better chance of exerting an influence during this phase of planning because the organization is actively seeking a variety of new ideas and it has not settled upon any specific framework, strategy, or tactic to be followed. Equally important is the fact that the most important people in the organization tend to be involved in strategic planning; as a result, this is the best time to attract the attention of important leaders, such as members of upper management.

In addition, during strategic planning, the organization is willing to focus upon a wider range of options, both internally and externally. Internal environment refers to the strengths and weaknesses possessed by the organization. On many occasions, an organization chooses a specific strategy in direct response to its assets and deficits. If the organization has certain strengths or weaknesses, a particular strategy might be particularly attractive or unattractive. Strengths include (but are not limited to) past track records, connections, relevant staff members, the demand of the target market served by the organization, and so forth.

Weaknesses, in contrast refers to any limitation that might exist, including financial issues, lack of expertise/experience, questionable reputation, prior obligations that must be honored, and the like. In essence, weaknesses involve anything that might prevent an effective and forceful effort or whatever might trigger delays in effectively pursuing an option.

If a course of action that is favored by the community builds upon the strengths of a potential partner or collaborator, that strategy might be especially attractive. In the case of weaknesses, if an organization cannot easily move in other directions, this internal limitation can result in an opportunity involving the host culture to be inviting by default. If this is true, the local community might gain an advantage in negotiations.

Planners seek to employ whatever strategy has the best prospects of a positive return; if the organization faces obstacles in one area, it will seek alternative opportunities. Thus, local negotiators should simultaneously speak of the dangers inherent in other opportunities while pointing to a culturally appropriate project as a relatively safe and lucrative alternative.

External environment (in contrast to internal environment) refers to the greater milieu in which the organization exists. What is the "market," for example, for the goods, and services the project aims to deliver?

All of these are important questions that local communities need to consider and address. Not only should local people evaluate their assets, deficits, strengths, and weaknesses, they need to simultaneously appraise others that are involved in the planning process. By doing so, accurately envisioning what can and cannot be gained in a negotiation becomes easier.

One of the classic tactical orientations of business is called the "niching strategy." If a powerful opponent exists, the organization will suffer if it chooses to compete directly against it. In this situation, smaller and weaker organizations typically wait to see what the dominant force decides to do. Once the rival's strategy is understood, the weaker organization focuses its attention in other areas to avoid unwanted rivalry.

In the Toledo district of Belize, for example, economic advisors from the outside encouraged local Maya farmers to invest heavily in order to make a transition from subsistence farming to specializing in Cacao (chocolate) growing. Although the farmers were uncomfortable doing so, many complied. Soon, thereafter, the price of chocolate fell dramatically and many of the farmers, who had borrowed in order to modernize, were financially ruined.

Afterwards, a smaller and weaker company known as Green and Black's (the brainchild of Craig Sams and Joe Fairley) approached the Maya. Known as the Maya Gold project, the goal was to buy organically grown Cacao that could be produced in small groves without fertilizer or heavy investment. This crop could be grown along with subsistence food products. And since it was organic, the product would sell at a premium, be somewhat insulated from drastic price variations, and the demand was more predictable than generic chocolate. To take advantage of this opportunity, the farmers banded together to form the Toledo Cacao Grower's Association. The project was successful because it produced a specialized crop that the dominant chocolate companies were not willing to produce. This minimized the competition that had to be faced. The local people have been very successful with this arrangement because, in addition to being lucrative, it meshes with the Maya way of life.

In general, external environment refers to any outside variable that either encourages or discourages the organization regarding a specific course of action. During the strategic planning process, any number of projects can be proposed. In addition, strategic planning tends to be less structured and the more flexible atmosphere creates broad and generic opportunities for local leaders (and anybody else) to forcefully mold the organization. It is also the time when organizations hire consultants.

Local leaders must be vigilant to keep mainstream consultants from subtly merging their own agendas and orientations into the strategic planning process. In many circumstances, consultants seek to introduce strategies in ways that preempt other options. If advisors appear to harbor unstated perspectives or hidden agendas, local leaders need to address these covert perspectives. If directives of this type are left unacknowledged and unchallenged, the orientations of others may be thoughtlessly conceded without adequate discussion.

Strategic planning is also a time when culturally sensitive individuals can make a bid for consulting assignments. In the final analysis, local leaders and their advocates need to do more than react; they should assume a leadership role.

Influencing long range planning

Local leaders should actively seek to influence strategic planning when the opportunity to do so presents itself. This process, however, does not occur very often. On most occasions, the organization or the business arrangement has already defined its strategic plans and its mission statement; usually, therefore, plans and decisions take place under the umbrella of an established strategic plan.

Although long-term plans are forged with a strategic plan or mission statement in mind, considerable latitude usually still exists. In other words, there tends to be a large, "gray area" within which culturally sensitive negotiation can take place. If the community has a particular goal, for example, a case can be made for it that is phrased in a manner that meshes with the strategic plan. Rivals, however, might simultaneously attempt to achieve their own agendas in order to tap the organization's limited resources. Remember, resources are scarce in any organization and various vested interest groups will fight for them.

If, on the other hand, strategic plans proceed in directions that do not reflect the needs and desires of the local community, attempts can be made to brake or postpone such actions as much as possible. Although it may be futile to attempt to permanently prevent a withdrawal of support or some other negative action, such unfortunate eventualities might be delayed or minimized. By portraying a long-range plan involving a host culture as viable and consistent with the overall strategic plan of the organization, furthermore, it might even be possible to redefine projects involving a host culture so they better mesh with the outsider's current strategic plan. Doing so might be possible even if such tactics appear, at first glance, to be contrary to the mission statement. Local leaders, however, will need to present a compelling rationale in such situations.

On many occasions, furthermore, strategic plans are so general that the priorities of a host culture (and almost anything else) can be nested under it. In situations, for example, where the organization's strategic plans call for "increasing market share" local leaders may be able to present a plan they prefer within such a mandate. By so arguing, culturally sensitive projects can emerge as viable and capable of helping the organization to achieve its goals.

When dealing with very general mission statements, however, others can also make a legitimate bid for the organization's resources.

Local leaders, therefore, must consciously justify their projects in terms of being the most effective opportunity for fulfilling the organization's mission. By phrasing a request for support from the organization in such a way, the project is presented in a manner that will be readily understood and appreciated by the ultimate decision makers within the organization.

Long-term plans are forged with certain well-defined strategic orientations in mind. By focusing on that reality, local leaders will be better able to forcefully present a justification of projects involving host cultures.

Operational plans and evaluations

Operational plans involve the short-term, day-to-day, operations of the organization. On the one hand, these actions stem from and are evaluated on a local level. On the other hand, the performance of the project is ultimately tied to operational successes or failures.

Simply because a project is skillfully pursued at an operational level does not inevitably mean that the organization will consider it to be successful. When asking for organizational support, local leaders must not promise what they cannot deliver. If they do, healthy projects may be evaluated as failures because they do not deliver what was promised. When competitors for organizational support are denied funding, they inevitably shift gears and try to get the winners to promise more than they can deliver so they look bad after the fact. If, for example, unrealistic projections are offered as benchmarks for evaluating performance, a project, even though successful, might fail to measure up to this unrealistic standard and, as a result, be ranked as a failure.

Remember, when projects do not perform according to expectations, rivals and detractors will be in a position to argue that the effort was a failure and that future organizational support should revert to them. As a result, rivals have a vital interest in getting their adversaries to "up the ante" as much as possible when seeking organizational support. It will be a hollow victory to win short-term support, by becoming saddled with unrealistic commitments that cannot be achieved. Thus, in the heat of negotiation, local leaders need to resist the urge to guarantee what cannot be delivered.

The opposite is also true; if others get the nod, make them commit to explicit and measurable results. Remember, evaluations are based upon stated and defined goals; if a competitor's project has an unreasonably easy criteria of evaluation, even a mismanaged effort will satisfy the stated guidelines and be judged successful. When competitors win organizational support and take funding from projects away from the local community, these rivals should not get off easy. If the project is successful, congratulations are in order; but rivals shouldn't get a free ride by having easy criteria to satisfy.

As a result, local leaders have a direct interest in helping to develop operational plans regarding projects and establishing criteria regarding how they will be evaluated, even if their projects are rejected. By insisting that competitors are judged via appropriate yardsticks, local communities may be in a better position in future years; if it can be shown that rival projects were not successful the argument can be made that they should be replaced with culturally sensitive programming that reflects the local community. Thus, lack luster performances by others (when properly documented), can be used as a justification for giving future funding to projects involving the local community.

Conclusion: using planning effectively

The goal of this chapter has been to provide local leaders and their advocates with a bird's eye view of the planning process as it has developed in policy science and the business disciplines. Although the reader may have been exposed to such concepts in the past, it is hoped that this concise discussion, focused around local communities and their needs, is useful.

Table 2.4 The planning processes compared

Issue	Strategic planning	Long-term planning	Operational planning
Opportunities	Focusing the organization around culturally sensitive projects involving the local community.	Presenting the case that it is in support of community goals is a good ad hoc tactic.	Including community goals in short-term plans even if doing so is not part of the organization's primary mission.
Dangers	The organization chooses a mission that does not reflect community goals.	Rival groups seek support.	1 Not Getting Support 2 Agreeing to be evaluated using unreasonable criteria.
Tactics	Justifications should be phrased in ways which mesh with the organization's strengths and weaknesses.	Tailor the justification for support in terms of the organization's mission statement.	1 Don't agree to be judged with unreasonable criteria. 2 Be sure competitor's projects are judged using appropriate criteria.

DISCUSSION

Different types of planning exist. Each has its own characteristics. Those involved in planning need to understand what type of planning is taking place and develop goals and tactics accordingly.

Participating within the planning process may be difficult because indigenous, ethnic, and rural communities often embrace orientations that differ significantly from those of mainstream decision makers. Local leaders must be aware of these differences and be able to effectively function within that environment.

One way of effectively meshing with organizations is to understand and work within the constraints of the established planning process as it has evolved in business and policy science. Thus, thumbnail sketches of Strategic, Long Term, and Operational Planning were provided (see Table 2.4).

As local leaders and their advocates gain clout, they become responsible for negotiating within various organizations and with a wide range of competitors. One way to be effective is to embrace the methods and rhetoric of planning as they have evolved in business/policy science. By doing so, negotiations can be more effective when dealing with a wide range of colleagues, partners, and rivals.

Relevant terms

Accounting: The business function which keeps records. Today accounting has expanded into "managerial accounting" which uses records for strategic purposes and for strategic planning.

Evaluation: When plans are made, projects are given criteria upon which they will be evaluated. Strategic planners should insist that projects are evaluated using fair and relevant criteria.

External environment: Any influence on the organization and its strategic plans that comes from outside the organization itself. Rival organizations, demographic characteristics of the population, and the economic situation are examples.

Finance: The business function which deals with raising capital and the cost of using money and resources. In recent years, this discipline has grown in power since money has become increasingly scarce.

Internal environment: Any influence inside the organization that impacts its strategic plans. Examples include the organization's strengths, key personnel, past experiences, reputation, etc.

Long-term planning: Using the mission statement or general strategic plans, long-term plans implement the organizations goals in fairly long-term ways.

Management: Originally the premier business discipline. Today, management shares authority with several other disciplines. Highly involved in strategic planning. Points to its general orientation as a qualification for strategic decision making.

Marketing: The business function which deals with the organization's customers.

Niching strategy: The strategy of finding a small market and catering to it. Niching firms often wait to see what large powerful organizations are going to do and then specialize in ways which avoid direct competition.

Operational planning: Short-term, ad hoc planning. The actual implementation of the organization's strategic plans. Due to the fact that it responds to circumstance, operational plans can be quickly changed and may stray from the avowed mission of the organization for tactical reasons.

Strategies: In a general sense, what the firm wants to accomplish and how it hopes to do so.

Strategic planning: The most primary area of planning. Mission statement set. Important members of the organization are involved. Other plans and tactics are based on the results of this activity.

Tactics: Short-term decisions which, while aware of strategic plans, are more flexible.

Discussion questions

1   Business organizations are divided into different disciplines which have distinct roles in the planning process. What are the four traditional business disciplines? Describe them. Why is it important to understand the diversity of the business disciplines? How will local decision makers most effectively operate within such a system? What concrete actions can be taken in order to better the situation?

2   Compare/contrast external and internal environment. How can both be used to justify the priorities of local communities? Give an example.

3   How might the actions of powerful, dominant organizations competing in a region create opportunities for weaker organizations? Use the concept of niching to discuss. Apply your ideas to negotiation strategies that might be used by local leaders.

4   What phase of the planning process results in broad general overarching strategies and mission statements? Why should local leaders be active in this phase of planning? How will their role decline if we do not participate in this phase of planning? Discuss with reference to long-term opportunities.

5   Operational plans deal with the day-to-day activities of an organization. How can local leaders use this phase of planning in ways that advance their communities? How can this phase of planning be used to an advantage even if the organization has made a conscious decision to move away from strategies favored by the local community?

Reference

Sisk, Henry L. (1969). *Principles of Management: A Systems Approach* (Cincinnati, OH: Southwestern).

Chapter 3

Remedies for conflict

Learning objectives

Disagreements and conflicts are natural, not abnormal, and various styles for dealing with divergences exist. Although the standard tools of negotiation and decision making are useful, alternative techniques (such as mediation and arbitration) are sometimes needed. Litigation might emerge as a last resort. In addition, processes of indigenous conflict resolution (that embrace local traditions) potentially have a role, especially within small-scale, rural, and/or ethnically distinct communities. By understanding these options, a wider range of tools becomes available to facilitate self-determinism as local peoples seek greater control over the decision-making process.

Specific learning objectives include:

1   Perceiving conflict as normal.
2   Conceptualizing different stages of conflict.
3   Acknowledging different styles for dealing with conflict and disagreement.
4   Understanding methods of conflict resolution such as mitigation, arbitration, and litigation.
5   Envisioning indigenous conflict resolution and its role in negotiation and decision making.

Accepting and recognizing conflict

Conflict and disagreement are natural, not abnormal, and inevitably arise when different stakeholders experience and/or are impacted by divergent goals, beliefs, vulnerabilities, circumstances, and so forth. If not dealt with effectively, conflict (and issues related to it) can trigger tensions that undercut or inhibit positive working relationships between individuals and/or groups. To minimize and control these hurtful potentials, conflict often needs to be anticipated, managed, and mitigated.

Conflict can arise when goals are uncertain and/or when they are changing. Such responses are likely to emerge as a natural response to ambiguity.

This is often the case when small and vulnerable communities experience significant and prolonged contact with outside intruders who offer disruptive, but seductive and possibly helpful, opportunities.

When new and unprecedented conditions trigger conflict, for example, two factions (one "conservative" the other more "progressive" or "modern") are likely to arise. Each bloc might embrace distinctive and mutually exclusive thoughts regarding how to deal with the situations before them. Those with a more traditional orientation typically prefer the older style of life, cling to their heritage, and hesitate to accept changes that are triggered by outside contact. More "progressive" members of the community, in contrast, often welcome a greater embrace or alliance with the outside world and are more likely to be attracted to the options that it offers. The resulting tensions between these factions can undercut the internal harmony of a community as well as complicating and/or disrupting its negotiations with the outside world or potential collaborators. Hurtful and counterproductive tensions, rivalries, and responses often result.

In the heat of contention, mutual misunderstanding can easily emerge. Communications may break down or be misinterpreted. Emotions might interfere with or prevent evenhanded communications between rivals. Such potentials exist internally in situations involving follow members of the community as well as when dealing with outsiders.

Different levels of conflict, of course, may also exist; in one well known and intuitive model, some conflicts are minor and inevitable disagreements pose little threat to cooperation and collaboration. Others are potentially disruptive and can destroy working relationships. This continuum of levels of tension can be viewed with reference to a well-known intuitive typology that ranges from minor disagreements, to chronic problems, to crises.

Whenever people are in contact, an array of trivial and commonly occurring difficulties potentially arise. An adage from the military observes that "A griping soldier is a happy soldier." On the one hand, this saying underscores that people are always experiencing some sort of tension. On the other hand, when people are willing to acknowledge their disagreements (instead of hiding or internalizing them) relationships tend to be good or at least workable.

If, on the other hand, an assortment of recurring trivial annoyances are ignored or left unresolved their disruptive potential can grow. Under these conditions, chronic patterns of disagreement may arise that, over time, take on a life of their own with disruptive consequences. Although no particular incident might be significant, ongoing tensions can fester, take a toll, and trigger distrust in ways that cause alienation, disunity, and so forth. Frustrations and the anger it spawns can cause one or both parties to begin to question the value of the relationship. More significant are full-blown crises in which conflict and disunity potentially disable the relationships between parties. The resulting responses can be hurtful and costly to all. If such a trend

Table 3.1 A continuum of conflict

Level	Analysis
Common	Some level of conflict or disagreement tends to be inevitable. Such commonly occurring differences are not significant problems.
Chronic	Minor problems repeatedly arise and/or minor conflicts habitually crop up in ways that are unhealthy for relationships. This situation can trigger more substantial tensions.
Crisis	Disagreements grow to a level that threaten the relationship. Forceful action tends to be needed to counter such feelings and responses. On some occasions, damage cannot be reversed.

DISCUSSION

Although conflict is natural and inevitable, it can also be disruptive and destructive. Lower levels of conflict include minor problems that create minimal threats to relationships. Should conflict becomes chronic, however, a recurring and hurtful potential can arise. When crises emerge, relationships are potentially undercut, requiring formal, forceful, and/or systematic attention.

continues, significant damage might occur. On some occasions, relationships cannot be mended. If less serious problems are addressed in a timely and equitable manner, however, disruptive tensions can often be minimized or mitigated. This is illustrated in tabular form in Table 3.1.

Thus, conflict is normal. It should not be viewed as an atypical twisting of relationships that are ordinarily completely harmonious. People have their own goals and attitudes. This reality needs to be accepted. By recognizing that the conflict is to be expected, dealing with it in a sensible and effective manner becomes an easier task. The goal should be to accept conflict where it exists, work through it in positive and constructive ways, and minimize its potentially harmful effects.

Conventional methods

A variety of strategies exist for dealing with conflict. One classic representation of an array of options is presented by Kenneth Thomas (1976) in his *Handbook of Industrial and Organizational Psychology*. Thomas discusses five basic strategies including "collaborating," "competing," "compromising," "accommodating," and "avoiding."

Collaborating can be characterized as "I win, you win." Different stakeholders work together to achieve objectives that, typically, are in their mutual interest. Although some disagreements may exist, these differences are addressed and mitigated; in the process, potentially hurtful impacts are reduced or mitigated.

Competition exists where an "I win, you lose" attitude prevails. It is characterized by a potential for the person, group, or organization to lose or gain coupled with the need to look after self-interests. The focus is upon winning and losing, not parity and equity. Many mainstream negotiations are based upon competition, with the results being judged by a standard suggested by the competitive model. Many small-scale societies, in contrast to this orientation, focus upon community-centered (not strategic and individualistic) orientations for dealing with the outside world. Where this situation occurs, competitive methods that are popular within the mainstream world might not suit indigenous, ethnic, and rural communities. By being aware of this possibility, the effectiveness of an "I win, you lose" strategy can be calculated and alternative strategies can be better envisioned.

In situations where a "You give, I give" attitude prevails, the spirit of compromise prevails. Doing so involves all involved parties giving up something of value, while each simultaneously gains at the other's expense. The common good (or at least the feelings and attitudes of the involved stakeholders) is considered and addressed. Under such circumstances, some issues might be left unresolved, because when people give in to the wishes or demands of others they are not totally happy with the results. Because these (often sensitive) areas of divergence are left unreconciled, reaching a workable compromise can often proceed quicker than if all issues had to be totally resolved before any agreement could be reached. Although compromise can be a good tactic, negotiators need to be careful not to give up too much. When dealing with diverse groups that might not understand each other, an objective social scientific appraisal may be an invaluable tool.

In accommodating, one party allows the other to win. This process can be described by the phrase "I lose, you win." On some occasions, a concession or accommodation might not impact one party very much even though it has great value to the other. Under these circumstances, accommodating can be a good strategy that makes others happy although the cost to the giver is minimal. Doing so can help maintain harmony and build goodwill. In other situations, one party might be wrong and, as a result, providing an appropriate accommodation is the proper course of action. Some battles, furthermore, just can't be won, so giving up without a fight can be an effective response. When negotiators are making concessions, they often need to conduct some sort of cost benefit analysis. A cultural analysis of all impacted stakeholders provides valuable information that is vital to the decision-making process.

In avoiding, there are "No winners and no losers." Under such circumstances, key and important issues might be left unaddressed in order to reduce strife in the short term. This tactic can make it easier to concentrate upon

Table 3.2 Styles of conflict response

Style	Analysis
Collaborating	I win, you win: Mutual goals are addressed. Work though differences. Find creative solutions. Satisfy both parties.
Competing	I win, you lose: The issues addressed are very important. A decision is needed immediately. Can't be a tie. Parties must stand up for themselves. Personal and very competitive.
Compromising	You give, I give: All stakeholders give up something. Common good facilitated. Some differences might be unresolved. Easier and quicker than other methods. But your position can be "picked away."
Accommodating	I lose, you win: You don't really care. You are wrong. You can't win. Maintaining harmony is important.
Avoiding	No winners, no losers: Key issue left un addressed or sidestepped, but postponing might make matters worse. If avoidance is employed, the ultimate resolution might not have your input.

DISCUSSION

The Kenneth Thomas models reminds us that a broad range of options for dealing with conflict exist. Cultural circumstances often influence what approach is most effective in a particular situation. Insightful negotitators have a significant role in analyzing how different styles of resolution are likely to function in specific contexts.

other issues that appear to be more important and/or resolvable. Although temporary harmony or ad hoc cooperation might prevail, the causes of tension can be left unresolved. On some occasions, putting off dealing with conflict might merely postpone future tensions; doing so can outweigh the immediate benefits. Thus, a wide range of strategies and tactics exist when responding to conflict (see Table 3.2).

Thus, a variety of methods for dealing with conflict exist. Understanding them can provide vital tactics for negotiating with others. People from specific cultural groups tend to respond in a certain, predictable manner; as a result their style of dealing with conflict can be viewed as a "default setting." A range of other default settings often exist; that is the next topic of discussion.

"Default settings"

In addition to the fact that various styles for dealing with conflict exist, individual people and specific groups tend to think and act in a predictable, systematic, and "pre-programed" manner. Computers, by analogy, tend to be "preloaded" with a variety of predetermined "default settings," that are not inherent or universal. The same is true when dealing with diverse people; to a large extent different peoples are "programed" by their cultures, traditions, and heritage. The social sciences, such as anthropology, provide tools for identifying these patterns of response.

Representative default settings exhibited by people are influenced by variables such as (1) the culture, (2) values, (3) and paradigms. Each is briefly discussed below. Other influences (such as needs) clearly exist but are not discussed here because they are considered elsewhere. The discussions presented here, therefore, should be viewed as representative, not exhaustive.

Culture: Viewed broadly, culture refers to the collective, learned knowledge that the human race, as a species, has acquired, preserved, and transmitted. Viewed more narrowly, culture refers to one specific way of being human. Different cultures possess their own distinctive rules, priorities, codes of behavior, and so forth. Thus, talking about "Japanese" and "American" cultures can be meaningful and appropriate. Terms such as "national character" are sometimes used to identify such phenomena. Acknowledging that these distinctions exist does not imply that all people totally embrace the culture of which they are a part, but merely that certain distinctive and recognizable patterns exist. In my *Rethinking Business Anthropology* (2013), such issues are discussed at greater length with reference to business strategy.

Cultures tend to provide their members with a wide array of default settings that encourage specific ways of responding and interpreting the actions of others. The resulting tendencies and reactions can become so ingrained that social actors are likely to assume that the type of responses they make are universal, inherent, innate, and exhibited by all people. Misreading others in such a manner can trigger potential clashes, or at least create an atmosphere of confusion and misunderstanding.

Values: Values are standards regarding what is important, acceptable, revered, easily dismissed, and so on. The cultural background of people has a significant role in determining what values they embrace or reject and why they do so. In addition, values can be influenced by other issues that transcend the generic culture (such as age and sex).

Baby boomers in the United States, as is widely known, have tended to be distinctive ever since they established their "youth culture" in the 1960s. As a significant faction of the population, baby boomers continue to be distinctive. Their patterns of response can be explained (1) with reference to the specific needs of this segment at particular times and (2) with reference to the fact that a large cohort of individuals from this age group share a variety of key values. In many cultures being a member of a particular "age grade" is even more important than in North America because relationships are more formally structured or institutionalized with reference to age groupings.

For whatever reason, specific clusters of stakeholders might possess values that are internally homogeneous, but distinctive from the broader culture or society. In the early 1990s, I met a colleague from the University of Leipzig at a professional conference. Greeting her, I said "I see you are from East Germany" but quickly corrected myself to "Germany" in order to acknowledge the recent reunification of the country. She responded in a cold and deliberate manner, "You were right the first time, I am from East Germany."

Thus, while many Germans were celebrating the reunification of their nation, some people of a certain age and from a certain region were not happy with the new state of affairs. Apparently, their default settings were based, at least in part, upon the values held by those who were opposed to the new political realities.

Similar to the people of East Germany who were dismayed by reunification, many indigenous, ethnic, and rural communities are also subjected to traumatic, albeit exciting and transformational, changes. Not all people respond to these emerging situations in the same way because specific segments possess distinctive values

Paradigms: People tend to embrace over-arching systems of belief that color the way in which they view the world. Even when these patterns are obviously "wrong," they can possess profound staying power and continue to wield a powerful influence. The plight of Galileo and his attempts to convince people that the earth moved around the sun is a case in point. The old belief that the sun moves around the earth was so strong that, in the short term, it could not be successfully challenged.

Another set of paradigms, that has proved to be irreconcilable in some circles (at least in the United States), is the dyad of "biological evolution" vs. "intelligent design." The concept of evolution, of course, assumes that the species alive today are products of what is usually envisioned as the "survival of the fittest" or, more accurately, today's living things are offspring of ancestors who were able to reproduce and pass on their genes to future generations. Over many generations, the resulting patterns of selective reproduction lead to evolution and change.

Intelligent design, in contrast, is the theory that a force beyond random events is at work (that is typically envisioned as an all-powerful, rational god that is actively involved in the world. This force is believed to have designed and created life. In the United States, both of these views are currently held by significant segments of the population. Although, over time, trends may shift, these beliefs are currently unshakeable among loyal adherents to both positions.

Neoclassical economics is another paradigm that provides an overarching interpretation of human response that asserts that economic behavior is rational and universal. The neoclassical paradigm can be challenged both by behavioral economics and by the substantive economic model.

Thus, paradigms (patterned ways of thinking that are often relied upon in a "knee jerk reaction" manner) are powerful, ingrained, and often resistant to change.

In general, default settings are not universal and inevitable. They are patterned variations that mold people to think and act in a certain way. Recognizing these default settings can be an important means of understanding how people think and react (see Table 3.3).

Default settings potentially limit objective and thoughtful discussions between people as well as covertly influencing their relationships. The fact that different people(s) possess distinctive default settings can create situations where those holding contradictory views and orientations may have trouble understanding and/or responding to each other. This possibility can exert hurtful consequences. By being aware of such default settings, however, finding ways to acknowledge and mitigate differences between people might become easier.

This observation (and other thoughts provided above) set the stage for a discussion of conflict as well as ways to envision and respond to it.

Table 3.3 Default settings

Setting	Analysis
Culture	From a micro perspective, "culture" refers to a particular way of life as practiced by specific people. The culture is learned, handed down, and typically embraced by people, although variation often exists among its members. Even when change inevitably takes place over time, recurring and predictable patterns make it possible to refer to "American," "Japanese," "Iroquois," "Maori," etc. cultures.
Values	Values involve what people believe is important, moral, significant, and so forth. Values can be based upon general cultural criteria as well as more circumscribed influences, such as age and sex.
Paradigms	Paradigms are general theories or perspectives that are embraced and form a systematic and relatively rigid way of processing information.
Others	This listing is meant to be illustrative, not exhaustive. A wide variety of default settings exists. When considering a situation, look for whatever important covert influences exist.

DISCUSSION
"Default settings" are largely covert influences upon thought and action. Analyzing these patterns of response can provide a better understanding of how people think and act.

Beyond conventional negotiation

Although a wide variety of methods for forging agreements exist, they are not always effective. Some disagreements are so great that the involved parties cannot easily form a working relationship even when doing so is in their mutual interest.

Within the mainstream world, three systems have arisen that expand beyond the usual processes of negotiation. They include, mediation, arbitration, and litigation. After these commonly employed options have been reviewed, a separate section is devoted to alternatives (collectively referred to as "indigenous conflict resolution") that arises from the cultural traditions of the people involved.

Mediation (Boulle 2009) is a system of resolving conflicts by employing the services of a mutually trusted third party(s) who helps others to resolve problems, disagreements, and so forth. Not serving as counselors or advisors for only one partisan group, the facilitator(s) maintains a neutral stance, striving to help all involved parties to better understand the situation and the options that are available to resolve it. In some circumstances, a mediator has expert knowledge regarding the specific issue under dispute. Under these circumstances, mediators are sometimes referred to as conciliators.

The proceedings that result from mediation or conciliation are typically not binding (as is the case in arbitration and litigation) unless the parties decide to forge a formal settlement when the mediation proceedings are successful. The matters under discussion, furthermore, tend to remain private (as opposed to legal proceedings where the facts and actions become part of the public record). In many places, mediation has emerged as a profession that typically requires formal training and certification.

Although parties enter into mediation with the hope and expectation of finding a workable solution, resolving the issue is not compulsory or mandated. Participants, therefore, may unilaterally walk away from the proceedings at any point and for any reason. The simple fact that the parties are willing to seek mediation, however, tends to indicate that they want a resolution and that a good chance of success exists.

In many pre-industrial, rural, and small-scale societies, local leaders, elders, or other respected individuals have long functioned in a role that closely parallels mediators. When this is true, such communities are likely to feel comfortable with this method of conflict resolution. Where this is true, local people may be willing to accept mediation instead of relying upon systems (such as arbitration or litigation) that are more formal and potentially alienating.

Styles of mediation can be developed that account for the distinctiveness of the participants. A method of mediation within education, known as "peer mediation," for example, employs fellow students as mediators. Being similar to the disputants, these peers are potentially better able to understand the situation and broker a solution. The same "peer approach" can potentially be adopted when people from distinct cultural backgrounds seek to resolve a conflict or dispute.

Mediation is a "non-adversarial" method of resolving disputes in which the goal is not to assign blame and responsibility, but to forge solutions. Indigenous systems of conflict resolution often follow this approach. Thus, Native American court systems tend to focus upon mitigating problems and reducing pain or tension instead of being preoccupied with who is "right" or "wrong" (personal knowledge from working with Alaska Native courts).

A key technique used by many Native American peoples is the "talking circle" in which all interested participants are given the floor and allowed to speak without interference in a manner that often leads to non-argumentative brainstorming regarding how to resolve the conflict. As the talking circle example suggests, indigenous, ethnic, and rural peoples might be comfortable with a mediation-style of conflict resolution because they tend to practice methods that are analogous to it.

An emerging and innovative approach to mediation that has evolved in the developed West is "party directed mediation" (Billikopf 2014) that involves the facilitator(s) dealing with each party separately in "pre-caucus" meetings in order to improve their abilities to effectively present their points of view. This preliminary coaching allows all the stakeholders to more effectively articulate their concerns and demands. This type of preparation can be of value to participants who need to be groomed and coached; many indigenous, ethnic, and rural people fall into this category because they are not experienced with dealing with the mainstream world and its methods in formal ways.

Transformative mediation (Bush and Pope 2002) looks at conflict as a crisis in communication. The goal of this specialized approach is to improve the abilities of the parties to communicate, understand the issues, and reduce negative and hostile feelings, while gaining the ability to interact in productive ways. Because cultural differences can lead to misunderstanding, this focus is of potential value.

Thus, mediation provides a range of practical techniques for resolving conflicts that are widely used in the Western and developed regions. It is voluntary and not legally binding, but it often leads to a fruitful resolution of differences. Although not a product of the indigenous, ethnic, or rural communities, mediation shares important characteristics of conflict resolution methods that are practiced by many such peoples. Table 3.4 depicts mediation.

Mediation, therefore, is a voluntary system that many indigenous, ethnic, and rural people can be comfortable with. The risks of involvement are low because no mandated actions will result from being involved with the process.

Arbitration: In arbitration (Steven and Sheffrin 2003), the participants allow a neutral third party to pass judgment regarding the matter under

Table 3.4 Mediation

Issue	Analysis
Characteristics	Mediation is voluntary, not binding. Parties are involved because they choose to participate. Not participating or withdrawing from mitigation are options. The action is private and details are not disclosed to the public.
Benefits	Parties have greater control over how the issues will be discussed and they are not obligated to accept a solution unless they choose to do so. Many indigenous, ethnic, and rural peoples might already practice methods that are analogous to mediation and feel comfortable with the process. A specific proceeding might be conducted in a culturally sensitive manner.
Drawbacks	There is no guarantee that the issue will be resolved. Parties cannot be forced to participate.

DISCUSSION
Mediation is a risk-free approach because there is no requirement to follow the suggestions or decisions made during the process. If the method is conducted in culturally sensitive ways, it might avoid intimidating or alienating participants.

discussion. The resulting decision, furthermore, becomes legally binding and enforceable by the courts. The term "non-binding arbitration" is sometimes heard, but is not employed in this discussion (where the term "mediation" is reserved for non-binding forms of alternative conflict resolution). "Arbitration" is used when referring to situations where definitive and obligatory rulings are made that cannot be rejected (except under extraordinary circumstances).

Arbitration is often used as a substitute for court actions, although (as with mediation) the findings are not public. A facilitator (or in some cases a panel) renders judgment. The format, process, and "feel" of the proceedings often resembles a trial, although typically streamlined and quicker. Nonetheless, rules of evidence, and so forth, apply. The arbitrating official (or panel) makes a decision that the parties are not able to reject. The judgments tend to be final.

In some cases, a contract or prior arrangement might stipulate that disagreements will be resolved via arbitration. Where such a requirement does not exist, parties are free to reject an offer to arbitrate. Once the parties choose to participate in arbitration, however, decisions are final, enforceable, and they cannot be denied or ignored.

Those who consider entering into this need to be very careful in order to ensure that the arbitrators who make decisions are culturally competent.

One advantage of arbitration is that the parties often have a degree of control over who will pass judgment. In court proceedings, in contrast, the parties probably have little control over who will preside as judge and they have only limited influence over the makeup of the jury. This situation might put indigenous, ethnic, and rural people at a disadvantage because the decision makers might not be adequately familiar with the cultural and situational context of the case. If arbitration is chosen, in contrast, those involved are likely to have a greater say in choosing who will render judgment.

As with mediation, arbitration is relatively speedy, cheap, and the findings are confidential (see Table 3.5).

Arbitration can be viewed as a middle ground between non-binding mediation and the court system. It operates outside the legal framework but does so in a manner that is reminiscent of legal proceedings. The system often provides a means of ensuring that culturally sensitive individuals will decide the case. It is relatively cheap and quick.

Litigation: In everyday language, litigation is said to take place when someone is sued in court. These actions are civil, not criminal in nature. In litigation, a "plaintiff" claims to have been damaged or hurt by the actions of a "defendant." As a result, some sort of remedy or compensation is demanded from the defendant.

If the plaintiff is successful, the court will require the defendant to do something that might range from providing compensation to adhering to the demand that requires the defendant to do (or not to do) something. A

Table 3.5 Arbitration

Issue	Analysis
Characteristics	Binding. Formal. Court-like. Findings are private and are not made known to the public.
Benefits	Quick and cheap. The ability to choose arbitrators that are culturally sensitive potentially exists in some cases.
Drawbacks	Some participants might not feel comfortable with the Western, court-like format. Care may need to be taken to ensure the arbitrator(s) is culturally competent. Appealing or overturning a decision is difficult.

DISCUSSION
Although arbitration outwardly resembles court action, it is distinct from it. It is a streamlined method of resolving differences that is not public.
Arbitration is often preferred because it is cheap and quick. Some contracts specify that disputes will be resolved via arbitration. Indigenous, ethnic, and rural people may need to be careful to ensure that if arbitration takes place, it will be conducted in a culturally competent manner.

"declarative judgment," for example, (Bray 2010) sets the record straight in order to prevent further disagreements.

Although people and organizations are typically sued, it is often possible for an individual or group to sue a government or public entity. The Maya of Belize, for example, have recently sued their government and won.

In general, a lawsuit begins when the court receives a complaint that asserts that the plaintiff(s) has been injured by the defendant for reasons that are provided and discussed. Selecting the particular court that will hear the case is often a key strategic move. This is known as "choosing the proper venue." In Alaska (USA), for example, Native, State, and Federal courts might all have potential jurisdiction if Alaska Natives are involved. Once a case has been started, furthermore, there is a tendency for the other courts to honor the jurisdiction of that court and not get involved. Because of this common practice, future litigants often initiate a lawsuit in the venue that is most beneficial to them. This tactic is known as "racing to the courthouse."

After this initial paperwork has been completed, the plaintiff is given a "summons" and a copy of the complaint that is officially and ceremoniously delivered to the defendant. This document notifies the defendants regarding the nature of the lawsuit and states details, such as when the individual must appear in court, and so forth.

The actual trial, of course, is a complicated matter that is typically the realm of professionally trained lawyers. No advice will be given here because a little knowledge is a dangerous thing. In general, the burden is upon the plaintiff to prove that damage was done by the defendant and the job of the defense team is to derail that effort. All sorts of complicated procedures exist that lawyers strategically use to accomplish their respective goals. Eventually a judge or a jury renders the verdict. After that, a lengthy and complicated appeals process potentially begins.

All of this is typically costly and time consuming. Lacking adequate funding, many potential plaintiffs are unable to take legal action. Large firms, for example, possess the resources needed to document wrongdoing and to sue individuals who violate copyright and intellectual property rights. Members of small indigenous, ethnic, and rural enclaves, in contrast, are often not able to gather evidence and fund a court action even when they have a valid claim. As a result, these small and weak entities are denied the protection that is readily available to large and rich organizations.

Those rendering judgments, furthermore, may not be familiar with the situations faced by indigenous, ethnic, and rural peoples. When those responsible for rendering verdicts lack adequate knowledge of the situation or the people involved, potential inequity can result that needs to be forcefully addressed and mitigated. Those considering lawsuits are urged to be aware of this potential problem and, where necessary, devise ways to diminish it.

Under some circumstances, furthermore, a court case may be a precedent setting and/or be used to clarify a law. Where such a situation exists, the

Table 3.6 Litigation

Issue	Analysis
Characteristics	Legal, formal, costly, time consuming, Appeal possible.
Benefits	Becomes part of the public record. If the "race to the courthouse" is successful, a good venue may be available. Decision can set a precedent.
Drawbacks	Costly. Time consuming. Appeals may stretch out over a long period. Relatively little control over who will decide the case.

DISCUSSION
Litigation (suing) is complicated, costly, time consuming, and risky. Court cases, however, may resolve issues in ways that set precedents that help other people in similar situations.

decision rendered in one litigation may help many other people to gain equitable treatment. This benefit does not occur when mediation and arbitration are used to resolve conflicts, because these proceedings are outside of the law. Table 3.6 describes litigation.

Thus, a variety of methods of conflict resolution exist in the mainstream world. "Alternative methods" include mediation and arbitration. Legal remedies and the court system are always available. A problem, however, may be that these options tend to be products of the mainstream culture and, therefore, they are potentially insensitive to the needs and perspective of indigenous, ethnic, and rural peoples.

Indigenous conflict resolution

Local people often benefit by embracing the techniques of negotiation and conflict resolution that have been developed by outsiders. An alternative exists in which the proceedings of a conflict resolution activity adhere to a peoples' traditional methods of social control and negotiation. This strategy has a long history and it has been effective in diverse places.

After the "fall of Roman Empire" in AD 476, for example, the Latin people were allowed to continue using Roman law among themselves (although special rules applied when others were involved). Odvacor, whose regime replaced the Empire, obviously understood that a people are subtly and intimately connected to their legal tradition and he allowed it to continue functioning.

Jumping forward to the modern colonial era, the British Empire's policies of controlling and administering its territories typically involved maintaining the existing regimes and methods of control as long as loyalty to England existed. Due to this administrative strategy, local and indigenous codes of law and conflict resolution were largely preserved.

In the United States, indigenous peoples are viewed as dependent, internal nations that retain the right to maintain their own systems of law and social control. All of these examples demonstrate that a long tradition of validating and nurturing local social control goes back to ancient times and survives to this day.

Depending upon the region or country where a dispute takes place, indigenous courts may or may not exist. Where they do function, however, certain limitations have probably been imposed by the sovereign government. In the United States, for example, the "Major Crimes Act" gives Native courts only limited authority in criminal cases, although in civil matters jurisdiction has not been significantly undermined.

An alternative to unique traditions, however, asserts that a universal and culturally free system of law and conflict resolution should replace the local heritage. The Age of Enlightenment, that dominated eighteenth century thought, provides a classic example of that policy. The justification for universal standards was based upon the belief that rational legal systems are superior to those that spring from tradition or emotion. These superior methods, the logic continues, should be universally applied.

A self-conscious experiment of policy and strategy that reflects the quest for universal and rational legal systems is the Napoleonic Code. After coming to power, Napoleon commissioned a panel of respected jurists to create a legal framework that would be rational, consistent, objective, efficient, and fair to all. When Napoleon conquered a territory, the resulting Code was introduced as the new law of the land. Of all his achievements, Napoleon was most proud of this legal system, observing, "My true glory is not to have won 40 battles ... what will live forever is my Civil Code" (Wanniski 1998: 184).

Nonetheless, dissatisfaction arose. Complaints emerged that laws are not merely rational, objective, and universal rules. Alien legal frameworks might also possess a specific cultural content that conflicts with the people and their ways of life. Speaking about Catalonia, Enric Prat de la Riba (1998) observes that people "spoke of law as a live entity, which is spontaneously produced by national consciousness.... They said that law and language were both manifestations of the same national spirit ..." In this way, the vision of an impartial, culture-free, and universal law was challenged. As an alternative, Napoleon's universal code of law was depicted as a thwarting and alien artifact, not as a universal and liberating tool. According to this view, local and cultural codes should be preserved.

Are mainstream methods of negotiation and conflict resolution following in the path of the Napoleonic Code? Apparently so, because they can easily be viewed as a generic system that strives for universal application while ignoring the full context within which decisions take place.

Alternatives to universal strategies include relying upon rules, codes of behavior and methods of conflict resolution that already exist in regions and communities. When talking about mediation, for example, the point was made that it is often analogous to the mechanisms that already exist and function within local communities. As a result, this type of approach may be successful in these environments. Despite parallels, however, mainstream mediation is an intrusive, outside set of techniques that are imported. As a result, mediation might not adequately mesh with local peoples and the challenges they face.

A more culturally and regionally sensitive approach is to employ techniques that exist locally instead of relying upon outside methods that resemble them in some ways. Initiatives that strive to do so are collectively known as indigenous conflict resolution. A useful review of these techniques is provided by Carlo Osi in his "Understanding Indigenous Dispute Resolutions and Western Alternative Dispute Resolution" (2008), a monograph-length article appearing in the *Journal of Conflict Resolution*.

Indigenous conflict resolution mechanisms employ local and traditional systems for dealing with problems between people. Doing so can be an effective means of sidestepping potential tensions that could otherwise be caused by outside governmental, court, military, or police involvement, and/ or interference. This tactic can provide significant benefits where political strife exists and/or where hostility to outside influences or pressures might arise.

This process (which tends to be tailored to particular regions, groups, and circumstances) often seeks to build a broad consensus through a process of open discussions. In many small-scale societies, for example, the opinions of respected elders typically exert significant influence. "Elders," of course, are not merely old people; they are revered role models who have won the respect of the community and, perhaps, serve as informal ambassadors for their cultures, societies, and traditional ways of life.

Disputants are often more willing to accept the opinions of esteemed local leaders than the advice of outsiders. Even though such homegrown advisors tend to have no formal "authority," they often wield great clout. When indigenous conflict resolution is successful (often with the involvement of such informal leaders), tensions may be resolved and unity built. Respected local leaders (elders and so forth) are often invaluable in this regard.

Caution may need to be taken under some circumstances because a wide range of initiatives (such as those involving the roles of women) might be at odds with local traditions. Such initiatives can fail if they attempt to accomplish too much too quickly. Today such issues are important points of contention and opinions are often heated. Great care needs to be exercised under such circumstances.

The United Nations Millennium Development Goals (United Nations ND), for example, was designed to alleviate poverty in developing countries. Part of its agenda involves advocating for women's rights in areas including education and health issues (including birth control). Doing so has caused some regions, where tightly defined sexual roles exist, to reject these goals.

Thus, if campaigns of indigenous conflict resolution (such as those involving women's rights) violate the norms of a significant segment of the population where they are being introduced, resistance might develop. When attempting to address reformist agendas using indigenous dispute resolutions, risks and potential tradeoffs might need to be considered.

Outside organizations (such as partnering companies), furthermore, may hesitate to use these systems because of a lack of familiarity with them. These outsiders might be especially leery if the judgments are binding. Outside organizations, however, might be willing to participate in such discussions if they function as a form of mediation that is not binding. In many cases, adhering to local traditions (even in a non-binding manner) can build greater understanding and trust on both sides (see Table 3.7).

Indigenous conflict resolution involves using local traditions to settle disagreements. It is often employed as a technique to help the people of a region to address their arguments in a familiar way that is understood and respected.

These methods can be of potential value when outsiders seek to address tensions, misunderstandings, and clashes with local communities. When doing so, the outsiders overtly show respect for the people they are dealing with. Although these outsiders will probably hesitate to use these grassroots forms of resolution in ways that result in binding obligations, these methods might be useful in building the rapport and understanding that can provide insights needed for constructive action.

Table 3.7 Indigenous conflict resolution

Issue	Analysis
Characteristics	Based on local traditions. Typically administered locally. Cultural leaders, such as elders, may play a significant role.
Benefits	Often more concerned with results, not determining who is right or wrong. Culturally appropriate. There is a greater chance the findings will be respected by local people.
Drawbacks	Not precedent setting. Outsiders might not want to be bound by findings.

DISCUSSION
Although other methods, such as mediation, may resemble or be analogous to it, indigenous conflict resolution embraces the mechanisms and traditions of a people. It deals with issues at a grassroots, local level and often gains local consensus as a result.

Conclusion and discussion

The usual techniques of negotiation are often unable to deal with all sensitive issues. Conflict is universal because people have different goals, needs, and vulnerabilities. Thus, disagreements between both individuals and groups are often inevitable. This is natural.

Poorly managed conflict can lead to hostility that undercuts cooperation. Well managed conflict, on the other hand, may foster understanding, mutual respect, and can lead to equitably resolving issues in a manner that leads to future harmony.

Mainstream methods of resolving conflicts include mediation arbitration, and litigation that range from non-binding discussions to legal actions with verdicts that are enforceable by law. Although these mainstream methods are well known, on some occasions, techniques based upon local traditions may suffice or be preferable. When this is the case, a system of indigenous dispute resolution may be most appropriate.

Relevant terms

Accommodating: A style of conflict typified by an "I lose, You win" approach.

Age of Enlightenment: An intellectual movement of the eighteenth century that focused upon rational thought and action.

Alternative conflict resolution: A general term referring to any means of resolving conflicts that does not rely upon legal or court procedures.

Arbitration: An alternative method of conflict resolution in which an arbitrator (or panel of arbitrators) is authorized to render a binding decision.

Avoiding: A style of conflict typified by a "No winners, no losers" approach.

Collaborating: A style of conflict typified by an "I win, you win" approach.

Competing: A style of conflict typified by an "I win, you lose" approach.

Compromising: A style of conflict typified by a "You give, I give" approach.

Culture: A "default setting" based on a wide range of learned behavior.

Default settings: People often respond in patterned and structured ways simply out of habit, inertia, or tradition. These actions can be viewed as "default settings."

Elders: Esteemed members of traditional cultures who serve as role models and whose opinions are respected, although they tend to have no official role. They often help to resolve conflicts.

Indigenous conflict resolution: A method of conflict resolution that exists in local communities, but is not recognized by the laws of the sovereign nation, nor is it a conventional alternative dispute resolution mechanism that is practiced by the mainstream population.

Litigation: An alternative to negotiation in which one party sues the other in court in order to seek relief for damages supposedly caused by the other party.

Mediation: An alternative method of conflict resolution that is voluntary. The mediator attempts to help the parties work through their differences to find a resolution.

Napoleonic Code: A code of laws, intended to be fair and objective, that were introduced in regions where France gained political power. Opponents complained that legal frameworks are culturally loaded and should not be universally applied.

Paradigms: A default setting that refers to the models or basic theories people use to view the world.

United Nations Millennium Development Goals: A statement of goals that focuses upon strategies to reduce poverty and sickness worldwide, especially in the Third World.

Values: Values are socially acceptable standards regarding what is important, acceptable, revered, and so forth. They are culturally defined.

References

Billikopf, Gregorio (2014). *Party Directed Mediation: Facilitating Dialogue Between Individuals* (Berkley CA: University of California Press).

Boulle, Laurence (2009). *Mediation: Principles Processes, Practice*, 2nd edition (Australia: Butterworth).

Bray, Samuel (2010). "Preventative Adjudication" *University of Chicago Law Review*, 77, 1275.

Bush, R. A. B. and Pope, S. G. (2002). "Changing the Theoretic Underpinnings of Mediation: Implications for Practice and Policy" *Pepperdine Dispute Resolution Law Journal*, (3)1, 39–65.

Prat de la Riba, Enric (1998). *La nacionalitat catalana*, 4th edition (Barcelona: Edicions 62), 46. Quoted from Jacobson, Stephen (2002). "Law and Nationalism in Nineteenth-Century Europe: The Case of Catalonia in Comparative Perspective" *Law and History Review* (summer).

Osi, Carlo (2008). "Understanding Indigenous Dispute Resolution Processes and Western Alternative Dispute Resolution" *Journal of Conflict Resolution*, 52, 164–229.

Sullivan, Arthur and Sheffrin, Steven M. (2003). *Economics: Principles in Action* (New Jersey: Pearson).

Thomas, Kenneth (1976). *Handbook of Industrial and Organizational Psychology* (Chicago: Rand McNally).

Walle, Alf H. (2013). *Rethinking Business Anthropology: Cultural Strategies in Marketing and Management* (Sheffield: Greenleaf).

Wanniski, Jude (1998). *The Way the World Works* (Washington, DC: Regnery Gateway).

Chapter 4

Creating an atmosphere of empowerment

Learning objectives

The term "indigenous" and its implications are expanding in ways that ethnic groups applaud and nations fear. Strategies of economic and social development, furthermore, often trigger hurtful and disruptive changes even while providing benefits. Strategies are discussed that offer empowerment and equity including **Community-based natural resource management** (that involves governments and local peoples co-managing resources in mutually acceptable ways). In other situations, ethnic enclaves are unilaterally asserting political, social, and economic rights that predate the authority of the current political regime. These strategies, practiced independently or in tandem, offer a potential for empowerment.

Specific learning objectives include:

1   Realizing that the term "indigenous" is evolving and expanding.
2   Recognizing trends towards local and equitable empowerment.
3   Be aware of the tragedy of the commons paradigm, critiques of it and their importance.
4   Identifying adversarial methods for gaining empowerment.
5   Placing these initiatives within a cultural and economic context.

The expansion of indigenousness

In recent years, initiatives have emerged that seek to increase and/or more clearly define the rights of indigenous populations. On September 13, 2007, the United Nations "Declaration on Rights of Indigenous Peoples" was passed by a vote of 111 in favor and four (the United States, Canada, Australia, and New Zealand) against (United Nations General Assembly 2007). Since the original passage, Australia has signed the agreement.

Key elements of the declaration include (The Charter of Human Responsibilities 2007):

1   Indigenous Peoples have the right to self-determinism and to determine their political status.
2   The right to distinct political, legal, economic, social and cultural institutions, while retaining the right to participate in the life of the state.
3   Right to establish educational systems and provide education in their own languages.
4   The Right to practice and teach spiritual traditions, to protect privacy of cultural sites and control ceremonial objects, and rights to repatriation of human remains.
5   Shall not be forcibly removed from their lands or territories.
6   The Right to development and to determine priorities for their lands, territories or other resources.
7   The Right to determine the responsibilities of individuals to their communities.

Although the declaration has no legal force, it does point to a growing concern regarding the rights of indigenous peoples.

In many parts of the world, indigenous people are "Third World" descendants of the original pre-colonial populations that remain in the majority in their land even though outsiders might dominate political, financial, and/or economic activities. Other geographic regions (sometimes called the "Fourth World") have experienced patterns of massive immigration that resulted in the indigenous population being reduced to a small minority in what was once their land. Although some writers use the term "Fourth World" to refer to the world's poorest countries, here it is used to refer to places where indigenous people who have been reduced to minorities due to outside patterns of migration (as is the case in the United States, Australia, New Zealand, Canada, and some other countries such as Belize). The fact that the dissenting votes regarding the Declaration on Rights of Indigenous Peoples all come from Fourth World countries indicates that different circumstances can cause divergent patterns of response regarding indigenousness.

The United States, for example, voiced concern with and voted against the declaration because a clear meaning of the term "indigenous" has not been agreed upon. In particular, the United States observed "[Because of] endless conflicting interpretations and debate about its application, as already evidenced by the numerous complex interpretive statements ... the United States could not lend its support to such a text" (United Nations General Assembly 2007).

Concern about a vague understanding and lack of agreement regarding the meaning of "indigenous" is problematic and potentially disruptive. The situation of the former residents of the Chagos archipelago, for example, demonstrates the uncertainty that exists regarding an operational definition of the term, its legal implications, and how it might evolve in the future.

In the 1960s, the residents of the Chagos Islands were evicted after the British government inappropriately depicted them as contract workers even though their ancestors had been in residence since the seventeenth century. The British goal was to depopulate the area in order to lease it to the United States for the construction of a military installation. Ultimately, the refugees took legal action and prevailed in court (although various obstacles continue that inhibit their return).

In court proceedings, the Chagos Islanders have routinely been depicted as indigenous. Thus, a document presented to the Parliament of the United Kingdom by Minority Rights Group International (2008) observed:

> Based on its 40 years of working with indigenous communities world-wide, MRG is of the view that the Chagossians do indeed constitute an indigenous people. The UK's duty towards the Chagossians must therefore be upheld in line with the rights of indigenous peoples' rights under international law.

This conclusion was reached after consulting criteria commonly used to evaluate claims of indigenous identity that includes:

1   Communal attachments to "place"
2   Historical precedence
3   Experience of severe disruption, dislocation and exploitation
4   "Historical continuity"
5   Ongoing oppression/exclusion by dominant societal groups
6   Distinct ethnic/cultural groups; and
7   Self-identification as indigenous peoples.

Having stated these criteria, the Minority Rights Group International continues by observing:

> It is commonly understood that most communities will not be able to satisfy all criteria; but such approaches create a sliding scale of indigenousness for the purposes of assessment. If a given societal group can establish its status as an indigenous people it will be able to access the evolving canon of indigenous rights in international law.

Governments, hoping to minimize claims involving indigenous status, in contrast, have long preferred a system of evaluation where if any single criterion does not meet the standard of "indigenous" the claim can be denied. Today, however, this rigid yardstick of evaluation appears to be weakening because judgments are increasingly based upon a balancing of the evidence, not the idea of a lone criterion invalidating a claim of indigenous status.

The further significance of the Chagos Islanders case rests on the fact that the people are descended from plantation workers who were imported to the islands by the French in the eighteenth century. Thus, members of this ethnic group have been viewed as indigenous even though their residence on the land does not predate the era of Western expansion and is, in fact, an artifact of it. Apparently, an indigenous status is becoming less related to pre-colonial ties to the land. This is a profound relaxation of a keystone criterion of indigenousness. With the "in residence prior to Western expansion" hurdle removed, a wide number of ethnic enclaves that were once merely viewed as distinctive ethnic minorities can make claims for an indigenous status that otherwise would be untenable.

Up until now, calculating who may be called indigenous has been relatively easy, especially when dealing with lands first visited by Europeans during the age of discovery. In the New World, for example, those living in the Americas when Columbus arrived (and their descendants) are candidates for indigenous status and no one else. In other parts of the world (Asia, Africa, the Middle East, etc.) where people have migrated freely over many centuries, the situation can become increasingly blurred and complicated. (Apparently, such concerns led a number of African countries to be leery of the "Declaration on Rights of Indigenous Peoples," although they eventually ratified it).

Nonetheless, until very recently the term "indigenous" has almost universally referred to cultures and peoples who have a long-term connection with a land that predates the modern era of political, economic, and demographic disruptions. No doubt, the more restrictive use of the term will not be abandoned by those who seek to minimize or defeat the claims that specific people are indigenous and deserving of rights and privileges as a result. Nonetheless, the obstacles in claiming an indigenous status appear to be weakening.

As Janet (2002: 121) has emphasized, the contemporary view of "indigenous" arose as a practical matter that was designed to deal with issues that existed after World War II when the United Nations was formed. Specifically, the impacts of Western colonialism and invasion were the prior issue being addressed in that era. In recent years, however, gaps have arisen in this arbitrary definition. Perhaps the time has come to rethink or expand what is meant by indigenous, its implications, and its significance.

All of this is a nightmare for governmental officials who, understandably, fear that although they may not have done nothing wrong or out of the ordinary, large chunks of their nation's sovereignty are suddenly up for grabs. This rising ambiguity and its consequences was dramatized when the United States voted against the Declaration on Rights of Indigenous Peoples precisely because of these problems. Such claims and counterclaims potentially impact many negotiations between indigenous (or self-proclaimed indigenous) peoples in their dealings with nations (and/or third parties operating under governmental authority).

In summary, the definition of indigenous is evolving and expanding. This situation places governments in an awkward and risky situation when devising strategies for resolving claims that are related to an indigenous status. In the past, governments could more accurately calculate if they had obligations to a specific people because who was eligible to claim an indigenous status was reasonably well defined and the criteria were not shifting. Given this security, governments felt comfortable pursuing economic development projects, making concessions to investors, and so forth. Today, a greater ambiguity appears to be emerging that might have a chilling impact upon economic development and the ability to attract investment capital.

This situation, however, may give people with an unresolved claim to indigenous status an added edge when negotiating with governments because they might be willing to resolve issues with compromises instead of risking a legal challenge in an adversarial action. Table 4.1 presents conflicting visions of indigenousness.

Thus, the definition of indigenous appears to be evolving in ways that potentially trigger significant power shifts. A broader definition and a relaxing of the criteria used to grant an indigenous status will benefit ethnic groups seeking the rights and protections that an indigenous status potentially provides. These people advocate for the establishment of such liberalized criteria. Governments, in contrast, tend to fear they will lose sovereignty and, as a result, they oppose such changes. Only time will reveal what eventually develops.

Community-based resource development

Even though the debate regarding the definition of "indigenous" and its implications continues, decisions must be made and initiatives pursued. On many occasions, sovereign nations (and those who work under their authority) need the cooperation of local people. Gaining collaboration, however, is often difficult especially if the priorities and habits of local people are ignored or at odds with governmental policies. This type of conflict often arises in conjunction with some type of conservation effort, such as initiatives to preserve wildlife by forbidding (or severely limiting) subsistence activities such as hunting.

When governments implement plans, gaining the cooperation of all relevant stakeholders is vital because otherwise local people can ignore, reject, and/or circumvent public policies. Policing these violations may be difficult and costly, if not impossible.

One promising approach for dealing with such challenges involves the government partnering with local people in order to better insure support and compliance. Community-based natural resource management (CBNRM) involves governmental strategies that empower local people by giving them a degree of self-determinism. These concessions are granted in order to enlist local cooperation and support.

Table 4.1 Visions of indigenousness

Issue	Analysis
Tradition view	The current use of the term "indigenous" was developed after World War II to deal with issues related to colonialism. As a result, "indigenous" came to refer to people who had connections to their homeland before the era of Western expansion. The definition possessed a number of criteria. In general, if a people do not meet all the criteria, the claim for an indigenous status can be defeated.
Emerging trends	The criteria needed to demonstrate an indigenous status are becoming less restrictive. Instead of a people being forced to satisfy all criteria, a more balanced view is being advocated in which claims of indigenousness are decided upon using a sliding scale. The key requirement that a people must have a connection to the land before the colonial era is being relaxed.
Implications	Long established benchmarks require a very high standard of proof in order to validate a claim of indigenous status. As a result, many people have been unable to satisfy these criteria and gain recognition as indigenous. Currently, less strict criteria are being suggested. Ethnic groups that aspire to indigenous status embrace these developments because they potentially enlarge their rights. Nations, fearing a loss of sovereignty, oppose them.

DISCUSSION

When the prevailing views of indigenous were codified, the United Nations was concerned with issues triggered by the colonial era, World War II, and its aftermath. Criteria which fit the needs of the late 1940s and early 1950s, appear to be obsolete. Attempts are being made to update and more accurately describe an indigenous status and its implications. Nations, understandably, are concerned that an evolving definition of indigenous potentially challenge their authority. People seeking indigenous status applaud these developments and hope to benefit from them.

CBNRM typically seeks grassroots compliance and participation for protecting vulnerable natural environments by (1) sharing the decision-making authority over how the land and its resources are to be managed and used while (2) allowing local stakeholders to benefit from the fruits of their home territory. These initiatives have often been successful.

Consider, for example, a largely untouched wilderness populated by exotic trophy animals, such as lions and elephants (much of this discussion is prompted by personal discussions with anthropologist Richard Lee). If the government unilaterally defines this area as a game preserve and outlaws all hunting, the local people will be denied their livelihood and traditional way of life. Under such circumstances, the indigenous population and the government can easily emerge as adversaries and poaching is likely to emerge as a locally condoned practice. The failure of the program is likely under such conditions.

If, in contrast, the government and local people work together, a win–win situation may be achieved. In Namibia, for example, the hunting of trophy animals continues, although the government sets strict quotas. Local people, furthermore, decide who will harvest the animals. Richard Lee recalls that in Namibia a small number of elephants are taken each year. Members of the community, furthermore, typically sell the hunting permits to wealthy sportsmen who pay a staggering sum for the privilege of "bringing down" an elephant. After the safari (which is also a source of revenue), these hunters tend to merely take the tusks or a trophy head. The meat is then distributed to the community. This arrangement keeps the number of elephants at an ideal level, interjects cash into the local economy, and provides free food to the local population. And because of management strategies and quotas, the arrangement is sustainable. The local people benefit as the continued existence of elephants in the region is ensured.

Not only is such an approach an admirable method of protecting the natural environment, it can also be used to protect cultural products such as the archaeological record by discouraging looting (Walle and Asgary 2015), As a result of the fact that these tactics can be used in ways that transcend the natural environment, it will be referred to as Community-based Resource Management (CBRM) (see Table 4.2).

Governments often enlist the help of local people in order to achieve goals and gain cooperation. Perhaps neither party will consider this to be an ideal situation, but view it as a practical compromise. In any event, greater cooperation and collaboration can occur.

CBRM in action

As discussed above, the use of CBRM tends to be viewed as the "devolution" or weakening of governmental and "top down" controls. In other words, decision making that previously took place within a purely governmental context by an administrative hierarchy is replaced by methods that are based on collaboration typically involving those who live close to and depend upon the resources being managed. This process is commonly called "co-management" and it is a crucial component of CBRM.

Berkes et al. (1991) emphasize that local-level management can result in responsible stewardship, contribute to cultural survival, and enhance social and economic development strategies. Unfortunately, barriers, such as distrust, patterns of dependency, paternalistic attitudes of outsiders, conflict of

Table 4.2 Community-based resource management

Issue	Analysis
Methods	A sovereign nation grants certain rights and incentives to local people so that they will be willing to participate in the co-management of assets and/or resources.
Goals	The sovereign nation seeks local cooperation in order to achieve its goals while the local community seeks the ability to use the resources of the region in productive ways that serves its needs.
Local gains	The elimination of strict governmental mandates and/or an opportunity to become part of the decision-making process.
Outsider gains	By giving local people a stake in governmental policies, the community can be enlisted as allies and supporters. As a result, achieving governmental goals becomes easier and more likely.

DISCUSSION
Creating alliances potentially provides benefits to both governments and local people. This arrangement can be used even if other disagreements exist (such as pending claims of an indigenous status). Each side gives up something while simultaneously gaining in ways that achieve mutual goals.

interest, etc. often exist. Due to the nature of indigenous life, furthermore, Berkes and Preston question the legitimacy of considering indigenous people to be just one of a long list of stakeholders and view them as a special group.

Richard Lee (personal communication) observes that while much good has come from co-management, it is primarily geared around the preservation of natural resources and strategies of sustainability involving the natural environment. Lee complains that this narrow focus can cause policymakers to turn a blind eye to cultural issues that simultaneously need to be addressed. Berkes et al.'s work demonstrates that the social, cultural, and economic health of indigenous people can be addressed via CBRM. Indigenous and rural people are urged to insist that cultural and social components are included in programs they are involved with.

CBRM seeks to achieve multiple goals that serve both local people and the larger nation. It does so by empowering communities to work with governments and the public sector for their mutual benefit. While the government has the ultimate say in how resources are used and harvested, its "top down" leadership is supplemented with "bottom up" decision making involving those who live in a region.

This type of shared decision making is particularly useful in situations where conflicting claims of ownership exist. Many indigenous people, for example, assert rights to the land that predate the current political regime. As a result, governmental intervention is viewed as an erosion of their heritage and an obstacle to their legitimate self-determinism. Nations, in contrast, are fearful that such trends will challenge their sovereignty.

CBRM potentially provides a mechanism that facilitates compromise and fruitful collaboration even if disagreements continue and have not been completely resolved. Indeed, this type of arrangement may encourage compromises that settle (or sidestep) claims and counter claims that, otherwise, would drag on in hurtful ways for years or decades.

CBRM allows indigenous and local people to reap the benefits of their homeland while simultaneously acting in accordance with public policies that reflect governmental strategies. The public sector encourages a responsible and sustainable use of the environment by partnering with the local people who live there. Such an arrangement is operationalized by combining a reasonable degree of governmental control over the land and its resources while granting an acceptable level of grassroots decision-making authority. Doing so encourages the collaboration of potentially rival stakeholders working jointly to satisfy the needs and goals of all interested parties

Indigenous and rural people are increasingly involved in CBRM initiatives. Although governments may be the ultimate decision makers, local communities help craft policies that serve their needs. Although the method may need to be expanded to more systematically deal with cultural issues, this approach demonstrates a means of empowering indigenous, ethnic, and rural peoples.

While this method has merit and potential, the "devil is in the details." What are the full implications of a CBRM program? How will it be implemented? Who will have authority over what? If disagreements occur, what mechanisms will be used to resolve them? When decisions are reached and letters of agreement are signed, great care needs to be taken. These details are outlined in Table 4.3.

In summary, CBRM is a method by which governments and local people collaborate in unified and constructive ways. On many occasions, harmony and long-term cooperation can be encouraged by doing so. In other situations, however, the government might maintain that the strategies used by local people are inherently destructive and must be opposed. The Tragedy of the Commons paradigm provides an intellectual justification for such conclusions.

The tragedy of the commons

Although working collectively has sometimes met with success, what potential problems exist when communities are allowed to manage resources? One of the seminal documents of contemporary environmental ethics and natural resource management is Garrett Hardin's provocative article "The Tragedy of

Table 4.3 Value and application of CBRM

Issue	Analysis
Description	Governments and local people co-manage a region or resource. In doing so, the government grants a degree of decision-making authority and the use of the resource to local people who, in turn, act in ways that mesh with governmental policies and strategies. The compromise can create a win-win situation.
Typical uses	Governmental actions potentially interfere with traditional uses of a resource. By partnering with local people, ways to avoid an adversarial relationship are developed.
Strengths	All stakeholders have a voice. Local people gain benefits. Tensions between the government and local people are reduced.
Weaknesses	Distrust and suspicion on both sides might continue.

DISCUSSION

CBRM is emerging as a means of reducing tensions and co-managing resources in ways that serve the needs of all impacted stakeholders. On many occasions, governmental policies are in conflict with the need, wants, and heritage of the local population. The resulting tension can lead to the failure of governmental policies while simultaneously undercutting cultural traditions, the local economy, and so forth. CBRM can provide a useful compromise that serves all stakeholders in an equitable manner.

the Commons" (1968). The basic message is that when a resource is communally or collectively owned and/or managed, it will inevitably be abused and degraded. Hardin presents his argument with reference to pasture land that is the common property of a community. According to Hardin, each herder, pursuing rational self-interest, will graze as many animals as possible. Such strategies invariably push the land beyond its carrying capacity, causing it to decline. Hardin suggests that alternative forms of ownership and land management are better able to ensure that the owner has a motive to treat the land in a responsible and sustainable manner.

Thus, if a specific herding family owns the land, its members will have an incentive to protect the resource and eliminate overgrazing. Or if the government dictates environmental policies, long-term strategies of sustainability could be more effectively pursued. As a result, Hardin's widely acknowledged paradigm can be used to suggest that collective ownership and management is likely to be non-sustainable; as a result, other options are more appropriate.

Because indigenous people often advocate collective strategies of ownership and management, "The Tragedy of the Commons" model seems to suggest that these traditional forms of resource management can easily result in degradation and ruin. As a corollary, eliminating communal arrangements and replacing them with alternative mechanisms (such as private ownership or strict governmental policies) seems to provide a better chance for true and lasting sustainability. Thus, the tragedy of the commons argument can suggest that traditional collective methods should be replaced by alternatives that grant ownership and/or control to specific groups that have a vested interest in sustainability.

In 1990, Feeny et al. reexamined Hardin's premise that collectively owned resources cannot be adequately sustained. Contradicting Hardin's predictions, specific cases were identified where collective ownership, usage, and/or management was compatible with sustainability. The discussion presents a taxonomy of property-rights systems and concludes that evidence made available since Hardin published "The Tragedy of the Commons" indicates that a range of local policies and strategies potentially encourage sustainability. That paper further emphasizes that issues, such as (1) the culture and traditions of a people and (2) the nature of the controlling institution, should be considered when the sustainability or non-sustainability of a particular option is being predicted.

These are important findings. Without them, it might incorrectly appear that collective ownership and decision making must be curtailed if sustainability is to be achieved. Apparently, however, this is not to be the case.

Continuing this chain of thought, Agrawal (1998) notes that many policymakers and governmental leaders tend to assume that local people typically act in ways that undercut conservation. This belief can lead policymakers to conclude that outside intervention, control, and even privatization are required. In other words, top down policymaking is viewed as superior to local decision making and control.

Agrawal provides another challenge to Hardin's conclusions. Analyzing forest management strategies of Himalayan villagers, he found that indigenous uses of the land can be rational and sustainable. Apparently, local people are capable of forging meaningful and effective solutions to the problems of sustainability.

The archaeological record also points to the fact that small bands may have the ability to create sustainable strategies of land usage even when larger and more complex societies cannot. Ancient Maya civilization, for example, proved to be unsustainable. Due to wide ranging factors, including the degradation of the environment, the ancient cities of the Maya world (Central America) collapsed and people adopted a new way of life based on smaller and more dispersed social units. Eventually, the damage caused by the unsustainable strategies of civilization were overcome as the environment renewed itself because people began living in greater harmony with their environment. In this case, small rural bands used the land in a sustainable fashion while advanced civilizations did not. The dialogue regarding the "Tragedy of the Commons" is presented as in Table 4.4.

Table 4.4 Tragedy of the commons

Issue	Analysis
Thesis	When assets are managed collectively, a situation exists where individual self-interest encourages people to treat the asset in a manner that leads to its destruction or degradation.
Argument for control	In order to prevent the destruction of the assets, strategies of management must be developed that mitigate the hurtful impacts that occurs when an individual exploits a collectively owned resource for personal gain. Options include private ownership or strict governmental controls leading to sustainability.
Alternative views	Evidence shows that indigenous and rural peoples do not inevitably act in ways that reflect the "Tragedy of the Commons" model. Examples exist where collectively owned assets are managed in sustainable ways.

DISCUSSION
The "Tragedy of the Commons" model has often been used to justify strict governmental controls and/or alternatives to collective ownership and management. Such conclusions and policies can easily be used to defend the extinguishing of local and indigenous rights. This theory, however, needs to be carefully evaluated before it is used to justify policy issues.

The "Tragedy of the Commons" model argues that collective ownership and management might lead to strategies of self-interest that result in resources being destroyed or degraded. This model appears to be closely aligned with the principles of neoclassical economics that involves rational actions that are designed to maximize individual gains. As we saw when discussing substantive economic systems, however, not all people operate in ways that reflect the neoclassical paradigm. It appears that where neoclassical responses do not dominate, the predictions of the "Tragedy of the Commons" model are likely to be in error.

Asserting local sovereignty

In the case of CBRM, the established government works with local people by providing a degree of decision-making authority to local people in order to gain their support and cooperation. The basic underlying strategy of this approach is that although the government does not officially surrender ultimate authority, it strategically chooses to share decision making and control.

Many indigenous peoples, in contrast, dispute the assertion that the current regime has legitimate sovereignty regarding them and the territory where they live. On occasion, such peoples seek to regain their rights and authority, asserting that these privileges predate the current political regime. In doing so, people claim an authority that overrides the sovereignty of contemporary nations.

Examples abound. In the United States, Native American groups (indigenous peoples of North America) are recognized as pockets of sovereignty within a larger nation. As a result, treaties and traditions regarding land use etc. are legally binding. Although the United States has its own distinct policies regarding indigenous claims, the basic principle that indigenous people possess distinct and un-extinguished rights because of their status is gaining wide international recognition.

In 2007, for example, two Maya villages in the Toledo District of Belize successfully sued their government to demand greater control over the land on which they live. The verdict upheld the Maya claim and concluded that their indigenous rights were stronger then the sovereignty of the nation.

While the Maya of the region believe that this test case sets a precedence that applies to the other Maya villages in the area, the government of Belize disagrees, concluding that the decision only holds sway over the two villages involved in the suit. As a result, additional litigation has taken place and legal proceedings continue.

The tactic the Belizean government uses in rebutting the Maya claims is to argue that the specific people in question are not indigenous people of Belize because they are descendants of immigrants who arrived in the 1880s to serve as plantation workers. As a result, the government reasons that although these people may be indigenous to Central America, they are not indigenous to Belize and, therefore, they are not eligible for special land rights and so forth. *The premise that indigenous people possess rights that trump sovereignty, however, is not challenged.*

In another example, the Mohawk Indians live in New York State and the Province of Ontario (straddling the border of the United States and Canada). Both countries have a history of demanding that members of this tribe declare their country of citizenship. Many Mohawks refuse to do so on the grounds that their identity (as Mohawks) predates the current political regimes and, therefore, their indigenous status takes precedence over USA or Canadian citizenship. In doing so, the Mohawk affirm that a new cultural and political entity has been superimposed upon their territory, but their rights remain. The debate goes on.

The Kurdish people of the Middle East face a similar situation. Their homeland (typically referred to as Kurdistan) is currently divided among a number of countries including Turkey, Iran, Iraq, and Syria. In each of these sovereign nations, the Kurds are a minority. If Kurdistan were united as a separate country, however, the Kurds would be in a solid majority. The Kurds, furthermore, have long pressured for the establishment of a Kurdish state (in a quest going back at least to the nineteenth century) and for a brief time after World War I a Kurdish country was established. Over the years, violence has periodically broken out over the issue of Kurdish independence with both sides suffering as a result.

In some cases (such as in Iraq), the national government has been accused of committing atrocities against the Kurds because of their ethnicity. Even when not treated harshly, many Kurds believe that their interests are not best served because of their minority status.

Many Kurds continue to pressure for the creation of a country of Kurdistan where the Kurds will have their own government and not suffer from a minority status. The nations that would have to give up territory to accomplish this goal, however, hesitate doing so. This situation is the cause of political unrest and international tension.

Nevertheless, the trend of local peoples to assert sovereignty is growing and can be presented in tabular form in Table 4.5.

Table 4.5 Asserting local sovereignty

Issue	Analysis
Description	Contemporary sovereign nations claim authority over their land. Indigenous people assert that they have rights that predate the establishment of the current regime that must be honored.
Typical uses	Indigenous populations assert rights challenging its sovereignty of the current regime in order to gain greater local control over the land, insure that certain rights are honored, and so forth.
Strengths	Increasingly, the definition of indigenous is being expanded in ways that potentially offers additional people the ability to assert local sovereignty. In addition, traditional patterns of land ownership and so forth are increasingly recognized as trumping the sovereign rights of nations that emerged in modern and colonial times. This trend often enhances claims of local sovereignty
Weaknesses	Even if a claim is upheld, actually gaining compliance can be difficult. The Chaos islanders, for example, have won their legal cases, but have still not been able to return home. Foreign countries challenging and interfering with the internal affairs of sovereign nations is highly unusual.

DISCUSSION

In the current era, indigenous, people are increasingly attempting to gain a greater degree of self-determinism. In addition, because the criteria used to define indigenous seems to be evolving, many people who were previously ineligible for indigenous status are seeking it. As a result, conflict regarding the sovereignty of nations and the rights of ethnic groups is growing.

Many peoples seek greater freedom and autonomy by claiming rights that predate the current political regime. In general, nations want to preserve the status quo while particular groups point to rights that they claim have never been extinguished, merely overridden and/or ignored by usurping regimes.

Proponents for indigenous rights speak of justice. A drawback is the fact that if the floodgate of claims and counterclaims is widely opened, nations and economies might be paralyzed because of the resulting doubt and indecision.

Strategic implications

Strategies and tactics involving indigenous, ethnic, and rural people need to adequately mesh with their goals, circumstances, and heritage. As a result, although standardized theories and methods provide valuable insights, they are not enough. Initiatives need to be envisioned with reference to the local, social, and cultural context.

Community-based Resource Management provides a route to empowerment that is offered by nations that are willing to share decision-making authority with local people. According to this sort of arrangement, the government abdicates a degree of ad hoc decision-making authority while officially maintaining sovereignty. On numerous occasions, local people have gained a degree of self-determinism and empowerment by embracing CBRM initiatives. Doing so, however, involves indigenous and rural people accepting (or at least not overtly challenging) the principle that governmental sovereignty prevails.

The alternative is for the people to declare that they possess rights that predate the existence of the contemporary nation that currently holds power. Although success can yield handsome results, failure can be painful, anger powerful forces that were unsuccessfully challenged.

In recent years, furthermore, the criteria used to define indigenous people appears to be becoming more relaxed, allowing a wider number of communities to assert unextinguished rights.

Although generic discussions of these options exist, they need to be considered from within a specific, local, and cultural context in which indigenous, ethnic, and rural people remain aware of the particular situation. A variety of methods for gaining empowerment and enhancing self-determinism exist. By choosing strategies carefully, the odds of success increase.

Relevant terms

Chagos Islanders: A people who have been declared to be indigenous even though their connection to the land does not predate the colonial era (and is actually an artifact of colonialism).

Community-based natural resource management: A method in which the government shares, decision making, and benefits deriving from the land with local people in order to gain cooperation and compliance regarding environmental and ecological issues.

Community-based resource management: A generalizing of community-based natural resource development that emphasizes that it can be used in ways that expand beyond, ecological, environmental, and natural resource initiatives.

Emerging trends of indigenous: A balanced view for determining indigenous status that views claims on a sliding scale.

Fourth World: A region where patterns of migration have made indigenous people a minority in their traditional homeland.

Local sovereignty: Local communities having control and decision-making authority over their region.

Third World: A region in which indigenous people remain in the majority even if they are socially and economically dominated by others.

Traditional view of indigenous: Indigenousness is determined by a number of variables that related to the fact that a people are an ongoing cultural/social entity that occupied the land before outside intervention (that typically began in colonial times). If any of the criteria cannot be verified, an indigenous status can be rejected.

"Tragedy of the Commons" model: Based on Garrett Hardin's work, the belief that communal ownership and management leads to resource destruction of degradation. This model can be used to justify outside control of resources.

United Nations Declaration on Rights of Indigenous Peoples: A non-binding resolution that attempts to clarify the rights that should be afforded to indigenous peoples. The United States did not vote in favor because the definition of indigenous was ambiguous.

Discussion questions

1   The criteria used to establish indigenous status appears to be changing. Why is this significant? Why do nations oppose such developments? What advantages do these trends provide to indigenous, ethnic, and rural peoples?

2   Discuss community-based natural resource development. How it is different from community-based resource development? How might nations benefit from using this method? How might local people benefit?

3   What is the basic argument of the "Tragedy of the Commons" paradigm? How can the perspectives derived from it be used in ways that undercut the self-determinism of local people? How has the "Tragedy of the Commons" model been challenged? How can this questioning be potentially important to indigenous, ethnic, and rural peoples?

4   On some occasions, peoples seek to use adversarial or confrontational methods in order to advance their rights. Discuss the pros and cons of

doing so. Indigenous people sometimes sue sovereign nations. What are the risks to the nations? What are the risks indigenous people accept when they do so?

5   Strategies of empowerment take place within a social and economic context. Discuss this reality with reference to a real or hypothetical issue involving indigenous people (or a group seeking indigenous recognition).

References

Agrawal, A. (1998). "The Community vs. the Market and the State: Forest Use in Uttarakhand in The Indian Himalayas." *Journal of Agricultural and Environmental Ethics*, 9(1), 1–15.

Berkes, F., George, P. and Preston, R. J. (1991). "Co-management: The Evolution in Theory and Practice of the Joint Administration of Living Resources." *Alternatives: Global, Local, Political*, 18(2): 12–17.

Charter of Human Responsibilities (2007). "UN Declaration on the Rights of Indigenous peoples." Retrieved March 24, 2010 from: www.charter-human-responsibilities.net/spip.php?article1411.

Feeny, D., Berkes, F., McCay, B. J., and Acheson, James M. (1990). "The Tragedy of the Commons: Twenty-two Years Later." *Human Ecology*, (1)19.

Hardin, Garrett. (1968). "The Tragedy of the Commons." *Science*, 162, 1243–1248.

Janet, Stephanie (2002). "Development, Minorities and Indigenous Peoples: A Case Study and Evaluation of Good Practice" (Minority Rights Group International).

Minority Rights Group International (2008). "Submission from the Minority Rights Group International." Select Committee on Foreign Affairs Written Evidence. Retrieved on March 24, 2010 from: https://publications.parliament.uk/pa/cm200708/cmselect/cmfaff/147/147ii.pdf.

Nafziger, E. W. (1977). *African Capitalism: A Case Study in Nigerian Entrepreneurship* (Stanford, CA: Hoover Institution).

United Nations General Assembly (2007). "General Assembly Adopts Declaration on Rights of Indigenous Peoples: Major Step Forward Towards Human Rights For all Says President." Retrieved March 24, 2010 from: www.un.org/News/Press/docs/2007/ga10612.doc.htm.

Walle, Alf and Asgary, Nader (2015). "Archaeological Tourism in the Middle East: A Community-based Resource Management model." *Journal of Middle Eastern Management*, 2(1).

Part II

Commonly used tools

Chapter 5

Strategic thought

Learning objectives

Two significant strategic activities involve deciding what business the organization is in and determining the degree to which outsiders will control, direct, and dictate important decisions. With these perspectives in mind, a representative sample of classic strategic orientations is discussed including (1) The Diffusion of Innovations Model, (2) The BCG Growth Market Share Grid, (3) The McKinsey Matrix, and (4) SWOT Analysis. These overviews are used to address issues regarding appropriate strategic planning choices that indigenous, ethnic, and rural people need to consider. In specific, the chapter will:

1   Focus upon what goals organizations seek to accomplish, the amount of autonomy given to specific divisions, and the degree to which upper management assumes control.
2   Introduce a representative sample of strategic tools that includes discussions of the contributions that they are designed to make and the limitations they might possess.
3   Consider the particular situations faced by indigenous, ethnic, and rural people and other relevant influences upon strategic planning.
4   Discuss ways to mitigate possibly negative side effects of particular strategies.
5   Examine useful alternatives that take the special needs of indigenous, ethnic, and rural people into account.

Introduction

Management guru, Michael Porter (1987) emphasizes that strategies improve when two basic questions are asked which can be paraphrased as (1) "What business is the organization in?" and (2) "How should the leaders or top management direct or oversee the organization's various activities?" Porter emphasizes that dealing with these issues in a self-conscious and appropriate manner is the key to success.

Properly answering these queries, however, can be difficult. Consider the challenge of fully understanding what business the organization is actually pursuing. Although seemingly self-evident, hurtful miscalculations can arise. In this regard, Theodore Levitt (1960) offers the example of the large railroads as they existed in the 1930s when people were just beginning to travel by air. In an attempt to establish themselves, the fledgling airlines sought to partner with the railroads that already possessed a network for attracting, serving, and booking passengers. Levitt observes that the railroad tycoons rejected such offers in the belief they were in the "railroad" not the "airline" business. In reality, Levitt emphasized, both the railroads and airlines are in the "transportation" business; rejecting the opportunity to participate in an emerging form of transportation led the railroads to abdicate the passenger portion of their industry to those who correctly saw a future in air travel.

After deciding (or, perhaps, coming to understand) what business an organization is pursuing, decisions should be made regarding the degree of control that top management assumes when strategies, tactics, and day-to-day planning takes place. The options range from allowing partners and subsidiaries to operate largely independently, on the one hand, to a centralized leadership that dominates the strategic and decision-making processes, on the other.

Having outlined these two issues, Porter (1987) discusses four basic tools of corporate strategy: (1) portfolio management, (2) restructuring strategies, (3) the transferring of skills, and (4) the degree to which activities are shared, In addition to these options, (5) outsiders might import models or strategies that were previously unknown in a region or community. Each of these alternatives is discussed below.

Portfolio theory: Those who follow a portfolio strategy pursue a strategic advantage through the process of diversification. In order to do so, organizations acquire a varied range of assets in order to spread risks and profit/loss potentials over a wide area. Under such circumstances, the role of top management is to invest broadly in order to widely disperse vulnerabilities in an attempt to stabilize profits over time. When such an arrangement exists, subsidiaries are often allowed a significant degree of autonomy as long as they perform in an adequate manner (however doing so is defined and evaluated).

A dominating outside organization that deals with indigenous, ethnic, and rural people using such a portfolio approach might not pressure people to change their manner of conducting business, their culture, traditions, ways of life, and so forth. As long as profit margins are maintained at an acceptable level, the status quo might be allowed to continue.

Although this "hands off policy" might permit or encourage organizational and cultural stability, it might also fail to benefit from the appropriate adoption of useful innovations, methods, and strategies that have been effective and productive elsewhere. Because innovative methods are often viewed as keys to success and effectiveness, a temptation to introduce these "improvements" often exists. As a result, dominant organizations typically seek to transform partners and subsidiaries by introducing refinements that were effective elsewhere. Three means of doing so are discussed below.

Restructuring strategies: On many occasions, a management team might seek to enhance performance or profitability by systematically and self-consciously introducing change. Thus, those who believe that the effectiveness of the organization is being held back by existing structures, procedures, and policies might mandate the use of new ideas and methods. Doing so is intended to unleash an unrealized potential. Under such circumstances, the relationships between people and the structure of the organization are overtly altered according to the demands of top management.

Modifications of this type are often appropriate, useful, and effective. A struggling business or organization, for example, might possess a strong potential for success but be relatively ineffective due to uncreative procedures, counterproductive organizational structures, and so forth. Outsiders, who envision this potential and possess a plan to introduce improvements might acquire the business at a low price due to its current lack-luster performance, facilitate needed changes, and see profits soar.

Hurtful ramifications, unfortunately, might arise if outsiders begin to manipulate important aspects in the lives of indigenous, ethnic, and rural peoples without understanding the full ramifications of doing so. Relationships between people are often structured in ways that transcend purely economic considerations; outsiders, however, might fail to recognize the relevance of these considerations. In such situations, undercutting or altering the status quo without adequate foresight and mitigation might be painful, destabilize the culture, and weaken local self-determinism. Regrettably, the outsiders who seek an economic transformation might fail to anticipate the disruption and pain potentially caused by their intervention. Although avoiding hurtful side effects needs to be a vital part of strategic planning, this important aspect of change can easily be overlooked.

Transferring of skills: Organizations often possess skills that can be applied in a wide variety of contexts. Because these abilities often provide what is perceived to be a competitive advantage, they are frequently introduced in a wide variety of contexts. Doing so is particularly commonplace when outside investors, decision makers, and consultants believe that they possess keys to success while assuming that others lack strategic savvy.

Although on some occasions, particular skills and methods might be usefully transferred, such options should be employed with care because existing patterns and traditions might be subtly intertwined into the social life of the community. When such social and economic interrelationships exist, introducing significant change might trigger unhealthy and painful side effects that need to be anticipated, avoided, and, mitigated.

Although introducing change may be a wise and viable strategy, the hurtful potentials of doing so needs to be recognized. Any likelihood for negative impacts should be identified and addressed. This possibility of undesirable ramifications is especially strong in situations where proposed changes are at odds with the traditions and heritage of the community.

A shortcut that is often used when introducing or transferring skills and methods involves hiring outsiders to dominate strategies, policies, and day-to-day operations. When indigenous, ethnic, and rural populations are not involved in such initiatives, the ability of local people to control their own destiny can be reduced. The opportunities for local people to rise to positions of authority under such circumstances can also be undermined. These trends can work against the best interests of the culture and the community.

Sharing of activities: Large organizations often gain a degree of efficiency by combining and/or sharing activities. An automobile company, for example, might operate more smoothly and efficiently by having all engineering activities performed to a centralized technical group, instead of allowing each division to maintain its own team. By doing so, the duplication of facilities and personnel can be eliminated and costs reduced.

The human resources function, is often more efficiently and cheaply managed when most of the work is conducted at one centralized location. Such a unified approach might provide upper management with a greater degree of control and access to information regarding personnel. In many cases, this kind of unified and centralized approach is cost effective and can be justified.

In situations where indigenous, ethnic, and rural peoples are involved, however, problems might develop. When specific groups of people are distinctive, they might not fit the mold of the workforce in general. As a result of these unique characteristics generic policies and strategies might be forced upon distinctive people in inappropriate ways. This hurtful potential can especially effect indigenous, ethnic, and rural people.

In passing, it is important to note that these last three tools (Restructuring, Transferring, and Sharing) are often employed in tandem with each other in ways that are potentially disruptive.

Outside intrusion: In addition to the methods outlined by Michael Porter, there is the possibility of introducing options into a region that are well established within the developed world, but are new to the people and the region where they are being employed. Consider the various extraction industries (such as logging, mining, drilling for oil, and so forth). Although these industries have carefully developed strategies and tactics, local people often have little experience with them. As a result, participating communities, people, and their leaders might not fully perceive the full implications of the decisions they are being asked to make.

In order to engage in the extraction industries, for example, profound alterations to the local environment and ecology might be necessary. After the economic intervention has been completed, the land may take generations to regenerate or, perhaps, be spoiled forever. The old gold fields around Dawson City, Yukon and Fairbanks, Alaska, for example, possess large stretches of wasteland consisting of "mining tailings" (waste products) from a century ago that have never rejuvenated.

The mining industry might envision all the costs and implications of extraction, but are the local people aware of the full consequences of pursuing this option? If the negative potentials are only understood after irrevocable decisions have been made unfortunately, however, local people might not be in a position to mitigate them. To the surprise and dismay of outside investors, local communities that are forewarned often oppose economic development and the resulting economic prosperity it offers in order to preserve their way of life. The battle regarding the Pebble Mine in Alaska is a specific example of this potential.

Tourism can be raised as another example. The large cruise lines routinely seek new "destinations" for their ships to visit. In the process of doing so, these large corporations often pursue relationships with indigenous, ethnic, and rural communities. The strategic planners of the cruise lines have developed sophisticated tactics that reflect their priorities. But do these models adequately take the needs of local communities into account? Although tourism might result in economic activity, how will it affect the community? Will the local economy become overly dependent upon the tourist trade? What side effects of participation in the tourism industry can be predicted? How can negative impacts be mitigated? Such issues that are of vital interest to indigenous, ethnic, and rural communities might not be adequately addressed.

Thus, when strategies are being forged a wide variety of issues can be envisioned. Michael Porter points to the portfolio approach, restructuring, transferring skills, and sharing activities. In addition, care often needs to be employed when outsiders introduce methods and strategies that are well known to the strategic planners of the developed world, but might not adequately be understood by local communities, such as indigenous, ethnic, and rural people. These issues are abstracted and compared in Table 5.1.

In general, a variety of specific approaches for establishing organizational strategies and tactics have been developed and are recommended. Most of them have been created for and tested within the Western and developed regions. As a result, they might not be appropriate when applied in other contexts. Indigenous, ethnic, and rural peoples need to be aware of this possibility.

A wealth of strategic orientations

In the discussions above, a number of options were analyzed with reference to indigenous, ethnic, and rural peoples. Although these tools have been widely tested and applied, they tend to be products of the modern world. As a result, they might not be well adapted for use elsewhere.

In addition to these general models, a number of classic and ubiquitous strategic models have been developed in the Western and developed sectors.

Table 5.1 Strategic tools

Issue	Analysis
Portfolio	The organization seeks to be involved in a variety of different activities in order to reduce risks and vulnerabilities. When doing so, various subsidiaries and/or partners may be allowed to function independently or with minimal outside intervention.
Restructuring	Organizations often function below their potential due to the way they are structured, the strategic plan being followed, and the relationships between people. Outsiders often seek to restructure organizations in order to remove these barriers to effectiveness.
Transferring skills	In order to be more efficient and effective, organizations often seek to transfer skills and activities from one division to others. The distinctiveness of many indigenous, ethnic, and rural people, however can limit the appropriateness of such tactics.
Sharing activities	Sharing activities often results in the home office or some centralized authority making decisions instead of local personnel. When indigenous, ethnic, and rural populations are involved, these strategic decisions might be counterproductive.
Outside intrusion	Although outsiders often possess sophisticated perspectives regarding an opportunity, local people might not possess the same degree of understanding. As a result, indigenous, ethnic, and rural leaders need to take care to be sure they understand the full implications of the decisions they are asked to make.

DISCUSSION
In addition to (1) understanding what business an organization is involved with and (2) perceiving the degree to which central management should control strategies and operational procedures, a wide variety of options exist including the portfolio approach, restructuring, transferring skills, sharing activities, outside intrusion. Indigenous, ethnic, and rural leaders need to be aware of these tactics and be able to respond to them in effective ways.

They should be used with caution when used with indigenous, ethnic, and rural peoples.

In order to address this important issue, a non-exhaustive sample of popular strategic models is discussed in order to provide a taste regarding how mainstream decision makers think and act. The particular paradigms to be considered include (1) the Diffusion of Innovations, (2) the BCG Growth Market Share Grid, (3) The GE McKinsey Matrix, and (4) SWOT Analysis.

Many other strategic and tactical approaches exist, but for reasons of space, only this representative sample is analyzed and compared. The variety of the sample chosen, however, demonstrates how different techniques differ in the ability to respond to the particular needs, vulnerabilities, and demands of particular people. Each is discussed separately before being compared and contrasted.

Diffusion of innovations: The diffusion of products and ideas from one group of people to another is a basic engine of social change. On some occasions, however, its importance has been overstated. In the early twentieth century, for example, archaeologist Grafton Eliot Smith (1911) theorized that the ancient Egyptians must have traveled to Central America because the Maya built pyramids. Smith reasoned that without the intervention of outsiders, these Americans could never have come up with that idea. Today, of course, social scientists recognize that the independent invention of products and processes is commonplace. Diffusion is a powerful force and it has an important role in both social theory and strategic planning.

In the field of agriculture, a significant body of research grew up in the United States regarding how the diffusion of innovations (such as the growing of hybrid crops) takes place. This body of research influenced the work of Everett Rogers and his seminal and highly regarded *The Diffusion of Innovations* (Rogers 1962, 1983). To his credit, Rogers' work is sophisticated and complex with his discussions pointing to the influence of a host of social and situational variables.

As typically applied within business, however, a popular abstraction of Rogers' model tends to focus almost entirely upon a typology of people who tend to adopt an innovation, when they do so, and who influences them. In summary, those who initially accept an innovation tend to be risk takers who are young, educated, and affluent. As time goes on, other groups that possess these characteristics to a lesser degree embrace the product. Those who are the last to accept the advance (or never embrace it) are depicted as ignorant, lacking in social status, and with little ability to influence others.

Innovators tend to be the first people to embrace a new product. They form a small sliver of the community (estimated at 2.5 percent) who are young and at the top of the cultural and status hierarchies. In addition, Innovators tend to be educated, informed, and financially well off (Rogers 1962: 282). Early Adopters, the second group to accept an innovation, possess these characteristics, but to a somewhat lesser degree. Approximately 13.5 percent of the population, they gain a tendency and willingness to accept the product from their social contact with the Innovators and, in turn, pass on information about and a desire for the product to the Early Majority (Rogers 1962: 283), a large group (34 percent of the population) that is attracted to the product after it has been adopted by the Innovators and the Early Adopters. The Early Majority possesses the traits that are associated with adoption, but to an even lesser degree than Innovators and Early Adopter. The Early

Majority, in their turn, influence the Late Majority (another 34 percent of the population) that possesses even less social status, intellectual wherewithal, and financial resources. Their willingness to innovate results from contact with those in the Early Majority, with whom they interact. Members of the last category to innovate are called Laggards (the remaining 16 percent of the population); they possess the lowest social status, are poor, uneducated, suspicious, and focus upon tradition. They embrace the product last, if they accept it at all. Laggards are depicted as having little influence upon others.

Those who use the diffusion of innovations model sometimes hedge their bets by acknowledging a group known as "Leapfroggers" who do not operate according to the model and often jump ahead to embrace an innovation outside of the predicted order.

This typology is what typically comes to mind when members of the business community discuss the diffusion of innovation. Nevertheless, the full Rogers model is much more complex and sophisticated than that, and can include "network" (Valente 1996a) and "threshold" (Valente 1996b) models which, for reasons of space, are not discussed here. This typology is compared and contrasted in Table 5.2.

The strategic value of such an approach is obvious. The typology not only predicts when particular types of people will accept an innovation, it also indicates who will influence them to do so. This information is of vital importance to those who want to encourage people to embrace an idea, product, or service. In graphic form this process of diffusion can be portrayed in Figure 5.1.

Thus, this model has obvious strategic significance because (1) it breaks the population down into subgroups that supposedly have somewhat homogeneous characteristics regarding their tendency to accept innovations, and predicts (2) how they can be influenced to do so by specific sorts of role models. Because of this practical value, the diffusion of innovations typology and its graph of presentation are often used as fundamental tools of strategic planning.

An assumption that is often covertly made is that adopting an innovation is a good idea or a smart choice and that those who do so are wise and well informed. But this might not always be true. Consider the introduction of mind altering drugs, such as cocaine, into a community. According to the Diffusion of Innovations model, the first to accept and use the drug would be Innovators, followed by Early Adopters, and so forth. Other segments of society might steadfastly refuse to use cocaine (reject the innovation). According to the Rogers' model, these abstainers would be pathetic Laggards. In reality, of course, these people might be insightful and wise. In addition, those who reject drugs might emerge as opinion leaders whose example impacts others in the community.

Table 5.2 Rogers' diffusion of innovations model

Category	Analysis
Innovators	A tiny percentage of young, educated, affluent, high status risk takers who are the first to embrace a new product.
Early adopters	A small, but more substantial, group that possesses the characteristics of the innovators, but to a somewhat lesser degree. Nevertheless, they interact with the innovators and develop a knowledge of and a desire for the innovation from these elite role models.
Early majority	A third of the population that possesses a moderate degree of social position and financial security. They are influenced by the early adopters and influence the late majority.
Late majority	A third of the population that possesses the characteristics that encourage innovation to a minimal degree. They adopt the product late in its life cycle. They are relatively uneducated, and in a financially weak position. They are influenced by the early majority with whom they are in contact. They exert little influence on others.
Laggards	The remaining minority is ignorant, poor, of low social status and do not serve as opinion leaders. They might never adopt the product because of their backwardness. Very few people are influenced by them.
Leapfroggers	Some people adopt the product in ways not accounted for in the model, typically by adopting out of order. They are called leapfroggers.

DISCUSSION

This models portrays a set of characteristics including wealth, social status, education, and opinion leadership as leading to a tendency to accept innovations. As these characteristics become weaker, the propensity to accept innovations is viewed as declining. Charting the influence of various groups upon others is a vital strategic consideration.

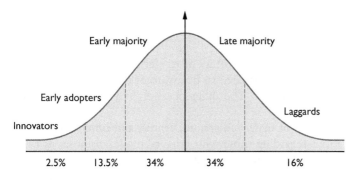

Figure 5.1 Diffusion of innovations model.

Extending the example, people in indigenous, ethnic, and rural communities who champion their heritage and are wary of what outside intruders offer seemingly might fit the description of Laggards even though they are influential role models who might possess useful insights. Thus, although Rogers' model might work fairly well within a homogeneous and mainstream cultural area in which a progression of wealth, sophistication, education, and influence exists, it might not be as appropriate when applied to distinctive cultural enclaves that are not reflective of these patterns. In fact, hurtful results might result from its application.

In the late nineteenth century, anthropologist Émile Durkheim (1997) noted a transition that was taking place as rural France become became increasingly urbanized. He demonstrated this shift by discussing two types of cultural solidarity that he dubbed, "organic" vs. "mechanical." Organic cultures have specialized parts (like the body of an animal in which various organs and components are distinct and serve specific functions). In an analogous manner, the various parts of an organic community all fit together, to form an interrelated, complex and functioning whole comprised of specialized parts. Durkheim notes that this pattern dominates complex, urban society. Thus, different social classes, professions, institutions, belief systems, and so forth combine in ways that help the society function more effectively. Durkheim also observed that as this organic trend becomes increasingly evident, the social and psychological needs of some people might not be adequately addressed. Thus, as the requirements needed for a complex society are addressed (specialization), the needs of specific individuals might be increasingly unsatisfied. This shift, according to Durkheim, can lead to social and personal dysfunction, such as an increase in the suicide rate (Durkheim 1951).

Mechanical societies (Durkheim 1997), in contrast, are small scale and there is little differentiation or specialization among its members. In such small rural communities, everybody knows and understands everybody else. The differences between people are less. Specialization is not as pronounced. Because the community is close knit; the degree of alienation, dysfunction, and misunderstanding is often reduced. Thus, many mechanical societies possess less of the stress and pain than a society that is making a transition towards an organic way of life.

On many occasions, the diffusion of innovations within indigenous, ethnic, and rural communities accompanies or triggers a shift towards a more organic way of life. Communities need to be aware of the potential for dysfunction as this transition occurs. The difference between these two is presented in Table 5.3.

The mechanical nature of many indigenous, ethnic, and rural societies has significant implications regarding those who Rogers' model dismisses as Laggards. According to the Diffusion of Innovations model, Laggards are written off as those who gain minimal respect from others and have little ability to influence others. These tendencies are often true in organic societies. Within

Table 5.3 Organic and mechanical societies

Issue	Organic	Mechanical
Description	The society is complex and made up of specialized parts. Intimate contact between different groups is reduced.	Community is close knit and homogeneous. There tends to be intimate contact among all members. People are similar and can relate.
Who is served?	In a complex society, specialization is needed. This specialization serves the needs of the culture.	Social, psychological, and economic needs of the people are served with an open and egalitarian social structures.
Limitations	The needs of local people are not addressed in order to serve the needs of the group.	Specialization and complexity are not accommodated in order to serve the needs of local people in intimate ways.
Tradeoffs	Achieving a more effective social organization is dominated in ways that might not take individual needs into account.	The social and intimate needs of people dominate. Social health and stability might be maintained as a result.

DISCUSSION
Durkheim's juxtaposition of organic and mechanical cultures demonstrates key differences in mainstream cultures (that are organic) vs. many indigenous, ethnic, and rural societies (that are mechanical). Both forms of organization have their strengths and weaknesses. Local communities need to be very careful when making a transition from a mechanical to an organic way of life.

many small-scale and homogeneous communities that possess a mechanical structure, however, such people are often revered, respected, and have the power to sway the opinions of others. They and their thoughts should not be ignored. Honored and esteemed traditionalists, for example, are often referred to as "Elders" in such communities. Although these informal leaders might have no official role within the society and its formal leadership hierarchy, Elders often possess significant respect and their opinions are widely respected.

Within indigenous, ethnic, and rural communities, furthermore, those who fit the criteria of Innovators might be largely outcast because they have rejected their heritage in order to embrace the attitudes and methods of intrusive colonialists or post-colonialists. Many American Indians, for example, write off such people by calling them "Apples" because they are depicted as being "red on the outside and white on the inside" and despised by traditionalists accordingly. Thus, individuals who resemble Innovators may be feared and resented by their own people even if they are the darlings of invasive outsiders.

In many parts of the world today, traditional cultures are experiencing a resurgence. As a result, traditional leaders who are connected to their heritage, are gaining increased clout. The typology of innovation associated with Rogers, however, does not account for such trends and responses. As a result, a rigid and unthoughtful embrace of the diffusion of innovations paradigm often needs to be tempered when used to explore the behavior of indigenous, ethnic, and rural peoples.

In conclusion, Rogers' Diffusion of Innovations model is a powerful and widely used tool for strategic planning. When applied to indigenous, ethnic, and rural peoples, however, it might provide poor counsel. This is true in part because many small-scale societies and communities are structured in mechanical ways. Such possibilities need to be recognized.

BCG Growth/Market Share Matrix: When managing assets, understanding the current and projected roles of each is vital. The BCG Growth/ Market Share Matrix provides a systematic way to do so. Some products and services, for example, are viewed to be the wave of the future, so current profits are of little concern. Older, fading products, in contrast, might serve the organization by providing profits that can reinvested in tomorrow. Other assets have outlived their usefulness and may be candidates for elimination. By evaluating products in terms of their current or evolving roles, the organization, as a whole, can be more effectively managed.

In order to provide this evaluation, The BCG Matrix employs two variables that are quantitative and empirical. The first is the rate of growth in the industry or product type. The second is the market share that is held by the product. Using these measures as benchmarks, specific products are placed into various categories known as 'Stars," "Question Marks," "Cash Cows," and "Dogs."

Stars are products in high growth industries that possess significant market share. In other words, they are in a dominant position in an industry that has a bright future. These industries, however, tend to be very competitive because many rivals are attracted to the industry or product type. Being relatively new, furthermore, participation in such arenas is likely to require a significant investment and/or involve substantial research and development monies. As a result, adequately nurturing Stars is often very costly, suppressing the current return on investment. Because the main role of Stars is to provide future profits, however, current financial performance is not viewed as vital. Just the opposite, the goal is to invest in the future, typically with large infusions of cash.

Like Stars, **Question Marks** exist in high-growth industries. Their market share, however, is lower, so they are minor, not major players. Nevertheless, because the industry is high growth, the possibility exists for Question Marks to emerge as strong competitors with significant sales and market share. Like Stars, the goal of Question Marks is not to generate current profits, but to gain strength, sales levels, and market share in order to be highly profitable sometime in the future. The immediate goal of Question Marks is to be transformed into Stars.

Cash Cows are dominant products in slow growth industries. Competition in these areas has often been reduced as competitors tend to be driven out of business or voluntarily withdraw from the industry. The level of required investment typically decreases because the product and the methods of production have been perfected and production facilities have been paid for. The role of cash cows is to predictably generate profits that can be reinvested in Stars and Question Marks (that represent the future of the organization). The expectation is that these cash cows are likely to eventually emerge as passé and the role of management is to generate profits as long as possible. By shifting the earnings of these old and fading products to future profit centers (Stars and Question Marks), the long-term health of the organization is insured.

Dogs are weak competitors in industries that are slow-growing or shrinking. Thus, they are feeble participants in unattractive businesses. A commonly suggested strategy for Dogs is disposal, either by selling them or liquidation. By doing so, the resources that formally supported these poor performers can be used for other, more lucrative opportunities.

Thus, using two quantitative measures, products are evaluated and placed into categories. Products that fall into specific categories are evaluated and managed according to particular guidelines and with reference to specific assigned roles. Presented in tabular form, these categories can be portrayed in Table 5.4 and a graphic form the BCG model is portrayed in Figure 5.2.

At an intuitive level, this model makes a lot of sense; as a result, it has emerged as a workhorse of modern strategic planning. On further inspection, however, the model might suggest or imply that healthy and robust Cash Cows with a long and productive future are destined to eventually decline into Dogs and face eventual extinction. The complaint is often raised that, if

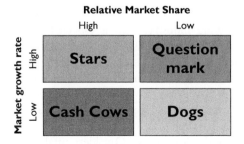

Figure 5.2 BCG Growth/Market Share Matrix.

Table 5.4 BCG Growth/Market Share Matrix

Category	Analysis
Stars	Strong products in high growth industries. The goal is to maintain or enhance position in order for stars to emerge as safe and profitable Cash Cows. Current profits are not a primary consideration.
Question Marks	Weaker products in high growth industries. The goal is to invest in these products in order to transform them into Stars. If management decides it cannot convert the Question Mark into a Star, elimination might be an option.
Cash Cows	Cash Cows are strong products in slow growing industries. In this environment, many competitors have withdrawn and costs are relatively low. As a result, profit levels are high. Profits from Cash Cows provide funding for Stars and Question Marks.
Dogs	Dogs are products with low market share in slow growing industries. They are candidates to be eliminated, if possible, either by liquidation of selling to other investors.

DISCUSSION
The BCG model presents a typology that is based upon two quantitative measures (industry growth rate and market share of a particular product). After doing so, the role of particular products is determined. Funding for the product and the benchmarks used for evaluating its performance reflect the category the product is placed in.

properly managed, many Cash Cows can enjoy long and fruitful lives unless they are undercut by inappropriate self-fulfilling prophesies that trigger failure and death. Thus, if the investment that the Cash Cow needs to be adequately maintained is withheld in the belief that the product is doomed to decline, it might not have the funds needed to remain competitive and eventually fail for that reason.

Many so-called Dogs, furthermore, remain profitable even if they have a small market share in a slow growing industry. This is especially true if a small, but loyal market niche is well served. Disposing of these products, might not be cost effective. When such circumstances exist, maintaining the Dog might be the best course of action. These realities need to be recognized.

When indigenous, ethnic, and rural people are dealing with mainstream partners, understanding their vision is vital. The community might want to rely upon a product or service for the long term. Outsiders might view it from a short-term perspective. Local people need to develop an understanding of the perspectives and motives of their partners or potential partners because these views might work against the community and its goals.

Consider the tourism industry. The cruise lines might be constantly seeking new destinations for its customers and view specific locations as moving through the BCG Matrix towards an eventual Dog status. If the cruise line manages it destination with this process in mind, a boom and bust cycle for the community might occur with a period of unhealthy growth followed by a hurtful economic slowdown that has traumatic implications. The cruise line, furthermore, might actually contribute to this hurtful process if it believes this process is taking place. When the cruise line becomes convinced that the asset is exhausted, furthermore, it will simply move on to another destination and reap the advantages on another Boom and Bust cycle. The abandoned community, however, would find itself in an unenviable position.

Members of the local community, in contrast, might view the opportunities provided by tourism to be permanent, if properly managed. Instead of mass tourism, the local people might seek to serve a smaller number of tourists by concentrating upon those who are more upscale, knowledgeable, truly interested in the community and what it has to offer. Tourists such as these might make return visits and are likely to spend significant money on high quality art works and crafts instead of buying cheap trinkets. Because the number of tourists being served is lower, the carrying capacity of the community would not be exceeded. Precisely because tourism is viewed as a permanent and ongoing economic asset and managed accordingly, it might survive as a viable economic activity for a long period even if the policies of the cruise lines would have triggered collapse.

Thus, viewing products as inevitably declining and planning strategies accordingly can be the kiss of death. If envisioned as permanent assets, these same products might have a long life. Communities need to be sure an inappropriate belief in inevitable decline does not covertly dominate the decision-making process.

Another blindspot of the BCG Matrix is that it focuses almost entirely upon customers and how to profit by catering to their demands. While doing so is important, the needs, wants, vulnerabilities, and so forth of local communities also need to be factored into the analysis.

In conclusion, the BCG model is rigid, inflexible and deals with two quantitative variables. In addition, it focuses upon the whims of customers and little else. The BCG Matrix has limitations that need to be recognized. When dealing with partners or potential partners who employ this model, indigenous, ethnic, and rural peoples need to carefully express their concerns and reservations.

The GE McKinsey Matrix: As indicated above, the BCG Matrix is based upon two empirical and quantitative measures (growth rate and market share). As a result, it is fairly rigid and it does not factor in personal judgment, intuitive, or qualitative variables. The GE McKinsey Matrix, in contrast, is better able to deal with such considerations. Like the BCG Matrix, the GE McKinsey Matrix evaluates products based upon two dimensions. The key measures employed, however, include more flexible and intuitive variables including (1) the attractiveness of the opportunity and (2) the competitive strength of the organization. Those using this mode of analysis are free to evaluate these considerations in any way they see fit. Doing so opens up a wide range of options.

Attractiveness refers to the benefits the organization will receive by being involved with a particular product, service, or other initiative. This degree of attractiveness can be evaluated from (1) some combination of business-like considerations such as the size of the opportunity, the growth rate, profit potentials, and so forth (2) along with a number of other more subjective evaluations such as "Is this the "right thing to do?," "Does the opportunity 'fit in' with other initiatives the organization is pursuing?," "What side effects are likely to occur?," and so forth.

This broader focus can be used to expand beyond the BCG model that rivets solely upon Market Share and Growth Rate. A particular business plan, for example, might trigger hurtful impacts within the community, result in a despoiled environment, and so forth. Using the GE McKinsey Matrix, dealing with these problems is possible and the desirability of a project can be evaluated accordingly. Doing so, however, is not possible when using the BCG method.

This flexibility allows the GE McKinsey Matrix to identify key implications of a proposed strategy because it can be expanded to address a wide number of issues that are of concern to indigenous, ethnic, and rural peoples. This can be an important strength of the method.

The second variable is business strength. As we saw with its treatment of attractiveness, this measure can be calculated in ways that expand beyond the quantitative evaluations. The community, for example, may have strengths of various kinds including people, legal rights, property, and so forth that cannot be easily quantified. The GE McKinsey Matrix is able to take all these variables into account.

The actual mode of presentation used to portray the GE McKinsey Matrix resembles the BCG Growth/Market Share Matrix. It, however, had nine instead of four cells and, therefore, is more complicated. It is presented in Figure 5.3.

As Figure 5.3 indicates, each cell in the Matrix is associated with a particular strategic option that, typically, is ideal for products and opportunities that fall into that category. Thus, opportunities that are high in attractiveness and competitiveness are exceedingly important and every effort needs to be taken to protect them. Products that are low in attractiveness and competitiveness, on the other hand, have little value and are candidates to be eliminated if doing so is a viable option. Between these two opposites, a range of possibilities exist.

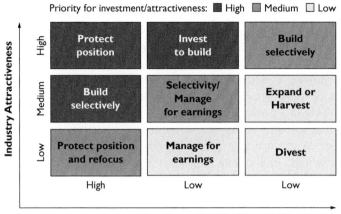

Figure 5.3 GE McKinsey Matrix.

Source: Kinsey and Company, Inc (2015).

The GE McKinsey Matrix offers indigenous, ethnic, and rural people the ability to factor in a breadth of issues when opportunities are being evaluated. This wide scope of analysis and evaluation can be very important, especially when communities seek to present their own points of view. Thus, an important feature is that the GE McKinsey Matrix is dealing with subjective data and perspectives in a way that will be understood by all. Most business leaders are familiar with this model; as a result, by using it, key points can be made in a manner that will be recognized as relevant. The model is also intuitive enough to be understood by members of the community with minimal business expertise.

SWOT Analysis: SWOT Analysis, (see Humphrey 2005) is a systematic method for evaluating strategies and tactics in order to predict their productiveness and effectiveness. It does so by examining the goals being pursued with reference to the (1) internal factors, including strengths and weaknesses as well as (2) external opportunities and threats. A SWOT Analysis can be narrowly used to evaluate specific products or be extended to deal with individuals, organizations, or communities. Almost all strategic planners are familiar with SWOT Analysis. In addition, it is straightforward enough to be understood by all interested parties. As a result, SWOT Analysis can serve as an invaluable analytic and explanatory devise.

As indicated above, SWOT Analysis is designed to deal with two juxtapositions: (1) Internal vs. External influences and (2) Helpful vs. Hurtful considerations. An overview of the four factors making up these juxtapositions (Strengths, Weaknesses, Opportunities and Threats) is provided below:

Strengths: Strengths are assets, resources and abilities that can be used to help achieve goals. Some of these properties might be tangible. Communities, for example, often own land or control other valuable commodities that have value and/or provide a strategic advantage. Tangible resources often open up opportunities or allow an organization, community, organization, or individual to compete in a particular arena.

Some of the assets held by the community, however, might not be factored in when evaluating a particular economic opportunity. A community, for example, might want to protect and preserve sacred land that it owns. As a result, this resource could not be sold or altered; as a result, these assets would not be evaluated as an economic strength. Mainstream partners and consultants, however, might not hold the same feelings of reverence regarding these assets and believe that such items should be viewed in terms of their potential economic or strategic value.

Other strengths might be intangible. Many tourists, for example, visit New Orleans because of the cultural and musical heritage that includes Jazz music. These strengths are intangible. Unfortunately, non-physical assets, such as cultural resources, might be ignored or not adequately maintained by mainstream strategic planners. Before Hurricane Katrina, for example, Garrison Keillor observed that although the airport, hotels, infrastructure, and so forth of New Orleans were receiving much attention and funding, nurturing the intangible cultural heritage that tourists visit New Orleans to experience was largely ignored by planners and policymakers (Walle 1996). Such an oversight, Keillor warned, could spell eventual disaster. Since indigenous, ethnic, and rural people are likely to possess a unique intangible heritage of significant value, Keillor's warning and its implications should not be forgotten. In general, strengths include a wide variety of variables including human skills and knowledge that exist only in the human mind or the collective thoughts of the community.

Weaknesses: Weaknesses are the internal qualities that prevent an organization or community from accomplishing something. They are often viewed as forces that inhibit growth and limit economic progress. They hinder an ability to reach goals or to achieve full potentials. Weaknesses are often associated with lacks or limitations that can be "corrected," typically through the infusion of money. Investments, for example, can be used to replace obsolete equipment, improve the infrastructure, engage in research and development, and so forth. If the organization is large and powerful, strategic planners often seek to control or eliminate weaknesses. Lesser organizations might not be able to do so. These weaker entities would be forced to develop strategic plans that acknowledge their limitations and develop strategic plans accordingly.

Communities, furthermore, might prefer to maintain what others perceive to be weaknesses. Some indigenous, ethnic, and rural peoples, for example, live in communities that lie beyond the road network. Mainstream people, who value freedom to travel, are likely to consider the lack of a road to be a weakness. And in many ways this might be true. Those who want to establish economic relationships with the community and seek better access would also seek a road. Members of the community, however, might believe that isolation is preferable and they might want to minimize their contact with outsiders.

Formerly isolated villages in Alaska (such as Minto) that have gained road access often note a growth in social problems as a result of greater contact with the outside world. As a result, some people are unhappy that the road exists (Minto residents (2002–2010). As a result, some segments of the population believe that the lack of a road is an asset. Communities need to overtly express what they consider to be weaknesses and strengths, because such preferences and evaluations might not be obvious to mainstream strategic planners.

Opportunities: Opportunities provide useful and desirable options to an organization, community, or individual. Benefits potentially arise from taking advantage of these prospects. Under many circumstances, however, an opportunity will only exist for a certain period of time. The term "window of opportunity" reminds us that the unique situation needed to successfully tap an option might be fleeting and require immediate action.

Opportunities arise in a number of ways. Sometimes, laws and regulations provide opportunities. In the United States, for example, indigenous tribes and bands are able to legally operate gambling casinos in states where games of chance are banned. In other words, unique legal rights held by indigenous nations provide economic opportunities. Geographic locations, the access to resources that are in demand, a workforce with specific knowledge or skills, and so forth can also provide opportunities. Many other types of opportunities exist.

Competitive advantages can arise from taking advantage of opportunities. As a result being aware of and acting in regard to opportunities can be vital. Evaluating the potential side effects and the long-term costs of some opportunities, however, can be difficult.

Threats: Threats jeopardize the organization, community, or weaken its initiatives, goals, or opportunities. Threats might also raise the degree of vulnerability that is faced. Outside partners and consultants are likely to see a lack of money, a shortage of qualified employees, a failure to act quickly and decisively to be threats. In addition, local communities might fear rapid and uncontrollable change, the arrival of outsiders, and unwanted transitions in the way of life. What is a threat lies in the eyes of the beholder. Outsiders tend to view threats as whatever undercuts profit-making potentials. Communities are often more concerned with the way of life, the environment,

Table 5.5 SWOT Analysis categories

Category	Analysis
Strengths	Strengths are assets and abilities that can be used to help achieve goals.
Weaknesses	Weaknesses are the traits that prevent an organization, community, or individual from accomplishing something.
Opportunities	Opportunities provide useful and desirable options to an organization, community, or individual.
Threats	Factors that jeopardize the organization, community, or individual, weakening its initiatives, goals, or opportunities.

DISCUSSION
These categories can be viewed, described, and evaluated from a subjective perspective. As a result, it becomes possible for people and communities to express their feelings, fears, and goals in a straightforward manner. Doing so enhances the ability of people to fully and subjectively express themselves.

the mental health of the people, and so forth. These local concerns are legitimate; communities need to overtly and precisely articulate what they feel are threats and why. On many occasions their view will be distinct from those of outsiders.

Thus, internal variables consist of Strengths and Weaknesses while external variables consist of opportunities and threats. They are presented in tabular form in Table 5.5.

A benefit of SWOT Analysis is that the categories used to evaluate opportunities are very flexible and subjective. The BCG Matrix, by comparison, is quite rigid and quantitative. That tool cannot factor in the wide range of variables that indigenous, ethnic, and rural people view as significant. SWOT Analysis, however, can be conducted in ways that are culturally sensitive and address concerns of interest to the community. A graphic presentation is portrayed in Figure 5.4.

SWOT Analysis, therefore, can be adjusted to deal with the values and concerns of local communities and indigenous, ethnic, and rural peoples. Doing so can be very important because outsiders hold their own opinions which may need to be countered using frames of reference that they will understand.

Discussion and conclusion

The purpose of this chapter is to introduce the strategic decision-making process as it takes place within the business community. By doing so, useful

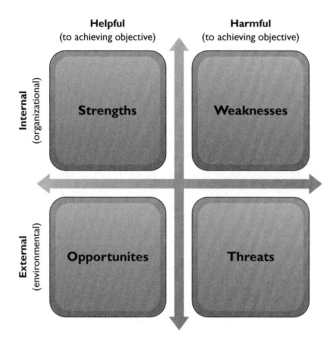

Helpful
(to achieving objective)

Harmful
(to achieving objective)

Internal
(organizational)

Strengths

Weaknesses

External
(environmental)

Opportunites

Threats

Figure 5.4 SWOT Analysis categories.

insights were offered to indigenous, ethnic, and rural peoples. The discussion started Michael Porter's observation that two basic strategic decisions are (1) "What business is the organization in?" and (2) "How should the leaders or top management direct or oversee the organization's various activities?" Having made this point, Porter (1987) outlines four basic tools of corporate strategy: (1) portfolio management, (2) restructuring strategies, (3) the transferring of skills, and (4) the degree to which activities are shared, In addition to these options, (5) existing business models or strategies might be imported into regions by outsiders.

The observation was made that although some approaches, such as the portfolio method might provide local freedom and empowerment, strategic planners often seek to implement significant change. As a result, indigenous, ethnic, and rural people need to carefully evaluate opportunities with an eye towards what transformations will likely occur if the plan is operationalized.

In addition, a sampling of popular strategic tools that are well known within the business community were discussed. Some of these methods are very rigid while others are broad, flexible, and able to deal with the unique concerns of distinctive communities and peoples. The examples examined, of course, are not exhaustive and many other paradigms and techniques could have been included if space had been available.

A basic issue addressed is that these methods differ in (1) their flexibility and (2) in their ability to deal with a wide range of issues. As a result, some of these tools might not be as appropriate when analyzing the needs, wants, and vulnerabilities of distinctive groups such as indigenous, ethnic, and rural peoples.

As was emphasized when discussing the BCG Growth/Market Share Matrix, only two quantitative measures are used when evaluating products. In addition, the model is totally centered upon customers and, therefore, it does not seek to address the needs, wants, and vulnerabilities of those who provide goods and services. SWOT Analysis, in contrast, can be implemented in a manner that takes the feeling of the community and its people into account. When local people are evaluating strategic plans, they can benefit from the use of strategic models that are flexible enough to deal with their needs.

From this point of view the strategic tools discussed are compared and evaluated in Table 5.6.

Table 5.6 A sample of strategic methods

Strategic tool	Analysis
Diffusion of Innovations	Predictions are made regarding when particular types of people are likely to embrace a product. The model tends to covertly imply that products will eventually decline and die. This orientation might work against communities that have limited opportunities and want to provide a good or service as long as possible.
BCG Matrix	Evaluation is based upon the quantitative measures of market share and growth rate. The evaluation centers upon customers and outsiders, not the community. Addressing a wider range of variables is not possible, making the method rigid.
GE/McKinsey Matrix	Evaluation is based upon two measures, attractiveness and competitiveness. Subjective and qualitative (not merely quantitative) analysis is possible. Specific concerns of interest to local people can be worked into the evaluation.
SWOT Analysis	Four variables (strengths, weaknesses, opportunities, and threats) are systematically considered. These variables can be considered in subjective ways and in a manner that transcends the whims of customers.

DISCUSSION

This non-exhaustive sample of strategic methods demonstrates significant differences in flexibility and in the ability to examine a wide range of variables of interest to indigenous, ethnic, and rural peoples. When strategic tools are being used to evaluate opportunities, decision makers need to be sure that they are appropriate for the community and the situations in which they are being used. If it appears, this is not the case, additional strategic evaluation using an appropriate set of tools is recommended.

As indicated above, some tools such as the BCG Matrix might inhibit a free-flowing discussion while others, such as SWOT Analysis, are more likely to encourage a broader and more robust evaluation. When local people are presenting their position and evaluating their opportunities, a broader approach is often preferable.

A number of variables might need to be considered when evaluating the strategic tools to be used. They might include criteria such as (1) Quantitative vs. Qualitative, (2) Rigid vs. Flexible, and (3) Universal vs. Specific.

Quantitative vs. Qualitative controversy: For many years, most business research tended to be quantitative and scientific, not qualitative and humanistic, in nature. Reasons for this preference include the desire to be rigorous and the fact that quantitative measures can be manipulated statistically in order to facilitate the decision-making process. In recent years, however, the business community has increasingly recognized the value of qualitative methods that focus upon how people think, what they feel, and so forth. Such evaluations can especially be of value when indigenous, ethnic, and rural peoples are interacting with mainstream counterparts who might not understand them or appreciate their concerns.

Rigid vs. Flexible: Much research is straightforward and conducted in explicit, direct, and preordained ways. Doing so can add rigor to the research process, provide standardized evaluative procedures, facilitate the comparison of various research projects, and so forth. Although these are significant benefits, the resulting rigidness can limit the data that can be gathered, the issues that can be considered, and how the data is evaluated. As a result, by being inflexible, rigor might increase, but the flexibility needed to explore an issue in all its complexity might be inhibited, The situations faced by many indigenous, ethnic, and rural peoples are very complex. In addition, mainstream partners might have trouble understanding the concerns, goals, and vulnerabilities of such people. As a result, a wide variety of data might be required in order to properly evaluate the situation. Gaining this data might require abandoning rigid strategies.

Universal vs. Specific: Some models that were established in the Developed West (and serve well there) might not be useful or appropriate when applied outside of that sphere. If a specific model or method that is designed for a particular people or region is applied outside of that context, problems can easily develop. Although decision makers tend to prefer standardized tools and methods, many indigenous, ethnic, and rural peoples are distinctive. As a result, models specifically developed in the developed West might not work well when dealing with these people. Local communities need to remember that they might need to draw attention to these limitations and provide alternatives analyses. These issues are presented in Table 5.7.

Strategic analysis, therefore, is complicated. The way it is conducted can have an impact upon the conclusions reached. Indigenous, ethnic, and rural need to take care to be sure the strategic methods used are appropriate.

Table 5.7 Criteria for evaluating strategic methods

Issue	Analysis
Quantitate vs. Qualitative	Quantitative methods can be useful in presenting empirical data in unambiguous ways. Qualitative measures are useful when seeking to understand what people think and feel. What kind of data is most needed for the analysis?
Rigid vs. flexible	Some methods are fairly rigid and limit the types of information that can be used in a strategic study. Doing so can focus the analysis, but at the cost of limiting the types of information that can be made available and evaluated. What are the tradeoffs of both options? Which method is most appropriate?
Universal vs. Specific	Some methods might be ideally suited for a particular environment (such as mainstream people or the developed world.) The model used needs to be appropriate for the purposes for which it is being used. What strategic model best fits these requirements?
Other variables	This is not an exhaustive list. Other key issues might need to be considered when evaluating and choosing strategic tools. Do so as required.

DISCUSSION
Strategic methods vary. Care needs to be taken to be sure that the methods being used reflect the particular problems and the concerns of the people being evaluated. Particular strategic method possess blind spots and, therefore, they might need to be supplemented. Indigenous, ethnic, and rural people are often concerned with self-determinism, a long-term focus, culturally sensitive analysis, and so forth. Care needs to be taken to ensure that the methods of strategic analysis employed address these issues and other community concerns.

Relevant terms

BCG Growth/Market Share Matrix: A strategic model that relies upon two quantitative measures (growth rate and market share) to predict marketability.

Cash Cows: With reference to the Diffusion of Innovations model, dominant products in low growth industries.

Competitive Strength: A component in the GE McKinsey Growth/Attractiveness Matrix.

Diffusion of Innovations: A strategic tool that predicts when particular people will adopt a products and who will influence them to do so.

Dogs: With reference to the Diffusion of Innovations model, weak products in low-growth industries.

Early Adopters: The first significant group to adopt a product. They are influenced by Innovators and influence the Early Majority.

Early Majority: About one-third of the population that is influenced by the early adopters to accept a product and influence the Late Majority.

Flexible: The methods used are broader and the methods used are not as tightly established. This can result in less rigor. The research gathered and manipulated, however, can be richer and more robust.

GE McKinsey Competitiveness/Attractiveness Matrix: A method of analysis that is able to consider both quantitative and qualitative data when assessing product marketability.

Growth: One of the two components in the BCG Matrix.

Innovators: a small component of the population that first adopts a product. The tend to be young, affluent, and high-status risk takers.

Laggards: People who might never adopt an innovation or do so very late.

Late Majority: About one-third of the population that is influenced by the Early Majority and have little influence over others.

Leapfroggers: People who adopt a product out of the usual order.

Market share: One of the two components in the BCG Matrix.

Opportunities: A component of SWOT Analysis.

Porter's two strategic questions: Michael Porter emphasizes asking "what business you are in" and "what power should top management have when decisions are made regarding specific subdivisions?"

Portfolio management: The strategy of acquiring a wide variety of products and subdivisions in order to reduce risks. These entities might be allowed to function independently.

Portfolio theory: A method of investment that uses diversity in order to limit risk.

Question Marks: With reference to the Diffusion of Innovations model, weak products in high growth industries.

Restructuring strategies: Introduce changes into subdivisions or partners in order to operate more effectively.

Rigid: The methods used or the data accepted for consideration are strict. As a result, "objective" observations are easier to defend. Less evidence can be considered, however, and this might limit the practitioner value of the findings.

Sharing activities: Attempting to build efficiency by combing certain activities so specialists can perform them.

Specific: Adjusting products, services, and other business activities so they mesh with the local community or culture. The goal is to win loyalty by carefully tailoring what the organization does to mesh with those being served, and their needs, expectations and demands.

Stars: With reference to the Diffusion of Innovations model, dominant products in high growth industries.

Strength: A component of SWOT Analysis.

SWOT Analysis: A qualitative method of evaluating opportunities that considers strengths, weaknesses, opportunities, and threats.

Threats: A component of SWOT Analysis.

Transferring skills: Transfer skills from one division to another in the hopes of enhancing effectiveness.

Universal: Universal thought and analysis emphasizes aspects of life and action shared by all people. Strategically, those who embrace such an approach might seek to standardize products, management strategies, and so forth over a wide area or the entire world.

Weaknesses: A component of SWOT Analysis.

Discussion questions

1   Michael Porter discussed four basic techniques of corporate strategy. One allowed for a degree of freedom from outside intervention. How could this affect organizations and communities? Three of these techniques call for greater control by top management or outsiders. How might this impact indigenous, ethnic, and rural peoples?

2   The chapter discusses a range of strategic models that differ in the degree to which they are flexible and can examine and process a wide variety of data. Do you think this is an important consideration for indigenous, ethnic, and rural people? Why or why not?

3   As an example of how strategic models diverge, important differences between the BCG Matrix and SWOT Analysis were discussed. What differences did the chapter focus upon and why were these differences considered to be significant? Do you feel this is a crucial issue? Why or why not?

4   Four basic strategic methods were discussed, but the author acknowledged that many others exist. Nonetheless, it was suggested that some general trends and differences could be discerned from comparing this sample. What are these trends and differences? Do you believe they are significant? Why or why not?

5   The chapter concluded with a discussion of criteria for evaluating strategic methods. Do you believe that doing so is important? Are strategic methods interchangeable? Why or why not?

References

Durkheim, Émile (1951). *Suicide: A Study in Sociology* (New York: The Free Press).

Durkheim, Émile (1997). *The Division of Labor in Society.* Trans. W. D. Halls, (New York: Free Press).

Humphrey, Albert (December 2005). "SWOT Analysis for Management Consulting." *SRI Alumni Newsletter* (SRI International).

Kinsey and Company, Inc (2015). *Valuation: Measuring and Managing the Value of Companies.* New York: John Wiley.

Levitt, Theodore (1960). "Marketing Myopia." *Harvard Business Review*, 38(4), 45–56.

Porter, Michael (1987). "From Competitive Advantage to Corporate Strategy" *Business Review*, May.

Rogers, Everett (1962). *Diffusion of Innovations* (Glencoe: Free Press).

Rogers, Everett M. (1983). *Diffusion of Innovations* (New York: Free Press).

Smith, Grafton Eliot (1911). *The Ancient Egyptians and the Origin of Civilization* (London and New York, Harper & Brother).

Valente, Thomas A. (1996a). "Network Models of the Diffusion of Innovation." *Computational and Mathematical Organization Theory*, 2(2), 163–164.

Valente, Thomas W. (1996b). *Social Networks*, 18(1), January, 69–89.

Walle, Alf H. (1996). "United States Encourages International Tourism." *European Business Review*, 96(3), 50–56.

Chapter 6

Organizational concerns

Learning objectives

In addition to providing a strategic orientation, the field of management is also concerned with organizational issues. The methods that have developed within business are somewhat distinct from humanistic perspectives and the context of reform. This chapter compares and juxtaposes different perspectives regarding the role of organizational and bureaucratic structures starting with alternatives to the industrial methods of the late nineteenth century. A discussion of formal and informal theories of bureaucracies and organizations follows, along with view of the evolution of American culture and business that might provide clues regarding indigenous people, ethnic groups, and traditional communities. Specific issues addressed include:

1 Understanding how some reform movements, such as the Arts and Crafts movement and the Appalachian Settlement Schools, reacted against the industrial revolution.
2 Envisioning corporate initiatives, such as paternalism, as additional responses to the inequities of impersonal and rational economic systems.
3 Perceiving how a focus upon formal organizations aimed to create a rational system that would be efficient and fair.
4 Recognizing how formal organizations overtook informal relationships that inevitably exist and exert a strong influence.
5 Appreciating how David Riesman and William Whyte envision changes in American culture that might or might not be mirrored among indigenous, ethnic, and rural peoples.

Introduction

As indicated in the last chapter, an important branch of management theory and practice focuses upon strategic choices that are designed to effectively achieve sought after goals. The branch of management that is discussed in this chapter, in contrast, considers (1) organizational and bureaucratic structures.

These important issues are often narrowly viewed from the perspectives of the developed and Western regions. Care needs to be exercised to ensure that the theories and methods employed are appropriate for the specific peoples being impacted.

To provide an intellectual foundation, a number of historic case studies are presented. Sometimes noble motives spawned these activities; on other occasions, they were self-serving or ethnocentric. On a positive note, a number of initiatives that were initially the products of outsiders eventually came to be embraced by local peoples who gained empowerment as a result. Transformations of this type can enhance self-determinism in positive ways.

Having dealt with these largely humanistic examples, theories of organization and bureaucracy typical of business thought are analyzed in ways that transcend the developed, Western, and mainstream regions.

Reformers and visions of a better life

During the last 200 years, many attempts have been made to enhance the quality of life that are experienced by people. In a variety of ways, these efforts have sought to transform the workplace, everyday personal experiences, as well as the nature of society. Initiatives of this type can be traced as far back as the age of Plato. In recent centuries, such efforts have become commonplace.

Typically, strong, powerful individuals or vested interest groups seek to provide unilateral leadership and direction. This has been true even when local leaders eventually emerged. A number of ambitious examples from the United States quickly come to mind. Some quickly failed, such as the 1840s Brook Farm of Massachusetts (a social experiment that sought to showcase New England's transcendental movement and early socialistic theories). Other examples, such as the Amana Colony, flourished for many decades. Two such experiments that will be briefly discussed include Elbert Hubband's Roycrofters of Upstate New York (in East Aurora, near Buffalo) and the Appalachian Settlement School movement that, starting in the early twentieth century, sought/seeks to bring rural mountain people into the modern world in appropriate and culturally sensitive ways.

Before beginning, let me observe that this discussion does not address the proliferation of new religions in the nineteenth-century America (such as the defunct Shakers and faiths that continue to thrive, including Mormon (Latter Day Saints), Christian Scientists, Seventh Day Adventists, and emerging Native American faiths (including the Iroquois' Code of Handsome Lake). In addition to acknowledging the sacred and spiritual contribution of these sects, they also appear to reflect secular concerns to restructure culture, and society in a more enlightened, productive, and sensitive manner.

Other utopian schemes, of course, existed outside of the United States, such as William Morris' work in England that sought to merge socialism with a reverence for rural life and handcraftsmanship. Significant interplay existed between movements in the United States and those that developed elsewhere. The Roycrofters (to be discussed), for example, were influenced by William Morris and his work. The Appalachian Settlement School movement, furthermore, was inspired by Jane Adams' Hull House of Chicago (founded in 1889) that, in turn, had been influenced by Toynbee Hall in the East End of London, which did similar work aiding the poor in Britain. Hull House, the first of many urban "settlement houses" in the United States, provided services to those in need, including recent immigrants. In addition, the settlement house movement provided a venue where early twentieth-century women could make powerful contributions in a world that was largely controlled by men. The Appalachian Settlement School movement emerged as a rural version of this initiative and was, likewise, the product of ambitious women seeking to make their mark on the world. Both the Roycrofters and the settlement school movement are discussed.

The Roycrofters

In the nineteenth century, the Romantic Movement challenged the dominant belief (stemming from the Age of Enlightenment) that science and rational thought should dominate social life and decisions regarding culture and society. An important rebuttal to this premise was Romantic Nationalism which argued that cultures, heritages, and traditions respond to the emotional needs of people and profoundly mold both society and individuals. Romantic ideas went on to provide the foundation for the Pre-Raphaelites, a movement that sought to recapture the intimacy of vernacular life and art that had existed before the Renaissance. A basic tenet of the Pre-Raphaelites was its belief that the intimate and rustic existence of earlier times was superior to the modern world that, in the nineteenth century, was transforming both everyday life and the increasingly impersonal ways in which factories and other workplaces were managed.

In the last chapter we discussed Émile Durkheim's portrayal of "organic" cultures as modern and impersonal with mechanical cultures being intimate and close to nature. The work of the Pre-Raphaelites and the theories that stemmed from their work are humanistic parallels to Durkheim's organic system published a full 50 years before his concepts appeared in sociology and anthropology.

Building upon the Pre-Raphaelites, Morris designed and marketed home furnishings that were inspired by the medieval era. Morris also championed methods for organizing the production of goods in order to tap the social and psychic benefits of handcraftsmanship. Morris felt that doing so was a positive alternative to the increasingly dominant procedures of mass production in mind-numbing factories. A social reformer, Morris wrote a highly regarded utopian novel, *News From Nowhere* that depicts a world where assembly lines and cities have been replaced by rustic, rural life and artistic craftsmanship. According to Morris' vision, more rural and less organic/modern methods would result in a better life for all.

In America, meanwhile, Elbert Hubbard had amassed a fortune working for Larkin Soap Company in Buffalo, New York. Larkin prospered as a result of Hubbard's strategy of providing generous premiums to those who bought the company's products. "Larkin Clubs" consisting of women who pooled their purchases in order to win the substantial premiums (that included furniture) brought prosperity to the firm.

Hubbard, however, increasingly fell under the sway of William Morris' vision of a rustic utopia where people embraced their work with joy instead of slaving in drudgery. He sold his stake in Larkin and went to East Aurora, New York to form a company based on Arts and Crafts principles that produced products of high quality and did so by hand.

An excellent marketer, Hubbard made the Roycrofters famous as well as popularizing the Arts and Crafts style of rustic home furnishings. He remained a national celebrity until his death when the Lusitania was torpedoed. With its founder dead, the Roycrofters experienced a gradual decline and went bankrupt in 1938.

During their high points, Hubbard and the Roycrofters exerted a profound influence upon social theory. Hubbard also championed methods of organization and motivation that expanded far beyond mere dollars and cents issues. Rustic life, handcraftsmanship, and their impact on psychic wellbeing were celebrated. An overview of the Roycroft Movement is presented in Table 6.1.

Thus, at the turn of the twentieth century, the Arts and Crafts movement celebrated rural life and portrayed rustic people in heroic ways. In America, Elbert Hubbard's Roycrofters emerged as a major tastemaker and social reformer that advocated a return to a more simple and rural mode of existence. Hubbard's example and philosophy (among other influences) helped set the stage for the Appalachian Settlement School movement.

Appalachian Settlement Schools

At the same time that the Roycrofters was emerging as a powerful force in taste, craftsmanship, and business organization, the Appalachian Mountains of the Southeastern United States were viewed as a backward and underdeveloped region that, due to isolation, had not adequately benefited from the advances of technology, industrialization, and the modern world. And yet, the people who lived there were simultaneously celebrated as living in close-knit communities that were rooted in rural life and took pride in their handiwork and crafts. After the region had been settled in the late eighteenth century by immigrants of Scots-Irish descent, the Appalachian people had largely stayed to themselves with minimal outside influence and contact; as a result, much of their distinctive heritage remained intact.

Table 6.1 The Roycroft Movement

Topic	Analysis
Basic description	The Roycrofters is an example of the Arts and Crafts movement that advocated rustic, rural life while emphasizing personal freedom, dignity, and handcraftsmanship. Hubbard's Roycrofters and the example it provided fueled a major social movement and popularized a style of architecture, home furnishings, and personal products.
Operational tactics	Decentralize the organization. Give workers freedom. Create an environment that is close to the earth and caters to personal needs. Encourage the participation of the entire work force in decisions involving people.
Motivational tactics	Allow people to do things that they enjoy. Help people to be creative. Provide an environment where people merge their lives with the work they do in positive and enriching ways.

DISCUSSION
An example of the Arts and Crafts movement, the Roycrofters helped popularize handmade furniture and furnishings while spearheading a social movement that celebrated rustic life. A powerful force in the early twentieth century, the Roycrofters exerted a strong and ubiquitous influence on organizations and methods of motivation.

Eventually these cultural survivals attracted the attention of British folk-song collectors such as Cecil Sharp (Karpeles 1967) who traveled to Appalachia to conduct fieldwork aimed at documenting aspects of English culture that had become extinct in their country of origin. These influential scholars and fieldworkers viewed Appalachia as a treasure trove of their heritage that could be recaptured in no other place (except perhaps in Canada's Nova Scotia, which also has a strong folklore and folk music tradition). As a result of this interest, a number of noted scholars (including Alan Lomax and many others) have continued over the years to visit Appalachia and conduct fieldwork. The region's rich musical tradition, furthermore, forms the foundation of modern country music.

The intellectual environment of the Arts and Crafts movement coupled with folksong fieldwork were powerful forces when the Appalachian settlement School movement was emerging. Seemingly inspired by the English folklorists, for example, Susan Chester (of the Log Cabin Settlement near Asheville, North Carolina believed that these mountain people were "the purest Americans to be found" (Special Collections n.d.). No doubt this sentiment was based on the fact rural Appalachians were direct descents of early settlers that had been impacted to a minimal degree by the waves of immigration that, in the nineteenth century, had made America a proverbial "melting pot" in which ethnic distinctiveness was diluted by contact with others.

Embracing this point of view, Chester sought to revive aspects of the Scots-Irish heritage, such as its weaving tradition. A veteran of urban settlement houses (similar to Chicago's Hull House) Chester was a graduate of Vassar College. What emerged as the Appalachian Settlement School movement can be understood as an extension of the urban Settlement House movement that dealt with rural people instead of city dwellers.

Chester is similar to many other educated and progressive Northeastern women who ventured into the Appalachian region in the early decades of the twentieth century to create and operate schools and provide other human services. Some of these settlement schools aimed at religious evangelicalism while others were secular. In most cases, however, the women who founded these schools were ambitious, aggressive, and they sought a niche where they could make their mark even though America at the time provided relatively few opportunities for women to exert a leadership role. Appalachia, however, was a place where their efforts, visions, and skills were appreciated; the settlement schools provided a venue for these female leaders.

In specific, settlement schools made a significant impact upon Eastern Kentucky. Two such institutions are Alice Lloyd College and the Hindman Settlement School.

Around the time of World War I, Alice Lloyd and June Buchanan settled on Caney Creek in Eastern Kentucky and founded an educational institution that today is known as Alice Lloyd College. Pippa Passes, the name of the town they established, was inspired by the Robert Browning poem that reads in part "God's in his heaven, all's right in the world" (Quiller-Couch 1919: 718). Working for decades, Lloyd and Buchanan built up a large residential school in order to provide mainstream educational opportunities to mountain folk while simultaneously striving to preserve Appalachian heritage and traditions and build local pride.

As a faculty member at Alice Lloyd in the late 1970s, the shadows of earlier times still prevailed when I was there. Although many new buildings had been constructed before my arrival, the old dining hall, abandoned but still standing in those days, was a reminder of the past. It was obviously a piece of folk architecture constructed without reference to formal blueprints. The structure was long and rambling with a lengthy porch and rolling, uneven floors. One could almost see the ghosts of the past when exploring the old, decaying structure.

Although the school on Caney Creek was the brainchild of progressive New England women, over time it became part of the community that built up around it. Eventually local people and their ideas began to exert an influence. The school's slogan is "A light unto the mountains"; to this day the settlement school turned college continues to train Appalachian leaders, even if it has begun, in many ways, to reflect the tenets and priorities of private higher education as much as local needs and wants.

The Hindman Settlement School, located in Hindman, Kentucky (only a few miles from Alice Lloyd), is often pointed to as the first true settlement school. Along with Alice Lloyd College, it is located in Knott County in the Southeastern part of the state. It was founded by May Stone and Katherine Pettit in 1902. When I first visited the school in the 1970s, I found much had changed in 70 years, but some of the vintage furnishings still in use provided clues regarding the vision of the founders. In particular, I spied a desk made by Elbert Hubbard's Roycrofters. Here was an artifact of the American Arts and Crafts movement that had been carted into the hills of Kentucky as part of the furnishings of an institution that sought to transform the mountain people, in some ways, while simultaneously preserving their legacy and customs.

These women (and those who worked with them) provided a basic education before the public school system had been established. In addition, efforts were made to revive local crafts and lore, such as music and weaving. The school had an important role in the collecting of traditional ballads. This attention to the cultural heritage of the Scots-Irish built local pride as well as creating markets for handicrafts that could be used to earn money by selling these products to outsiders.

Over time, the Hindman Settlement School survived and evolved. Local intellectuals, such as James Still, a poet laureate of Kentucky, exerted strong influences. Recording artist Jean Ritchie, a member of the ballad-singing Ritchie family, became intimately involved with the school. A store that showcases local crafts was established.

Many of these initiatives were the brainchild of Mike Mullins, a local and home-grown leader who served as the executive director from the 1970s until his untimely death in 2012. More than anyone else, Mullins took an institution that had been created and directed by progressive Northeastern intellectuals and transformed it into an organization that was locally managed and truly reflected the community. Today, this venerable organization continues as an important part of the community that, over time, has come to be directed by local people, not altruistic outsiders.

Although the Hindman Settlement School was initially controlled by elites from the Northeast, its methods and goals are not to be confused with those of the Bureau of Indian Affairs boarding schools that overtly and systematically sought to destroy the local heritage, traditions, and culture of the people who were being served. Even though the settlement schools sought to provide a mainstream education, they simultaneously worked to build local pride as well as preserving the culture, heritage, and traditions of the people.

Over time, other organizations emerged. A few miles from Hindman and Caney Creek is the little town of Whitesburg, Kentucky. Since the early 1970s it has been the home of the Appalshop, a nonprofit organization dedicated to preserving and celebrating Appalachian culture. The original idea was to train local people to be film makers in order to provide skills that could lead to employment outside of the region. The opposite occurred as the Appalshop emerged as a magnet that drew creative people to Whitesburg who wanted to document, explain, preserve, and advocate for Appalachian culture. Today, the Appalshop continues as a band of film makers, record producers, event managers, and champions for the region that use their vision and skills in a quest to gain parity, equity, and self-determinism for Appalachian people and their culture.

As with the settlement schools, the Appalshop was founded by an outsider:

> ... a young Yale graduate, Bill Richardson, arrived in 1969 as a poverty worker. By this time, Appalachian poverty had become a fixture of network television.... Fathoming the resentment that these images engendered among ... [local people] Richardson helped local young people start the Appalachian Film Workshop whose declared purpose was to give mountaineers power to determine how the region's image was projected to the larger society.
>
> (Williams 2002: 360)

Today, the Appalshop stands as a resource that local people use to tell their own stories, better control their lives, and assert greater control over the region where they live.

Many years ago when I interacted with the Appalshop (more specifically Juneappal Recordings, a subdivision), the recording studio was on a main street and ambient noises from large trucks and so forth often ruined recordings. Young local people manned the microphones under the direction of Jack Wright, one of the founding members of Appalshop. In spite of challenges and the fact the staff were novices, the final recordings were sharp and good. In the process, local youth gained the skills they needed to preserve and transform their heritage as well as developing the perspectives and attitudes that encouraged them to do so.

Thus, another organization was started by outsiders but came to be controlled by local people. This variety of organizations is compared and contrasted in Table 6.2.

The discussion above revolves around a small sliver of Eastern Kentucky that I personally know. It, in microcosm, demonstrates that although outsiders typically provide initial leadership, local people may be able to ultimately emerge as leaders who assume a vital role in controlling their destinies. Thus, on many occasions, outsiders have entered indigenous, ethnic, and rural regions with their own perspectives. Over time, however, local leaders have sometimes been able to gain positions of power, decision making, responsibility, and empowerment. When this happens, a greater degree of self-determinism can emerge as the torch of leadership passes to the communities being served.

Table 6.2 A range of options

Institution	Description	Analysis
Alice Lloyd	Started as a settlement school. Eventually became a college. Continues to exert an influence.	While embracing the region and its heritage, Alice Lloyd College has emerged as a component of private higher education and largely acts accordingly.
Hindman	The first real settlement school. Initially controlled by outsiders, it has evolved its mission and is increasingly directed by local people.	Mike Mullins, a local leader, became the director. The school is active in promoting the Appalachian people and way of life. Artists, writers, craftspeople are involved.
Appalshop	Formed by poverty worker. Emerged as an institution that showcases and advances Appalachian culture.	The Appalshop empowers Appalachian people by providing a local voice and by training local people to preserve their heritage.

DISCUSSION
A number of organizations have been formed in Eastern Kentucky to help empower local people to control their own destiny and celebrate their heritage. Although there is a tendency for such organizations to be established and initially directed by outsiders, local control might eventually emerge.

Industrial paternalism

In addition to social reformers of this type, many industrial leaders have also dabbled in social engineering in the hopes of transforming those who worked for them. Somewhat similar to movements such as the Roycrofters and the settlement schools, these efforts are often described as industrial paternalism because those in charge ran their businesses (and related social activities) in ways that resemble parents making decisions for their ill-informed and under-age children. In the process, economic power was used as leverage in order to control the minds and behaviors of those who depended upon the organization for their livelihood.

I lived for a number of years in Binghamton, New York, a city that during the late nineteenth and twentieth centuries was intimately connected with paternalistic styles of management.

Endicott Johnson Shoe Company, for example, is known as "the Home of the Square Deal" because during the early twentieth century the company's management was committed to treating people fairly. Johnson City, a suburb of Binghamton, was the corporation's company town. A wide array of parks was established for the workers that included Merry go Rounds housed in weatherproof structures. The company built cozy homes that were sold to workers at a fair price. The goal was to organize and manage the company (and the surrounding community) in a humane manner that the corporate leaders believed would enhance the quality of life for all.

The original manufacturing facility for IBM, furthermore, was located in nearby Endicott, another suburb of Binghamton. Thomas J. Watson, the mastermind who created the IBM we know today, attempted to establish a cocoon of healthy and harmonious living for his employees. The benefits employees enjoyed eventually included country clubs, recreational facilities, appropriate activities sponsored by the company, and so forth.

IBM emphasized the establishment and maintenance of a strong espirit de corps by, among other things, singing company songs (El-Sawad and Korcynski 2007). Such a regulated environment, however, might have simultaneously caused people to sacrifice their personal freedom in order to receive a wealth of benefits that the company offered. As a former employee observed, "At IBM, you always had to impress somebody" (*Business Week* 1993: 199).

Impressing others included conforming to Watson's vision of a good life. Because Watson was very much against alcoholic beverages, for example, employees were well advised not to drink in public where a company snoop might see and report such behavior. As late as the 1960s (personal observation), there were restaurants in the greater Binghamton area where the complimentary water in restaurants was served in amber colored glasses. That way, an "IBMer" could order what was called a "water glass cocktail": an alcoholic beverage served in a tinted container normally used for water. The waiter could provide a drink (such as bourbon and water) on the sly and the fact that the patron was imbibing could not be easily detected.

I worked for a time at the Endicott plant in the early 1970s in a subcontracting role during the installation of an automated warehouse. Although I found the atmosphere to be somewhat confining for established "IBMers," most were willing to conform because of the benefits they received. A 1993 article in *Business Week* recalls this system of paternalistic management just when it was beginning to fade:

> [Y]ou can see IBM's influence everywhere.... On the right is the IBM credit union, where workers get their mortgages. A bit farther up is the IBM Conference Center, a country club for IBM employees. Then, along the river, the old clock tower of the IBM plant peers through the trees ... "IBM was like a family," says Ted Wolf, a 25-year IBM veteran ... IBM's paternalism – the company songs, the company clubs, the no-layoff custom – might have seemed like a quaint anachronism to other companies. Here, it was the fabric of the community.
>
> (*Business Week* 1993: 199)

At first glance, this paternalism might simply appear as an American version of the celebrated management practices commonplace in Japan that intimately integrate workers with their organizations, encourage the participation of all, and inspire comradery, as well as emphasizing a strong corporate responsibility for employee wellbeing. There is a significant difference, however. The behavior of Japanese companies reflects the culture, heritage, and traditions of their society and country. American paternalism, in contrast, was independently envisioned by powerful industrialists who forced their wills upon people who were vulnerable and dependent upon them.

Companies such as Endicott Johnson and IBM, nevertheless, were organized in ways designed to help employees even if they did so in a heavy-handed and autocratic manner. Such noble examples of paternalism are not to be confused with other company towns and stores such as those that existed in the Appalachian coal fields during the early part of the twentieth century (and later). Throughout the Appalachian region, coal operators routinely built "company towns" and operated "company stores" that catered to the miners and their families.

Instead of being altruistic, such activities delivered additional sources of profit while simultaneously providing leverage against those who might oppose the mine operators' wishes, goals, and methods of operation. Thus, troublesome employees who aggressively fought for better wages and working conditions could be fired, evicted from company housing, and banished. For a time, such tactics reduced the degree of unionization in the coal fields (George Davis, personal communication 1978–1979).

The coal mines, furthermore, preferred to pay their employees in "script" (a form of private currency that could only be spent at company stores or to pay rent for company-owned housing). By compensating employees in such a manner, additional profits resulted. Workers often complained that the prices at company stores were inflated because the script they were forced to accept as wages was not good elsewhere, giving the company store a monopoly advantage (Personal communication with George Davis, other veterans of the coal mines 1978–1979).

Thus, some business organizations were tightly controlled by visionaries who acted in benevolent ways while others were exploitative. They all, in their own ways, however, tended to limit the self-determinism of local people. This, of course, is a major concern of people who seek to control their own destinies. An overview of paternalism can be portrayed in Table 6.3.

Discussing this wide range of examples (ranging from the Arts and Crafts movement, to the Appalachian Settlement Schools, to paternalism, and pseudo paternalism, helps identify the backdrop or environment in which early theories of managerial organization emerged. Some, such as those related to the Arts and Crafts movement, were overt reactions against the corporate system of the late nineteenth and early twentieth centuries. Others

Table 6.3 Paternalism

Topic	Analysis
Basic orientation	Corporate leaders envision a better world and a means to achieve it. These leaders use their economic power to coerce people to comply.
Typical tactics	Benefits are provided in ways that influence people to act in a manner that the leader believes is in their best interest.
Difference from Japanese	Japanese organizations often reflect the traditions and heritage of Japanese culture. Paternalistic management reflects the personal belief and whims of powerful industrialists.
Pseudo paternalism	Some industrialists manipulated workers in order to boost profits and/or enhance control. Company towns and company stores of the Appalachian coal mining region are examples.

DISCUSSION
Paternalist management altruistically sought to benefit workers and advance their quality of life. Acting in such a humane manner, however, often stripped people of self-determinism and the freedom to make their own decisions.

recognized the value of small-scale ethnic enclaves. Paternalists were altruistic but dominated people in ways that undercut self-determinism. A few pseudo paternalists were exploitative.

Most of this thinking, however, stems from a humanistic perspective and was not greatly influenced by the strategic disciplines, such as business. Extending beyond this intellectual environment, modern theories of organization and bureaucracy began to develop as a distinct intellectual tradition. Most of these theories and practices were developed within the Western, developed, and "modern" regions of the world. This pedigree raises an important question: are such tools appropriate when dealing with indigenous, ethnic, and rural peoples?

In order to deal with this issue, a small subset of organizational theory is analyzed. Specifically, the differences between formal vs. informal organizations are discussed. Although management theory and practice is much richer and more complex than this small range of topics, narrowing the topics covered focuses the discussion in ways that deal with the challenges faced by indigenous, ethnic, and rural peoples.

Formal and informal organizations typically exist side by side. Although sometimes ignored or not adequately appreciated, informal organizations often wield significant power. This can be especially true of indigenous, ethnic, and rural communities. In order to provide an evenhanded view of how people interact in the workplace and beyond, both types of organizations are discussed.

Formal organizations

In the not too distant past, relatively few people "worked for somebody else." Almost completely depending upon wage labor for one's livelihood was not typical. Economic reality was not inevitably tied to trading one's time to outsiders for cash money. People lived close to the earth and subsistence was the norm.

Under those circumstances, economic activities were largely based upon self-sufficiency. Certainly, trade and economic exchanges with outsiders existed, but it was not the major economic mainspring it is today. People lived in small communities, specialization was minimal, self-reliance dominated, and face-to-face relationships were the norm.

Wherever the industrial revolution took hold, that pattern has changed. In most of the world today, large impersonal organizations have replaced intimate, informal relationships. The subsistence lifestyles that once dominated have been supplanted by specialization, cash, and trade. Interconnected and intimate rural life has given way to a detached urban existence, typified by large and impersonal organizations that operate according to complex and complicated rules.

Managerial specialists make decisions from a distance and expect subordinates to adjust accordingly. Over time, most of the world's people have become (directly or indirectly) dependent upon (and a part of) this sort of economic and organizational system. Increasingly large and dominant organizations expect workers to adjust to their demands. Managers and supervisors have become intolerant of those who do not.

Although this trend impacts the majority of the world's people, many indigenous, ethnic, and rural people experience life (or did so until recently) in a manner that reflects the old ways that Durkheim referred to "mechanical solidarity." These people participate in largely egalitarian relationships, face-to-face contact, and decision making by consensus. The economic system is often small scale and subsistence in nature. The requirements and expectations of modern organizations are not normal to these people. As a result, it is important to briefly discuss key aspects of modern formal organizations in order to appreciate their distinctiveness.

The field of organizational theory and behavior, of course, is very complicated. Here we will focus upon Max Weber, a pioneering theorist of complex organizations and a strong advocate for them. Dying in 1920, much good work has been accomplished since his time. Nevertheless, Weber set the stage for modern organizational thought as it has developed in the modern, Western, and industrial regions. Weber's thinking continues to exert a profound influence upon those who expand upon his work and critics who challenge it. Thus, by focusing upon Weber, relevant insights can be gained.

Early in his career, Weber studied the laws and bureaucracies of Ancient Rome. He found the Roman system to be rational and impersonal, focusing upon the tasks to be performed, not the personal feelings and/or partisan leanings of those involved. Apparently, Weber was impressed with how well these systems operated; his vision of the ideal bureaucracy closely reflects these characteristics.

Weber speculates that before Rome, people relied upon irrational traditions that were not organized, predictable, codified, and organized. The Roman system, in contrast, brought order and predictability in ways that provided an efficient and equitable means of harnessing people and their efforts in productive ways. Indeed, Weber's views of bureaucracy and organization is clearly reflective of Roman precedents.

Weber, furthermore, was writing just when the industrial revolution was expanding in the West to such a degree that administrative problems were arising that needed to be addressed. Governments, corporations, and other organizations were growing increasingly large. Many of these organizations had, offices, factories, or other subdivisions located in multiple locations. Often only sporadic contact was possible. The management of such massive organizations required techniques that were more formal and methodical than traditional relationships based on face-to-face contact. Although the old systems of communication and control might be sufficient within a small rural community, by the twentieth century they were often not effective.

Nonetheless, some organizational specialists attempted to recapture the rural ambience of earlier times. As we have seen, in the late nineteenth and early twentieth centuries, the Arts and Crafts movement attempted to deal with the threats of impersonal industrialization by recreating the rural ambience of earlier times and applying it to the modern world. Instead of adjusting to the industrial age, they wanted to reject it and return to the intimacy of an earlier era.

Weber ventured in the opposite direction in a quest to forge a more rational and efficient alternative. He reasoned that, as the industrial age took hold, the informal and intuitive traditions of the past needed to be replaced.

In their place, Weber offered formal organizations that were consciously planned and rationally created with specific tasks and goals in mind. He envisioned a system where the structures of authority could be easily described (and concretely presented in a chart that typically took the form of a pyramid). Instead of being based on friendship or privilege, impersonal organizations would prevail. Employees would be given assignments based on merit. When performing their tasks, employees would be expected to make (and act upon) objective decisions that most effectively advance the goals of the organization. Weber believed that employees must do so if they want to or not.

Weber, for example, believed that bureaucrats should not allow their partisan views to direct their decisions and actions. In Chapter 1, for example, we discussed that Weber advised public servants to act according to the demands of the job, not with reference to their personal feelings. By doing so, Weber believed a rational and well-ordered organization with a specific purpose and direction would more efficiently operate in the public interest. We also saw how the New Public Administration model pointed out that adhering to organizational dictates without reference to feelings or personal morality could result in hurtful and inequitable decisions; as a result, civil servants were urged to stand firm for what they felt was right even if doing so challenged the status quo. Weber's rational and systematic organizational methods possessed significant benefits, while also possessing a dark side that sometimes needed to be transcended. In spite of advocating rational organizations, Weber recognized this downside.

Weber's ideal bureaucracy

Thus, Weber felt that a systematic and rational bureaucracy was needed in an increasingly industrialized and complicated world. He realized that such a system presented a host of dangers and problems, but he felt that the benefits outweighed the problems. Weber envisioned a number of traits that characterized an ideal bureaucracy or organization including (1) a division of labor, (2) a hierarchy of authority, (3) objective recruiting and advancement, (4) formal rules and regulations, (5) impersonality, and (6) a career orientation. Each is discussed below.

Division of Labor: In small scale, traditional societies and organizations, people tend to be generalists; thus, in a rural farming village, most people perform the same sort of tasks. As a result, little specialization or division of labor is typically present. Even the few people who are specialists tend to fit the mold of the majority; thus, the local preacher or shaman might simultaneously run his own farm, providing spiritual guidance as a second profession. In small villages, furthermore, the assigned tasks are often adjusted around the specific person; the aged and those with disabilities, for example, are often given chores or assignments that they were able to perform.

The industrial revolution changed this age-old pattern. Work became more complex and the need for specialists arose. Some jobs (such as carpentry and plumbing) became very specialized and required practitioners that possess particular skills. A managerial elite arose. Manufacturing operations, such as assembly lines, typically demand that workers do precise things in an orchestrated and timely manner. The resulting division of labor enhances efficiency and quality allowing large and complicated organizations to get the most from their members, exercise greater controls, and gain the resulting efficiencies. Weber believed that complex bureaucracies with a clear division of labor should be the norm.

Hierarchy of Authority: In small villages composed of indigenous, ethnic, and rural people, an overt chain of command might not be obvious;

under such conditions, decisions are often made according to some sort of informal consensus. Older, respected individuals (often referred to as Elders) typically garner respect. Although they usually possess no overt authority, such people often have a covert ability to influence opinions and decisions. In small face-to-face communities, informal and communal decisions of this sort can be effective.

In the modern world, however, word of mouth and casual "gentlemen's agreements" are usually ineffectual. Weber believed that in complex environments, formal bureaucracies are required, especially in large organizations where the leadership operates from a distance and/or are different in significant ways from the rank and file.

Instead of seeking consensus, Weber envisioned leaders who possess the authority to unilaterally make unchallenged decisions. Power is allotted through a hierarchy of authority that explicitly states the particular authority possessed by specific individuals. This ability to act and control stems from their niche or position within the organization. In general, people have power because of their job and position. Under this system, they wield authority over those below them in the organizational hierarchy and they report to those who are above. Because different people have different levels of power, a pyramid of authority can easily be envisioned.

Objective Recruiting and Advancement: Adam Smith in his *Wealth of Nations* (1776) advocated a laissez-faire economic system in which the government stands by and allows the efficient to prosper and the inefficient to fail. Doing so was advocated as a way to enhance productivity and competitiveness. It also provided a method to reduce the tendencies for kings and other high-ranking royalty to give special economic privileges to friends, relatives, and bastard sons.

Under this system of sentiment and privilege, the lucky (but often inept) individuals were given authority over significant economic resources because of favoritism, not their competence. In many cases, unfortunately, these individuals lacked the ability or willingness to effectively develop and manage the opportunities they were given. When this happened, the economy failed to operate according to its potential and everyone, except the undeservedly advantaged, suffered as a result.

What was needed was a system where those who were truly competent and dedicated could rise to positions of authority. Weber totally agreed with this idea and advocated the establishment of systematic, fair, and objective methods for recruiting new members into the organization and for promoting and rewarding these achievers once on the job. He advocated a system where all organizational members are selected and rewarded based upon qualifications, competence, and contributions.

In this way, the best people would be put into positions that were well suited to their abilities, dedication, and drive. Under these conditions, organizations would be more effective and competitive.

Formal Rules and Regulations: In traditional cultures, informality and consensus tend to dominate. Tensions and problems are addressed as they arise, often in subtle and hazy ways. A significant artifact of this system is that people might never totally really realize what the rules really are. In a small face-to-face situation involving a homogeneous population, such a situation might be workable. Large organizations, however, are very complex and the members are probably not in regular and on-going face-to-face communication with each other. In addition, people in complex organizations often come from different backgrounds and, as a result, they can be less able to intuitively understand each other and/or anticipate the needs, demands, and obligations that exist. Such division and confusion can cause problems that potentially undercut the organization. The remedy that Weber recommends involves developing formal rules and regulations that are understood by all. When confusions or disagreements arise, these codes and codicils can be relied upon to resolve complex and difficult issues. Thus, explicit rules can help reduce organizational tensions and dysfunction.

Impersonality: Tensions, resentments, and dissention are likely to arise if people feel that they are not being fairly treated or if they suspect that others enjoy unjustified favoritism. These feelings can easily undercut the effectiveness of the organization.

In order to reduce this possibility, Weber suggests that organizations implement rules that are impersonal. Doing so can ensure that all members of the organization are treated in similar ways and loyalty and morale can be increased, as tensions and hard feelings are tempered. By applying these rules in a uniform and consistent manner, nepotism and providing friends with unfair advantages can be reduced in ways that benefit the organization.

Career Orientation: People who give their loyalty to organizations are likely to simultaneously lose important benefits that derive from being closely linked to their community. This can be especially true for those who live in indigenous, ethnic, and rural settings. Thus, giving loyalty to an organization can create significant risks and costs. Why should someone accept this vulnerability by becoming strongly identified with an impersonal organization?

Weber suggests that to compensate people and to win loyalty, organizations need to offer job security and a permanent career path. Such intangible assets can reward people for the security they give up when they endanger or compromise their relationships within their community or culture.

Thus, providing an environment for people to build a career, protecting employees from arbitrary dismissal, and offering permanent employment are vital benefits that may be required in order to recruit high quality talent from local communities. Besides providing incentives to local people, such a policy can potentially work to the advantage of outside organizations. Hiring local people instead of expatriates, for example, can be cheaper and help the organization to mesh with the local community in positive ways.

Thus, Weber advocated formal bureaucracies and organizations. He also identified a wide number of characteristics that can lead to greater effectiveness. In many ways, these characteristics transcend the more informal methods of organization and control that have long been present among many indigenous, ethic, and rural communities. Table 6.4 provides a summary of these characteristics.

Perhaps an understanding of Weber's view of organizations and bureaucracies can be clarified by examining his understanding of the city as an economic and social force (as presented in his *The City* (1921, 1958 English translation)). Weber argues that in the West urban centers or cities became the center for economic and political life and decisions making. He argues that this Western role was distinct from other regions, such as Asia.

In 1924 these ideas were incorporated into Chapter 16 "Non-legitimate Domination)" that appears in his posthumous *Economy and Society*. Weber views the city as an autonomous organization characterized by the specialization of individuals who are in close contact with each other and are separated from those who are beyond its bounds (such as those who live in the

Table 6.4 Weber's criteria for ideal organizations

Criteria	Analysis
Division of Labor	Particular people in an organization perform specific, assigned tasks. The organizations gains efficiency as a result.
Hierarchy of Authority	A clear understanding exists regarding what authority and decision making clout specific people possess, who must obey them, and who they answer to.
Recruiting and Advancement	People are given assignments based upon their abilities, not upon other factors, such as favoritism.
Rules and Regulations	Rules and regulations exist that apply to all people. They should not be applied unilaterally, with partiality, or without warning.
Impersonality	Decisions and actions are an artifact of the situation and are not based on personal relationships.
Career Orientation	People believe that if they join the organization they will gain entrance to a career path. Thus, the job is more than a short term, ad hoc relationship.

DISCUSSION

To be effective, organizations require a number of characteristics that are effective, take people into account, and make all feel they are being treated fairly. If these conditions are met, viable organizations can result.

hinterland). Weber describes their influence as "non-legitimate domination" that was based upon the power amassed by the city.

In certain circumstances, large organizations or companies might resemble the type of city that Weber complained about and exhibited "non-legitimate domination." Given these parallels, it appears that Weber intuitively sensed that large organizations and corporations that venture into the hinterland might exert hurtful and unjust impacts. Thus, although Weber made many positive remarks about formal organizations, he seems to have been aware that a dark side exists.

Today, the basic tenets of the Weberian bureaucratic model survives. Nevertheless a number of criticisms have arisen. Large impersonal organizations are likely to ignore personal needs. Weber's conceptualization is rational but people possess an emotional essence. Rules that serve organizations might not adequately take individuals, their needs, and their responses into account.

As will be discussed, informal relationships are also important. As a result, a system that fails to take these factors into account is incomplete. This can be especially true if tensions arise and differences between rival stakeholders need to be resolved.

Nonetheless, Weber's view of bureaucracies and organizations (and the work of others who build upon it) continues to serve an important role. Many other researchers since Weber's time have contributed to this perspective, but the rational and systematic focus has largely been maintained. It will continue as an important tool even though the formal conception of bureaucracies and organizations is limited and imperfect.

Informal organizations

Thus, although formal conceptualizations of organizations and bureaucracies (such as those provided by Weber) are useful, they do not present a total picture of how people function and operate. Unfortunately, some practitioners and theorists concentrate upon modern organizational life to such a degree that they tend to view anything but a formally structured hierarchical organization as limited, or even a perversion of the natural order of things. Thus, some argue that informal organizations rise up when formal organizations are inept, weak, or unable to take on their rightful responsibilities. In this regard Mescon (1959: 35) observes "it can hardly be questioned that the ideal situation in the business organization would be one where no informal organization existed."

Another possibility exists. As we saw in the discussion of the Arts and Crafts movement earlier in this chapter, informal and egalitarian relationships can be viewed as positive, ordinary, and normal. According to this perspective, formal and rigid organizations are arbitrary and abnormal, not vice versa.

As time has gone on, there has been a recognition that informal relationships are an inevitable fact of life. In addition, they typically provide a wealth of benefits as well as potential threats. In that regard, I am reminded of a conference I attended in Italy that was sponsored, in large part, by an important local corporation. At a luncheon I attended, the top executives of the host company (consisting of four brothers and one close friend) observed that key decisions were made in the most informal of ways. Perhaps a major "strategy meeting" would take the form of a nice meal served with the best of wines. Over fine food, informal chatting and brainstorming would continue until a consensus was reached.

The executives concluded that although this informal system sometimes led to costly mistakes, the organization was nimble and could quickly respond in order to take advantage of fleeting opportunities that companies with sluggish bureaucracies fail to tap. On balance, these key executives concluded that their informal system worked fine.

In other words, formal and hierarchical systems with elaborate checks and balances are not the only sources of effective decision making. Informal organizations can also excel. They incidentally tend to be more powerful and prevalent within small scale societies and organizations.

At the same time that Weber's work was gaining influence by touting formal organizations and bureaucracies, other scholars and practitioners began pointing to informal structures that existed, even if they sometimes went unrecognized. Although humanists had long been aware of this reality, it remained for Elton Mayo to introduce such thinking to business thought. He did so in his breakthrough research that is now known as the Hawthorne Studies. Mayo noticed that in a controlled experiment he was conducting, workers performed well above expectations. Curious, he created increasingly difficult obstacles to further inhibit good work, but nothing he did was able to reduce productivity. Ultimately, Mayo discovered that the workers realized they were being watched and collectively banded together to ensure that production levels did not drop. Here was an informal organization, invisible and unsanctioned, that was impacting the quality of work.

This example of informal groups working together, which Mayo discovered by accident, has led to a wide variety of research projects involving informal organizations. The current state of such investigations involves systematically mapping or charting these informal structures in order to benefit from a greater understanding.

As far back as 1993, Hanson and Krackhardt argued that formal organizational charts do little to reveal the importance of informal organizations and their complicated networks of relationships that interconnect the entire organization. In order to tap into this source of power and influence, the authors suggest analyzing or diagramming these relationships in order to better perceive their power and influence. Thus, the power and influence of informal organizations was recognized and suggestions were made regarding how to better understand and utilize these casual structures in an effective manner.

Increasingly, consultants and management teams are seeking ways to diagram and understand these informal structures in the belief that access to this knowledge can enhance performance. Companies, for example, have:

> surveyed its ... employees, asking them which colleagues they consulted most frequently, who they turned to for expertise, and who either boosted or drained their energy levels. Their answers were analyzed in a software program and then plotted as a web of interconnecting nodes and lines representing people and relationships.
>
> (McGregor 2006)

The consulting firm Katzenbach Partners, for example, is dedicated to exploring informal social networks in the belief that effectiveness can result from understanding the "constellation of collaborations, relationships, and networks" that exist among people and within organizations (Reingold and Yang 2007).

This multi-pronged research initiative, of current interest to those who study organizations, clearly expands far beyond examining and bolstering formal and overt organizations such as those studied by Weber and other researchers who were influenced by him. In today's world, a robust interest in both formal and informal organizations has developed.

Social impacts of informality

In addition to these aspects of informality, it is useful to assess shifts in the way people relate to each other due to social change. Two classic views of the United States that deal with such transformations include *The Lonely Crowd* by David Riesman, Nathan Glazer, Nathan, and Reuel Denney (1950) and William Whyte's *The Organization Man* (1956). Together, they demonstrate how changes in the way people are organized (both culturally and institutionally) can exert significant psychological impacts, stress, and possible pain.

The basic argument of *The Lonely Crowd* is that three different types of people (or methods of response) exist that can be categorized as "tradition-directed," "inner-directed," and "other-directed." Each is influenced by distinct influences and pressures and each responds to life and its challenges in a particular way.

Tradition-directed people embrace their heritage (what they have intellectually, socially, and morally inherited from prior generations). In America, early settlers such as the Pilgrims were often composed of religious sects that migrated to the New World in order to follow their religious heritage and their traditional ways of life without outside intervention. As we have seen, the Arts and Crafts movement attempted to create a social environment that nurtured traditional ways of life by duplicating the lifestyles of earlier eras. Many indigenous, ethnic, and rural peoples continue to act in this way.

Inner-directed people, in contrast, are less effected by their heritage or traditions, and are more influenced by who they are individually as well as how they think, feel, and act. Riesman et al. argue that eventually the dominance of tradition-directed people weakened and the inner-directed gained dominance. Historian Fredrick Jackson Turner (1893/1961), for example, suggests (in his "Frontier Thesis of American History") that the American spirit of rugged individualism had been honed on a wild frontier that demanded self-reliance that is reflective of what Riesman et al. later identified as inner-directed. Although perhaps overstated, Turner's vision of American history suggests that the rigors of frontier life transformed Americans from effete Old World traditionalists into virile and self-contained achievers. According to Turner, this experience caused American culture to evolve into the powerful and influential force it ultimately became. (Today, scholars temper and qualify the Turner's frontier theory; although it is not totally rejected, these forces are viewed as but one of several key influences upon American civilization).

The Lonely Crowd went on to conclude that, over time, other-directed people emerged as the norm. These people are primarily influenced by what other people think about them. Other-directed people, furthermore, tend to judge themselves through a comparison with others. Wanting to be accepted, the other-directed are more willing to adjust in order to gain approval than the tradition-directed or inner-directed. In addition, other-directed people more easily mesh with large organizations; as a result, the workplace is better able to mold them. Writing in the early 1950s, Reisman et al. noted that by the 1940s, this type of person was beginning to dominate American life. Today, in the twenty-first century, the case can be made that in the United States the shift towards other-directed has progressed even further (in spite of the fact that the counter culture of the 1960s moved in the opposite direction for a while). The other-directed style, furthermore, is the complete opposite of the traditional orientation of many indigenous, ethnic, and peoples.

Over time, informality and tradition have been weakened. Reisman et al. discuss how this was true in American society in the years immediately following World War II. Writing at approximately the same time, William Whyte concentrated upon these trends within organizations and the world of work.

Whyte starts his book by stating that he is not just writing about people who work for organizations. Instead, he is discussing those who have become part of an organization and identify with it to the degree that they lose their own sense of self. Viewed from the perspective of Riesman et al., people appear to have become other-directed with the organization and its members emerging as the others to be emulated.

In Chapters 7 and 8, Whyte discusses the education that business students and workers were receiving in the 1950s when he wrote *The Organization Man*. Earlier in this book we discussed how World War II led to a transition in business training away from the liberal arts and towards practical skills as taught by practitioners with focused skills. That trend was gaining traction when Whyte was writing, and he laments that business schools were trying so hard to effectively train future leaders that their effort was botched because they failed to introduce students to an adequate breadth. What students need, Whyte concludes, are the insights of the fundamental disciplines, not an endless array of specialized courses taught in an intellectual vacuum. And he predicted that this situation would get increasingly worse as universities responded to the suggestions of generous corporations that provided grants, scholarships, and other funds. History has proved that Whyte was correct in that regard. Whyte then goes on, in Chapter 11, to depict the modern executive as a "non-well-rounded-man."

For our purposes, however, the keystone to the book is presented in Chapter 2 "The Decline of the Protestant Ethic." In essence, Whyte argues that in the past Americans had been taught to work hard and wait for good things to come. That was religious advice. It was also the counsel young boys received when they read Horatio Alger stories in the late nineteenth and early twentieth centuries. People embraced ruggedly individualistic role models. Such visions became ingrained.

With the rise of massive organizations, however, living by that code of individualism became passé. Being a strong and self-reliant individual became a detriment, not an advantage when working in large organizations or bureaucracies. Social skills and the ability to adapt or compromise were more useful.

Nevertheless, Whyte wrote in an era when people were still being raised to think in terms of self-reliance and judged themselves accordingly. Young boys worshipped and sought to emulate role models such as ruggedly individualistic cowboy heroes. Ultimately, embracing this code led to a double bind that provided little comfort. People could remain true to their ingrained character and probably fail or, as an alternative, they could abandon their beliefs and cherished codes of conduct in order to succeed. Both solutions were unfulfilling and alienating.

In recent years I have talked to undergraduate students about this observation. They tend to find this chain of thought to be passé and not relevant. Their responses might reflect changes in character and expectations of younger generations who came of age after *The Organization Man* was published many years ago. Thus, the United States seems to have shifted away from individualism and towards a more collective ethos and existence. Fewer people believe that they have the ability to change the world. Compromise and adaptation to circumstances are more acceptable. Among today's emerging generations, the individualistic spirit appears to lack the power it once had in the United States.

In many parts of the world, however, the type of alienation described by Whyte might continue to be a powerful, disruptive, and dysfunctional force. This is because these peoples and cultures have not passed through a transformation towards organizational life that Americans have experienced and largely accepted.

Reisman et al. (1950) and Whyte (1956), therefore, present a warning regarding the tensions of economic development. As society, organizations, and businesses became more organized and systematic, people have responded accordingly. In America, this has resulted in a transformation away from tradition and informality and towards formal and systematic ways of living and acting. Influences and implications of this process are portrayed in Table 6.5.

Thus, both formal and informal methods of dealing with people are powerful tools. Their relative effectiveness is influenced by the nature of the particular community or society which might be evolving over time. In many developed regions, more formal social and institutional relationships has become the norm. Among indigenous, ethnic, and rural communities, however, informal and traditional ways of life are likely to persist. Numerous peoples, furthermore, are going to great lengths to preserve their heritage, ways of life, and methods of organization. Thus, the old evolutionary models that predict the inevitable decline of traditional ways of life is weakening. This trend and its potentials need to be acknowledged; the power of tradition and the self-determinism of people, needs to be acknowledged and celebrated.

Table 6.5 Psychic and social shifts

Book	Analysis
Lonely Crowd	A shift in American society has occurred (1) away from tradition and unique individual needs or potentials and (2) towards the influence of others. This has resulted in a major transformation in the way Americans respond to life, decisions, and other people.
Organization Man	In America, rugged individualism has been replaced by a collective orientation. During the period of transition, many Americans continued to embrace an individualistic ethos that was ill suited to the circumstances faced. The power of the old ways has weaken in America, but might continue among many indigenous, ethnic, and rural peoples.

DISCUSSION

Since the 1950s, American culture and economic life has been significantly transformed. As a result, the issues analyzed by Riesman et al. (1950) and Whyte (1956) are not as pressing as they once were. In many circumstances, however, this shift away from tradition or the individual and towards formal and impersonal organizational life is a major force. Indigenous, ethnic, and rural people need to be aware of these shifts and pressures.

Comparison and conclusion

The ways in which people interact with each other can be crucial to both the community and the individual. As the Arts and Crafts and the Appalachian Settlement School movements demonstrated in the early twentieth century, methods of managing people can be developed that take the desires and feelings of people into account. One way to do so is to acknowledge the needs and heritage of the people and not let the prerequisites of the organization overshadow the individual and the community. Initiatives, such as the settlement schools and Appalshop motivate people to acknowledge and respond to their essence and heritage. Other forms of organization (such as paternalism) have often been used even though they might be coercive in nature.

When looking at people and their interactions, both formal and informal phenomena can be examined. Formal organizations are concerned with consciously created structures while informal organizations are more grassroots in nature. For many years, business practitioners and theorists focused on the formal and largely overlooked the informal. Today, in contrast, informal organizations are receiving the attention they deserve. This trend can benefit indigenous, ethnic, and rural people because they are often structured and function in informal ways that are based upon their heritage and traditions, not formal rules and procedures introduced by outsiders.

The work of David Riesman et al. and William Whyte, although perhaps dated when applied to the United States, may provide useful counsel to those who are dealing with people who continue to live in small-scale societies and communities. Thus, although formal organizations are important and have their place, so do their informal counterparts.

This raises questions regarding the extent to which generic methods of formal organization can work effectively among indigenous, ethnic and rural peoples. The business community loves a ready-made solution that can be easily transferred from one situation to another. Unfortunately, under many circumstances strategies of organization and bureaucracy might not be effectively transferred. The distinctiveness of the community, not universal management tools, often needs to be the focus.

Relevant terms

Adams, Jane: A leader of the Settlement House Movement. Operated Hull House in Chicago.

Alice Lloyd College: A college in Eastern Kentucky that began as an Appalachian Settlement School.

Appalachian Settlement Schools: These involved a movement during the late nineteenth and twentieth centuries involving progressive women who travelled to the Appalachian Mountains of the United States to help relieve the poverty and ignorance that existed there.

Appalshop: An artistic and activist collective in Eastern Kentucky that extends the mission of the Appalachian Settlement School movement.

Arts and Crafts movement: An economic, political, and artistic movement that sought to recapture the benefits of small scale rural communities as an alternative to the industrial revolution.

Career Orientation: A component of Max Weber's ideal bureaucracy that emphasized offering employees careers and permanent employment in return for their loyalty.

Company stores: Stores operated by industrialists to serve their workers. Commonly used in the Appalachian coal mining regions.

Division of Labor: A component of Max Weber's ideal bureaucracy that emphasized specialization on the job in order to gain benefits such as efficiency.

Formal organizations: A component of Max Weber's ideal bureaucracy that emphasized that formal organizations with precise rules are superior to informal systems that are ambiguous.

Formal Rules and Regulations: A component of Max Weber's ideal bureaucracy that emphasizes that organizations operate more effectively when people know exactly what is expected of them and how they will be judged and treated.

Frontier Thesis: The theory advanced by Fredrick Jackson Turner that suggest that life on the rugged frontier transformed effete Europeans into virile and self-reliant individualists.

Hierarchy of Authority: A component of Max Weber's ideal bureaucracy that emphasizes that formal and understood power relationships (typically presented in organizational charts) provide the most effective way to deal with decision making and internal conflicts.

Hindman Settlement School: An Eastern Kentucky settlement school in which the external control of outsiders was replaced by local and home-grown decision makers.

Hubbard, Elbert: A leader of the Arts and Crafts Movement in American that founded the Roycrofters in East Aurora, New York.

Hull House: The first settlement house in American that was run by Jane Adams.

Informal organization: A means of organization that extends beyond Weber's vision of formal methods of organization.

Inner-directed: A component of motivation proposed by David Riesman et al. in *The Lonely Crowd* that emphasized the influence of personal characteristics.

Morris, William: A British leader of the Arts and Crafts movement and the author of the rustic utopian novel *News from Nowhere*. Influenced America's Elbert Hubbard who founded the Roycrofters.

Objective Recruitment and Advancement: A component of Max Weber's ideal bureaucracy that emphasizes setting and adhering to standards when hiring and advancing employees. Doing so serves as an alternative to favoritism.

Organization Man: A book by William Whyte that argues that a shift has occurred in America from rugged individualism to a more collective orientation.

Paternalism: A strategy in which industrialists use their economic power in order to mold employees in what that are believed to be healthy and moral.

Pre-Raphaelites: An artistic movement that attempted to recapture the essence of rural life and the traditions of pre-Renaissance Europe. Influenced the Arts and Crafts movement.

Protestant Ethic: According to Max Weber, the desire to succeed as an end in itself. Weber believes the resulting drive helped trigger the industrial revolution and modern capitalism.

Roycrofters: An Arts and Crafts organization owned and managed by Elbert Hubbard. Exerted a great influence in taste and in social theory during the early twentieth century.

Settlement House movement: A movement involving urban social services agencies that helped people in need. Associated with Jane Adams and Hull House in Chicago.

Settlement School movement: A movement in Appalachia that attempted to simultaneously bring the modern world to a rustic people while preserving and celebrating their heritage.

The Lonely Crowd: An analysis of American society by David Riesman et al. that emphasized a shift in influence from tradition, to individual feelings, and eventually to external role models.

Toynbee Hall: A settlement house in Britain that inspired Jane Adams to establish the Settlement House Movement in America.

Tradition-directed: A component of motivation proposed by David Riesman et al. in *The Lonely Crowd* that emphasizes the role of traditional attitudes and ways of life.

Turner, Fredrick Jackson: The author of the Frontier Thesis of America culture.

Weber, Max: An advocate of formal organizations. Proposed a number of components of ideal bureaucracies.

Discussion questions

1   Discuss the Arts and Crafts movement and the Appalachian Settlement Schools as economic and personal responses to industrialization. Do these movements provide useful clues regarding how indigenous, ethnic, and rural people can cope with a changing world? Why or why not?

2   Discuss industrial paternalism as a corporate response to the inequities of late nineteenth century and early twentieth century industrialism. How are these initiatives different from systems such as Japanese management?

While paternalism was altruistic, some other industrial developments were more self-serving. Discuss.

3　Max Weber and those who advance his work advocate formal, rigid, and static organizations. What are the benefits and deficits of such a system? How might they impact indigenous, ethnic, and rural peoples?

4　What are some of the benefits of informal organizations? How are contemporary business scholars and practitioners seeking to explore their influence? Do you feel this movement is important? Why or why not?

5　David Riesman and William Whyte both envision changes in American culture. Do you feel that these changes are inevitable and will eventually transform all of humanity, including indigenous, ethnic, and rural peoples? Why or why not?

References

Browning, Robert (1841). "Pippa Passes." *Bells and Pomegranates.*

Business Week (1993). "In Poughkeepsie, A Bitter Family Breakup." *Business Week* April 4, 199.

El-Sawad, Amal and Korcynski, Marek (2007). "Management and Music: The Exceptional Case of the IBM Songbook." *Group Organization Management*, 32(1), 79–108.

Hanson, Jeffrey R. and Krackhardt, David (1993). "Informal Networks: The Company Behind the Chart." *Harvard Business Review*, 71, July/August, 103–111.

Karpeles, Maud (1967). *Cecil Sharp: His Life and Work* (Chicago IL: University of Chicago Press).

McGregor, Jena (2006). "The Office Chart That Really Counts." *Business Week*, February 26.

Mescon, Michael H. (September 1959). "Comments on Organization." *The Journal of Educational Sociology*, 33(1), 34–36.

Morris, William (1890 [2009]). *News From Nowhere.* Reprinted by Oxford University Press.

Reingold, Jennifer and Yang, Jia Lynn (2007). "Hidden Workplace." *Fortune*, July 23, 2007.

Riesman David, Glazer, Nathan, and Denney, Reuel (1950). *The Lonely Crowd: A Study of the Changing American Character* (New Haven CT: Yale University Press).

Schein, Edgar H. (2004). *Organizational Culture and Leadership* (San Francisco: Jossey-Bass).

Smith, Adam (1776). *Wealth of Nations* (London: Strahan and Cadell).

Special Collections (n.d.). "Insider and Outsider, Fresh Air, Quare Women, and the Country Life Movement." Special collections and University Archives, University of North Carolina, Asheville.

Turner, Fredrick Jackson (1893/1961). "The Significance of the Frontier in American History," in Frederick Jackson Turner, *Frontier and Section: Selected Essays*, pp. 37–62 (Englewood Cliffs, NJ: Prentice Hall).

Weber, Max (1921). *The City* (New York: Free Press).

Whyte, William (1956). *The Organization Man* (New York: Simon & Schuster).

Williams, John Alexander (2002). *Appalachia: A History* (Chapel Hill NC and London: University of North Carolina Press).

Chapter 7

Motivation

Learning objectives

Besides developing strategies, managers seek to motivate. In the developed and industrialized West, a number of techniques have been developed to do so including X that assumes that workers are lazy, not to be trusted, and must be motivated by material rewards or the threat to withhold them. Theory Y, in contrast, insists that workers potentially like their work, can be loyal, and are best motivated with non-material rewards. Theory Z focuses upon cultural dimensions while David McClelland emphasizes the specific role of innate needs in particular cultures. This non-exhaustive discussion of motivation is presented with reference to indigenous, ethnic, and rural peoples.

Specific issues addressed include:

1   Understanding how Scientific Management and Theory X view employees in a way that leads to views of motivation that concentrate upon materials gain.
2   Viewing Theory Y as an alternative that views workers as intelligent, motivated, and in search of interesting and challenging assignments.
3   Perceiving Theory Z as one example of motivational theories that are concerned with social and cultural concerns, not merely the individual.
4   Envisioning a wide range of motivators (such as the need to achieve, the need for power and the need for affiliation as discussed by McClelland) that impact people to varying degrees depending upon the circumstances and environment.
5   Gaining the ability to choose methods and strategies that are appropriate to the situation.

Introduction

Devising appropriate, equitable, and effective ways to motivate people is of obvious importance to the health, wellbeing, and effectiveness of organizations (ranging from businesses to communities). An early theory of motivation stems from the work of Fredrick W. Taylor and his Scientific Management. A review of this theory sets the stage to juxtapose later perspectives; They vary significantly by depicting employees as (1) lazy and untrustworthy, (2) curious and potentially loyal, or as (3) "social animals." Finally, the work of David McClelland suggests that all people possess certain innate needs, such as the need for achievement, power, and affiliation. The power and influence of each of these needs, however, varies; a person's cultural background often determines the strength of each in relation to the others.

This representative and non-exhaustive array of motivational options is discussed with reference to the situations faced by indigenous, ethnic, and rural peoples.

Scientific management

In the late nineteenth/early twentieth century, Frederick W. Taylor dominated what is referred to as "Scientific Management." Taylor rose to prominence as an industrial engineer who devised efficient ways to perform specific tasks that could be standardized in order to increase production.

Once optimum methods of production were devised, workers were mandated to adhere to these strict protocols. Taylor insisted that such uniformity was the best way to guarantee the highest output from workers. In an increasingly mechanized world, Scientific Management sought to transform people into living machines and gain the efficiencies of standardization by doing so. Taylor is primarily remembered for his belief that that (1) research could determine the one best way to accomplish a goal and that (2) forcing people to act accordingly is a good strategy.

Although this approach could lead to rote efficiencies, it could also be mind-numbing. This, of course, is exactly the hurtful consequence of the industrial age that rival methods of production such as the Arts and Crafts movement (discussed in Chapter 6) sought to mitigate. Although Taylor wanted management to do the thinking and for minions to follow orders without question, the Arts and Crafts movement emphasized nurturing people, responding to their personal needs, developing a strong internalized work ethic, and offering fulfilling careers that gave people a sense of purpose.

This vision is, perhaps, best depicted by a short essay entitled "A Message to Garcia" that was written by Elbert Hubbard (1899), the Arts and Crafts leader who founded the Roycrofters. An inspirational parable, this celebrated essay recalls the efforts of Andrew Rowan, an American soldier who, during the Spanish–American War, was instructed to deliver a message to Garcia, a rebel leader that the United States wanted to enlist as an ally. Rowan took the letter and delivered it. Hubbard's essay went on to celebrate Rowan not for the contribution he made to the war, but because he asked no questions, simply took the letter, and using personal initiative and intelligence completed the mission.

Having done so, Hubbard juxtaposes Rowan's actions to those of typical employees who possess little initiative, must rely upon superiors for advice and leadership, and lack an ability to think for themselves. He concludes:

> My heart goes out to the man who does his work when the "boss" is away, as well as when he is at home. And the man who, when given a letter for Garcia, quietly takes the missive, without asking any idiotic questions.... Civilization is one long, anxious search for just such individuals. Anything such a man asks will be granted. He is wanted in every city, town and village – in every office, shop, store and factory. The world cries out for such: he is needed and needed badly – the man who can "Carry a Message to Garcia."
>
> (Hubbard 1899, n.p.)

This little piece, written as "filler" to complete a magazine issue, quickly took on a life of its own after it was reprinted by a railroad and given to employees and passengers. It has been translated into many languages and given to military recruits throughout the world. Many million copies have been produced. It has been made into two motion pictures (one silent, the other with sound).

As a result of this little essay, Hubbard became a darling of the robber barons of the era and his little epistle was celebrated as a tribute to the spirit of individualism that many in the era equated with American greatness. The lesson of "A Message to Garcia" is that people are best motivated by something that is inside them that will arise if people are allowed to show personal initiative as invoked by a fulfilling challenge.

In spite of the wide acclaim Hubbard received from business leaders, Taylor's Scientific Management (coming to prominence in the exact same era) was the complete opposite. In the early twentieth century, ideas of motivation associated with Taylor were widely employed in factories in Britain, the United States, and other developed regions. Without it, a key assumption of Scientific Management, affirms that if people are paid enough and if the threat of losing their job looms large, employees will be motivated; nothing else is likely to be effective. Scientific Management also assumed that because people cannot be trusted to think for themselves leaders need to mandate exactly how every aspect of work will be conducted. While Hubbard advocated a type of motivation represented by Rowan's inherent drive to succeed, Taylor acted as if such internal incentives did not exist.

Hubbard and the Arts and Crafts movement, in contrast, suggested that the "Rowan spirit" could prevail if work is fulfilling and inspiring. By providing this positive environment, a highly motivated workforce would result. Thus, Taylor viewed work as something external that people merely tolerate, while the Arts and Crafts movement proclaimed that work could and should be merged into the flow of life in empowering and enriching ways. If this was done, Hubbard believed that people would gain internal motivation and work with skill, purpose, and efficiency.

The methods of Scientific Management, however, were long used in the modern, Western, and developed realms. In places where impersonal factories dominated, many people who toiled under such conditions became accustomed to methods influenced by Scientific Management and learned to tolerate them. In more traditional and less developed regions, however, people have often continued to be more connected to their work in personal and intimate ways. Not having been trained to accept a tedious existence as cogs in industrial machines, many of these people have trouble adjusting to such conditions. These peoples seem to parallel Hubbard's Rowan, not plodding workers who let others do the thinking and are able to tolerate a dreary and unfulfilling work life.

Theory X

As management theories developed in the West and developed regions, a shift away from humanistic perspectives, such as those provided by Arts and Crafts movement, took place. Scientific Management that advocated the use of managerial control, emphasized material rewards and paid scant attention to spiritual and psychological needs. Eventually, as we shall see, these ideas were tempered. In spite of this progress towards more enlightened views, Douglas McGregor (1960) affirms that many managers continue to intuitively follow Taylor's advice that motivation is best accomplished with reference to material wellbeing coupled with a tendency to distrust or even fear workers.

In his *The Human Side of Enterprise* (1960), for example, McGregor points out that many managers underestimate the potentials of their employees and/ or have little recognition that workers have (or can be groomed to develop) a strong work ethic. Those with these jaundice attitudes are said to embrace what McGregor refers to as the Theory X of management and motivation.

Theory X asserts that employees tend to be lazy, seek to avoid work, hate their jobs, possess little ambition, avoid responsibility, and so forth. In other words, those who follow Theory X hold views that are similar to those advocated by Taylor and Scientific Management. As a result of these characteristics, the model assumes that employees must be motivated by monetary rewards and/or job security. McGregor acknowledges that those who embrace a Theory X style of motivation and management have a number of options available to them ranging from so-called (1) "tough" management that sets down strict rules and stiff punishments to (2) "soft" management that seeks to create harmony at work. Viewing these options as poles on a continuum, a wide range of specific tactics can be developed. Nevertheless, they are unified by their focus upon material benefits and the tendency to pursue few attempts to make the work rewarding, inviting, and/or compelling. McGregor insists that all of these tactics are ultimately unsuccessful because effective methods of motivation need to expand beyond financial rewards; Theory X fails to do so.

Theory X managers do not seek out heroic "Rowans" destined to excel. The belief that employees are lazy, exploitive, and untrustworthy justifies motivational guidelines that are closely linked to providing tangible rewards for a job adequately completed. Because Theory X portrays employees as being indifferent to the best interests of their organization, managers who embrace this perspective must rely upon providing adequate material rewards and/or threaten to remove these incentives. Enlisting (1) employee loyalty and (2) nurturing an internal desire within workers to do a job well is not seen as a viable strategy. This situation can be graphically portrayed in Table 7.1.

Thus, Theory X embraces a negative view of employees and suggests that managers need to protect their organizations from them. As a result of this belief, strategies are centered upon reducing the vulnerability of the organization to subversive forces that must be kept in check. The end product of this thinking is an adversarial model that views management and workers as opponents pitted against each other.

Theory X can be seen as preserving Taylor's views of motivation. Although Scientific Management has largely been replaced and repudiated,

Table 7.1 Theory X and motivation

Issue	Analysis
Attitudes towards workers	Workers are lazy, untrustworthy, and not interested in the needs of the organization.
Threats to firm	Because of their attitudes, employees may act in ways that serve their personal and short-term goals at the expense of the organization.
Coping strategies	Recognize that employees have goals and agendas that are best achieved by shortchanging the organization. The organization must protect itself by confronting this threat as required.
Motivation	Since employees will not be inspired or motivated by a sense of loyalty to the firm or a striving for personal achievement, methods of motivation should be based upon providing adequate material rewards or threatening to withhold them.

DISCUSSION

In many ways, McGregor's depiction of Theory X is a caricature of inept and uninformed managers who fail to view employees with regard to their potential. Although such thinking is not state of the art, it does reflect the attitudes of many managers.

McGregor suggests that many managers continue, at least covertly, to embrace its premises.

The work habits of indigenous, ethnic, and rural peoples might be envisioned in ways that, at first glance, appear to reflect Theory X. In regions of the United States where a significant Native American population exists, for example, the term "Indian Time" is often used to suggest that Native people are lazy and not to be trusted. In reality, many of these indigenous people possess multiple commitments that prevent them from honoring some requirements associated with regularly scheduled jobs. This is especially true when people continue to live a subsistence life in which the rhythms of nature, not the clock, dictate what people do and the schedule that should be followed. When the salmon are running in Alaska, for example, subsistence people must be on the river; that is not negotiable. It is not easy, however, for mainstream managers to understand the necessity of their employees to follow the patterns of nature, not the ticking of the clock.

Instead of understanding why employees fail to show up for work, frustrated managers are likely to doubt the sincerity of those who are absent, question their work ethic, and punish absences. Many of these employees, however, want to be good workers and will perform well and with loyalty if their needs are more fully taken into account by the organizations they work for.

Thus, remnants of Taylor's Scientific Management continue to exist. Over time, however, autocratic styles of management and motivation that assume employees are lazy, dishonest, and do not care about their work have lost popularity. Let us hope that those who deal with indigenous, ethnic, and rural people will become equally enlightened.

Theory Y

As an alternative to Theory X, Douglas McGregor (1960) pointed to Theory Y which was inspired, to a large degree, by the work of Abraham Maslow. While Theory X concluded that employees are lazy and not to be trusted, Theory Y recognizes that under the proper conditions employees can become loyal and hardworking. If people are treated appropriately, their motivation can grow in powerful and productive ways. Thus, while Theory X is preoccupied almost exclusively with end results (such as meeting quotas or adhering to a schedule), Theory Y is equally concerned with the process of work and how to engage employees in creative and productive ways. If these intrinsic needs (such as the desire to grow and learn) are taken into account in an equitable manner, Theory Y predicts that the results are likely to be positive.

Theory Y managers also believe that all people, not just supervisors and top management, have an innate potential to be creative and use their imaginations in a dynamic and fruitful manner. To achieve this potential, a work environment must be created that grooms and nurtures employees so they are willing to fully use their abilities when completing assigned tasks. In other words, people are most effectively motivated by expanding incentives beyond satisfying physical needs or threatening to withhold support.

Such a system of management, of course, is the complete opposite of Scientific Management and Theory X. McGregor concluded that, unfortunately, the methods and tactics associated with Theory X often dominate; as a result, employees often fail to achieve their full potentials on the job.

According to Theory Y, work is natural and under the right conditions, people will be drawn to it. A basic premise of those who embrace a Theory Y perspective is that modern industrial environments often fail to acknowledge and build upon the inherent goals, talents, needs, and initiatives of employees. The potentials of employees, however, can be tapped by responding to their ambitions, motives, and talents; doing so is an effective tool of management, supervision, and motivation.

Those who embrace a Theory Y approach believe that if properly groomed and nurtured, many, if not most, employees will work hard, willingly embrace responsibilities, gain the ability to act independently, perform well, and want to contribute. In a nutshell, when properly managed, employees can evolve to act like Andrew Rowan in Hubbard's "A Message to Garcia."

In short, McGregor argues in *The Human Side of Enterprise* (1960) that managers need to embrace a more positive and respectful view of workers. By doing so, potentials that are often unrecognized and unrealized can grow and mature. Perhaps, the negative views of Theory X create a self-fulfilling prophecy that leads people to develop lack luster habits and attitudes. If so, such managerial theories and habits hold back human potentials and keep them from flowering.

Being treated in a way reflective of Theory Y, however, may be able to reverse hurtful tendencies created by Theory X environments. If organizations and managers assume that their workers have an inherent drive to work hard, (1) a potential to be productive team members, and (2) an ability to develop into successful independent thinkers are likely to materialize. Managers and supervisors can create an environment that helps channel employee behavior and thinking in those positive directions. This is an important lesson of Theory Y. An overview of Theory Y is presented in Table 7.2.

Earlier in this chapter, we saw how managers who operate in communities with large American Indian populations might complain about what they call "Indian time." Supervisors might be outraged when work schedules are disrupted if employees fail to show up for work as scheduled. As a result, Theory X managers might conclude that Indian workers are lazy and undependable. In reality, as discussed above, many Native people rely to a large extent upon subsistence hunting and fishing for their livelihood. Loyal workers, or not, they must participate in these vital activities or go hungry.

Table 7.2 Theory Y and motivation

Issue	Analysis
Perspective	Workers have the potential to be trustworthy, hardworking, dedicated, and self-motivated.
Benefits to firm	Having a loyal, hardworking, and dedicated workforce is of obvious value.
Strategies	Eliminate self-fulfilling prophesies held by management that assumes that people are lazy, unmotivated and untrustworthy. Create a work environment where non-material goals, motives, and needs are addressed.
Motivation	People have an inherent desire to work hard, succeed and see positive results. The urge to work is just as basic as the desire to play. By providing an enriching environment and by treating employees with respect, workers will gain motivation that can be channelled in ways that benefit the organization.

DISCUSSION
While Theory X seeks to protect organizations from lazy, untrustworthy, and passive employees, Theory Y assumes people want to work hard, accomplish goals, and contribute. By embracing a Theory Y orientation, the organization will be better able to tap the full potential of employee's and gain their loyalty.

People in developed and industrial regions tend to look at their job as their primary (if not their only) bread-winning activity. As a result, these workers have developed a willingness to adjust to the needs of the organization.

This situation of the modern and developed regions does not reflect the lives and economic realities of many indigenous peoples. They have one foot in regularly scheduled work and another firmly planted in subsistence activities that do not adhere to a completely predictable timetable. These people often find it necessary to postpone regularly scheduled work because "the fish will only be running for a few days" or because "the Caribou herd is nearby." Decisions about not going to work are often based on such immediate and time-sensitive concerns.

Organizations and managers who embrace a culturally incompetent, Theory X perspective will have trouble understanding the perspectives of these employees and conclude that they are untrustworthy and lazy. Theory Y managers are more likely to view a situation from an employee point of view, acknowledge they might be loyal, and work to avoid conflicts that can trigger tensions. Such tactics are likely to be more effective when dealing with indigenous, ethnic and rural peoples.

Theory Z

In pioneering discussions of informal organizations in management thought, Elton Mayo's work at the Hawthorne plant focuses upon social and interpersonal relationships, not the dictates of upper management. Delving into motivations, Mayo advanced the theory that financial rewards, alone, were not sufficient to adequately motivate employees. In doing so, Mayo pointed to social needs, recommending that employers respond to workers in humane and caring ways. When treated in such a manner, Mayo believed that the quality of work would increase. Mayo's research led to the establishment of what is known as the Human Relations School of Management. Although evolving in contexts that are a distinct form this classic paradigm, Theory Z embraces a similar point of view.

Over the years, the term "Theory Z" has been used in several contexts by different researchers. This discussion refers to the work of William G. Ouchi. In the early 1980s, Ouchi published *Theory Z: How American Business Can Meet the Japanese Challenge* (1981) that attributes the success of Japanese industry to a distinctive style of managing by paying special attention to a strong corporate culture that grooms and develops employees over a long period of time and involves the entire workforce in the decision-making process. Ouchi demonstrates the effectiveness of this approach, by pointing to low employee turnover, strong job commitment, and higher productivity within Theory Z firms.

Ouchi used his analysis of Japanese management in order to argue that employees prefer intimate working relationships with both their companies and in their relationships with fellow workmates. Ouchi also suggested that employees need the support of their company to help them in situations that transcend work (such as family needs, social life, crises, and so forth). He also predicts that this kind of treatment leads to a strong work ethic, group identity, trustworthiness, and tendency to work to the best of their ability.

Organizations that operate according to Theory Z principles encourage participatory management. As a result, employees are involved in the decision-making process with resolutions and demands seldom being dictated unilaterally from above. Even if job promotions typically come slowly in Theory Z companies, Ouchi reports that employees tend to be loyal.

In Chapter 6, the point was made that the principles of Japanese management are distinct from the coercive practices of paternalism because the Japanese approach reflects the traditions of people and it gains wide acceptance as a result. Paternalistic practices, in contrast, are the brainchild of upper management and typically implemented in an authoritarian manner.

As an alternative, Ouchi emphasizes that quality and productivity tend to increase if organizations embrace a long-term commitment to their employees, develop a nurturing environment, offer a greater degree of participation, as well as freedom within the workplace. Under these conditions,

Ouchi suggests employees are often more willing to sacrifice and tolerate greater flexibility in ways that benefit the organization.

As with Theory Y, Theory Z is an overt alternative to Theory X. It embraces a concern for innate psychological needs and melds a social perspective to it. Thus it merges the concerns of Mayo and the Human Relations School with those of McGregor and proponents of Theory Y. An overview of Theory Z is presented in Table 7.3.

Because it is based upon a Japanese style of management, however, certain applications of a Theory Z orientation may be culturally bound. Nevertheless, in situations where the method seeks to address and satisfy human universals, such an approach may be useful and applicable under a wide variety of circumstances.

Although Theory Z emerged in a specific place (Japan is a highly developed industrial power that, at least until recently, encouraged intimate relationships between people and organizations), it might reflect the functioning of many Indigenous, ethnic, and rural peoples. Where this is true, a Theory Z orientation might be appropriate for smaller, face-to-face communities. In the typical Japanese organization, for example, subordinates and supervisors tend to interact in intimate ways, often spending considerable

Table 7.3 Theory Z as organizational model

Issue	Analysis
Attitudes towards workers	Workers are viewed as social creatures and as people who have feelings. By encouraging greater participation, in addition to addressing the social and psychological needs, employees will develop loyalty to the organization and work harder.
Organizational theory	Organizational structures can be more effective by empowering employees, involving them in the planning and decision making functions, and by developing strategies that help and nurture employees, both inside and beyond the workplace.
Strategies and tactics	Involve workers in a wide range of decisions. Allow them to help determine how a particular task is to be performed. Create an environment that satisfies social needs. Involve the organization in a manner that resolves psychological tensions.

DISCUSSION

Theory Z seemingly combines elements of Mayo's Human Relations School and McGregor's Theory Y. By doing so both internal and social motives are addressed. Doing so has positive implication both for employees and the organization.

time in after-work social activities. The goal of this contact tends to be bonding and camaraderie. The style of interaction employed is typically as egalitarian as possible, even in situations involving people possessing different ranks and degrees of authority.

Such a style and mode of organizational structuring and functioning appears to be reflective of cultures that embrace Mechanical Solidarity that was analyzed in Chapter 5. As discussed above, many small-scale indigenous, ethnic, and rural communities possess patterns of culture and organization that are mechanical in nature with the members exhibiting relatively little differentiation or specialization among members. In small, rural communities, for example, everybody knows and understands everybody else. People in all walks of life are in intimate contact with each other. Differences between people are deemphasized. Specialization is not as pronounced. Because the community is close knit, fellowship is emphasized.

Japanese principles of management appear to be closely aligned to a mechanical orientation and the harmony of the group that it fosters. We can speculate regarding why this is true. Perhaps it is nested in inherent aspects of Japanese culture. Is it an artifact of Japan's rapid industrialization in the late nineteenth and early twentieth centuries? In any event, the Theory Z method of management and motivation appears to be well suited to indigenous, ethnic, and rural people because many of these communities are organized in ways that are reflective of mechanical solidarity. As a result, the lesson of Theory Z expands beyond the context in which it was created. This theory focuses directly upon the fact that on many occasions, people do better when working in an empowering manner in which their social as well as their psychological needs are taken into account.

This discussion has dealt with three well-known theories of organization and motivation. Theory X views employees as lazy, unmotivated, and even enemies of the organization. Theory Y points to innate psychological needs. Theory Z acknowledges group (including cultural) considerations. The views of motivation discussed above, of course, are representative and not exhaustive. The paradigms discussed were chosen in order to develop a specific chain of thought that might be useful to indigenous, ethnic, and rural peoples. Many other perspectives could have been added if more space was available. The work of Abraham Maslow and Frederick Herzberg, for example, are conspicuously absent. Maslow's and Herzberg's listings of specific needs that motivate people at different times and under different circumstances, however, influence McGregor's work.

In conclusion, Theories X, Y and Z relate motivation to certain tendencies people are believed to possess. Theory X assumes people are lazy and untrustworthy. As a result they can only be motivated by material rewards and/or the threat of removing them. Theory Y affirms that people have innate psychological needs that can trigger a willingness to work hard, take responsibility, and so forth. Theory Y management seeks to motivate people by offering an environment that provides the ability to learn, achieve, and be part of something that is significant. Theory Z combines a concern for innate human needs with social perspectives. Even though Theory Z reflects Japanese culture, this method appears to reflect the ways in which small-scale communities function because it emphasizes intimate interaction with others in an egalitarian way. As a result, Theory Z is reflective of mechanical cultures that are so common among indigenous, ethnic, and rural communities.

Achievement, power and affiliation

Max Weber, a German sociologist of the early twentieth century, along with France's Émile Durkheim, is a towering figure of social theory. Methodologically, however, Weber was at odds with Durkheim and the way sociology developed in the late eighteenth and early twentieth centuries. In Weber's era, mainstream sociologists increasingly embraced the empirical method, typically adopting statistical analysis. Weber, in contrast, was a humanist who focused upon what people thought and felt, not merely what they were observed doing.

This subjective and intuitive approach is clearly present in Weber's masterpiece *The Protestant Ethic and the Spirit of Capitalism* (2002) which explored why the first great flowering of industrialization and modern capitalism occurred in northern Europe (especially Britain) and not somewhere else. In line with his humanistic leanings, Weber believed that this great economic shift took place where it did because of the distinctive feelings and beliefs of the people who lived there. In a nutshell, the Calvinist doctrines of early Protestant Christianity emphasized predestination. In other words, God already knew who would be blessed with a trip to heaven after death and who were inevitably condemned to a fiery, painful, and eternal hell.

As a result, Weber argues that many Calvinists sought riches and material success as an end in itself in the belief that God would favor his "chosen ones" in this life as well as in the next. Thus, in order to dispel the fears of everlasting suffering, many Calvinists of Northern Europe became preoccupied with gaining material successes in this life in order to gain evidence of God's favor. Money, wealth, and worldly attainments emerged as a way of keeping score: they provided a clue that people with a record of achievement were blessed by God in this life and the next. Such an emotional preoccupation with heaven and hell gave rise to an urge to accumulate and maintain great wealth which, in turn, was reinvested, resulting in a spiraling effect which culminated in power, economic clout, the rise of modern capitalism, and a flowering of the industrial revolution.

Weber also believed that in the Catholic countries this compulsion for material achievement, reinvestment, and capital accumulation was weaker precisely because the religious views of these people were different. As a result, industrial capitalism emerged more robustly in the North instead of in the South. Weber used his theory to challenge one of Karl Marx's favorite premises that religion was influenced by economic conditions and the means of production (as summarized in his "Religion is the opium of the masses" slogan). Weber argued just the opposite, suggesting that humanistic feelings and beliefs (in this case stemming from religion) trigger economic trends and relationships, not vice versa.

Most basically, Weber's point is that the feelings that people embrace exert a profound impact upon their economic lives. This same issue was taken up in the 1950s and 1960s by anthropologist David McClelland and is most fully expressed in his *The Achieving Society* (1961). Building upon Weber and psychologist Henry Murray (1938), McClelland asserts that all people have three basic needs (the Need to Achieve, The Need for Power, and the Need for Affiliation). McClelland believes that although these three needs are universal, they exist in varying degrees within different people. As Weber before him, McClelland maintains that the culture plays an important role in determining the power of each need (or motivation) as well as helping to determine which dominates. Thus, McClelland assumes that cultural patterns and the socialization process have major roles in determining the strength, impact, and influence of various motivational influences. They are discussed below.

Need to Achieve: According to McClelland, all people have a need to achieve that includes a desire or urge to accomplish challenging tasks, adhere to prescribed standards, "being successful," and so forth. McClelland, however, acknowledged that some people possess a stronger desire to achieve than others. The strength of this urge can impact the choices people make as well as the effort and sacrifices they are willing to endure. As Weber suggested, this trait can stem from a cultural background as well as other stimuli, such as the family, the socialization process, and so forth.

McClelland acknowledges that different people will indulge their need to achieve in their own ways. Some might seek out easy tasks that promise a good chance of success at a minimal effort and/or risk. Others with a need to achieve might take risks that push their abilities to the limit. In any event, achieving a goal tends to be more important than the tangible reward for doing so.

As indicated, McClelland's depiction of the Need to Achieve mirrors Weber's theory (discussed on p. 139) that industrialization and economic development in the West was triggered by the need to achieve. In essence, McClelland and his work extended Weber's theory, tested it in a laboratory setting, added additional dimensions (power and affiliation), and expanded the paradigm to include a greater cross-cultural dimension.

I have been told that a Japanese proverb observes "A nail that sticks out is nailed down." Apparently, this process involves putting those who egotistically "stick out" in their place. Such a tendency can be juxtaposed with life in the United States where notoriety associated with individual achievement is often sought and celebrated.

The achievement motive exhibited by indigenous, ethnic, and rural peoples who live (or historically have lived) in small scale communities, might be very different from what is observed in modern, industrial, mass societies, and especially within cultures like the United States that appear to be preoccupied with personal success and accomplishments.

Thus, in smaller communities where people are likely to relate to each other in more egalitarian ways and/or interact on a face-to-face basis, the need for people to flaunt their success may be less or not exist. In fact, in some cultures, people go to great lengths to avoid standing apart from others in any meaningful way. Other aspects of the culture and its traditions or mores might also undercut or reduce the need to achieve, as discussed by McClelland.

Need for Power: People with a strong desire for power seek to control or impact others. McClelland believes that although innate, a strong desire for power is acquired and learned. It might be (and often is) an artifact of the culture and/or the socialization process.

The fact that someone is driven to seek power does not necessary indicate that the person is selfish or bad. Those who seek a dominate position, for example, might want to help people and act in the public interest, as is the case with many politicians. Nevertheless, those with a strong need for power seek to wield control over others and they possess a strong desire to do so.

In certain circumstances, these power-driven individuals might be argumentative or at least willing to raise disputes in order to advance their point of view and/or get their way. People who seek power are not likely to place a high priority on reaching a consensus. Their goal is to control the situation by one means or another.

In some countries or cultures (such as the United States) a strong sense of individualism and individual initiative prevails. In such environments those with a strong need for power might be understood, acknowledged, or at least tolerated. In many other countries or cultural areas, however, a much more collective orientation might prevail. In such environments, those who forcefully seek power may be out of step with their fellows and emerge as ineffective or even outcast.

In contemporary business discussions, Japanese culture is often discussed as being more collective/consensus seeking while the United States is portrayed as individualistic and power focused.

When dealing with indigenous, ethnic, and rural peoples, determining the culture's and the people's relationship to individual vs. collective power can provide important clues regarding how business can best be conducted and how people can be most effectively motivated. On many occasions, the culture determines the role of power and who should wield it. As Margaret Mead (1935) demonstrated when examining the cross-cultural responses of women among a variety of indigenous peoples, attitudes towards power can be very different from community to community and from culture to culture.

Many indigenous, ethnic, and rural peoples live in small-scale communities that are characterized by face-to-face relationships and egalitarian relationships. They are organized in ways that resemble what Émile Durkheim depicted as mechanical in nature. Such communities are likely to deemphasize personal power and reflect the collective will. As social and economic transitions take place, however, the role, credibility, and legitimacy of personal power might increase. When dealing with indigenous, ethnic, and rural peoples, the traditions of the culture as well as emerging trends triggered by outside influences might need to be acknowledged and taken into account.

Need for Affiliation: McClelland uses the term the Need for Affiliation when discussing a person's need to be a part of and mesh with a social group. As intuitively understood, affiliation can be characterized as a positive relationship with another person or group. It is likely to be intimate. As Byrne has observed, affiliation typically involves "concern over establishing, maintaining, or restoring a positive affective relationship with another person or persons" (Byrne 1961).

People with a strong need for affiliation tend to seek and desire approval from others and positive contact with their fellows. In other words, relationships are very important. Those who are primarily motivated by the need for achievement or power, in contrast, might be relatively indifferent regarding what others think about them. This drive for affiliation, in contrast, can cause the need for achievement and power to be reduced.

People with a high need for affiliation tend to seek approval from those with whom they have regular contact. Having a strong bond with others can make these people feel as if they are a part of something that is important and more meaningful than they are individually. People who place a high emphasis on affiliation tend to be supportive partners or collaborators, but they might shy away from leadership positions that separate them from others.

Based upon personal anecdotal evidence, I have observed a strong need for affiliation among indigenous, ethnic, and rural peoples over wide cultural and geographic areas.

Thus, these three needs are distinctive and they might conflict with each other. The message of Max Weber and David McClelland is clear. The actual feelings and emotions possessed by people exert a profound impact upon what they do, want, and how they are motivated. For a variety of reasons, business theory and practice has tended to center upon empirical studies that are typically examined using statistical analysis. Weber and McClelland point to the need for a more humanistic and qualitative approach.

Thus, people tend to be motivated by feelings, such as the need for achievement, power, or affiliation. Perhaps this listing is not exhaustive and other needs (such as curiosity or issues such as "self-actualization" as proposed by Abraham Maslow) might also impact people and the motivations they experience. The goal here is not to provide a complete overview of all motivating influences. Instead, the emphasis is upon the fact that people can be motivated by a wide range of influences and desires, and understanding these feelings within a proper context is vital. The feelings of one group might not easily correspond with the sentiments held by others.

Most of the research concerning organizations and motivation was conducted in the modern industrial developed world. Perhaps, what has been learned in that context does not easily transfer elsewhere. When dealing with distinct cultural and social groups, keeping this warning in mind is vital.

Choosing the right motivational option

When dealing with people, determining ways to appropriately motivate them is crucial. Early theories of motivation, such as those embraced by advocates of Scientific Management and Theory X, concentrate upon incentives that are solely based on material gains. Theory Y emphasizes that employees have a richer and more complicated set of motivators that are related to personal, not merely material, needs. Theory Z adds a social element. The last paradigms considered focus upon an array of needs proposed by Max Weber and David McClelland, their relative power, and influences upon them such as culture. This non-exhaustive survey of theories and methods demonstrates diversity and complexity.

Of these four methods, Theory Z and the McClelland model are best able to deal with social and cultural traits. When dealing with indigenous, ethnic, and rural people, acknowledging and responding to their distinctiveness is vital. Although each culture is distinct, many of these cultural enclaves are (or recently have been) characterized by small-scale, face-to-face communities that Durkheim depicts as "mechanical" in nature. This fact may provide vital clues regarding the best way to motivate these cultural enclaves.

It is hoped that the discussions above provide insights regarding how to tailor motivational methods around specific people as they actually exist. Hopefully by doing so, it might be possible to avoid the mistakes that arise from attempting to motivate people in generic ways based on theories and methods that emerged in the Western, modern, and developed worlds.

Relevant terms

Achieve (Need to): A component of motivation proposed by David McClelland that dealt with the inherent need for people to achieve.

Achieving Society, The: A book by David McClelland that suggests people have three inherent needs (for achievement, power, and affiliation), but culture determines the relative power of these needs.

Arts and Crafts movement: An artistic and social movement that emphasizes that people are best motivated by responding to independence and desire for creativity.

Affiliation (Need for): A component of motivation proposed by David McClelland that states all people have an inherent need for relationships with other people.

Herzberg, Frederick: A motivational specialist influenced by Abraham Maslow who influenced Douglas McGregor.

Hubbard, Elbert: Author of "A Message to Garcia," an essay that emphasized the value of independent and self-motivated people. Provided a message that counters the motivational assumptions of Scientific Management.

Human Side of Enterprise, The: A book by Douglas McGregor that juxtaposed Theories X and Y.

Indian time: Drawing attention to the fact that many indigenous people will sometimes avoid scheduled work in order to fulfill subsistence obligations. Often pointed to as evidence that Native people are lazy or undependable. In reality, they simply must take advantage of unscheduled opportunities.

Japanese management: A managerial strategy associated with Theory Z that emphasizes collaboration and responding to a broad range of human needs.

Maslow, Abraham: A humanistic psychologist who influenced Douglas McGregor.

McGregor, Douglas: Author of *The Human Side of Enterprise* that argued that people can become trusted and hardworking employees if treated in an appropriate manner.

"Message to Garcia": An influential article that emphasized the value of independent and self-motivated people. Brought fame to Elbert Hubbard and the Arts and Crafts movement.

Power (Need for): A component of motivation proposed by David McClelland that asserts all people have a need for power.

Protestant Ethic and the Spirit of Capitalism, The: A book by Max Weber that argues that cultural factors led the people of Northern Europe to be motivated to develop modern industrial capitalism.

Scientific Management: Fredrick W. Taylor's attempts to find the one best way to do things. Believed motivation was based on material gains or the threat of losing them.

Taylor, Fredrick W.: The leader of Scientific Management.

Theory X: The belief that employees are lazy, untrustworthy and must be tightly controlled.

Theory Y: The belief that employees can become eager, productive, and self-motivated if managed in ways that cultivate these traits.

Theory Z: The belief that employees exist in a complex cultural milieu that exerts a strong impact upon their motivations.

Discussion questions

1   Compare and contrast Scientific Management and Theory X. What do they have in common? What type of motivation do these theories recommend? Why? Do you feel this view is limited? How might these views not be appropriate for indigenous, ethnic, and rural peoples?
2   How is Theory Y distinct from Theory X? Can you mention some circumstances where Theory Y is a superior means of motivating employees? Why or why not?
3   Theory X and Theory Y both focus upon individuals. How is Theory Z distinct from them? What is the relevance of culture and collection action? Do you believe that the basic message of Theory Z is limited to Japanese methods? Why or why not? Do you feel that Theory Z provides any useful strategies for dealing with indigenous, ethnic, and rural peoples in particular? Why or why not?
4   A wide range of motivators exist that impact people to varying degrees depending upon the circumstances and environment. Discuss with reference to indigenous, ethnic, and rural peoples.
5   How can methods of motivation be chosen in ways that respond to specific peoples and their environment? Discuss with reference to a real-life example. If an actual example does not come to mind, invent one to stimulate thought and conversation.

References

Byrne, D. (1961). "Anxiety and the Experimental Arousal of Affiliation Need." *Journal of Abnormal Psychology*, 63(3), 660–662.

Hubbard, Elbert (1899). "A Message to Garcia." *The Philistine* (East Aurora, NY: Roycrofters).

Mead, Margaret (2003 [1935]). *Sex and Temperament in Three Primitive Societies* (New York: Perennial).

McClellend, David (1961). *The Achieving Society* (Princeton, NJ: Van Nostrand).

McGregor, Douglas (1960). *The Human Side of Enterprise* (New York: Barnes and Noble).

Murray, Henry A. (1938). *Explorations in Personality* (New York: Oxford University Press).

Ouchi, William (1981). *Theory Z: How Americans can Meet the Japanese Challenge* (New York: Avon Books).

Weber, Max (2002). *The Protestant Ethic and The Spirit of Capitalism* translated by Baehr, Peter and Wells, Gordon C. (London: Penguin Book).

Chapter 8

Accounting and other tools of evaluation

Learning objectives

Accounting involves record keeping expressed in monetary terms. Financial accounting evaluates the health and performance of the organization, while managerial accounting manipulates financial information in ways that facilitate strategic and tactical decision making. Other, more robust forms of evaluation, however, also exist. The Triple Bottom Line, for example, evaluates social and ecological issues as well as financial information and profits. Thus, the three modes of evaluation concentrate, respectively, upon people, planet, and profits. To be most effective, these alternative methods of evaluation can be tailored to the community and its circumstances. This chapter will aid the reader in:

1   Viewing financial accounting as a useful and essential record-keeping process.
2   Understanding the basic financial statements and their significance.
3   Appreciating the mission and value of managerial accounting.
4   Recognizing other tools of evaluation such as the Triple Bottom Line.
5   Learning to tailor methods such as the Triple Bottom Line to reflect the local community.

Introduction

Accounting, most basically, is a form of financial record keeping and evaluation. It is usually divided into the subfields of "Financial Accounting" and "Managerial Accounting."

Financial Accounting begins with bookkeeping: a detailed recording of all the transactions that involve money (and other items that can be presented in monetary terms). Accountants also prepare a variety of "financial statements" that systematically report monetary information of interest to various stakeholders.

When creating, recording, and providing this information, certain standards referred to as Generally Accepted Accounting Principles (or GAAP) are typically mandated. The goal of adhering to these conventions is to ensure that financial data is presented in a standardized and transparent manner that is trustworthy and easy to understand (see Meeks and Swann 2008). A certain amount of leeway, however, is allowed. A parallel system of guidelines that operates internationally is the International Financial Reporting Standards (IFRS) that provides procedures regarding how financial data should be presented when multiple countries are involved (see Alali and Cao 2010). The goal of these systems is to ensure that reliable facts are provided in an honest, unambiguous, and actionable manner. This data is typically demanded by a wide variety of interested parties who tend to be outsiders.

Managerial Accounting, on the other hand, manipulates the available financial accounting records in order to provide insights and information of value to the organization's leadership team. Although financial accounting data is typically made available to outsiders, the fruit of managerial accounting tends to be private and proprietary. The information gained is kept secret and used to provide a unique competitive advantage to the organization.

Accountants talk the language of money and their discussions are very important. This significance, however, is not an inevitable indication that accountants have all the relevant information or that what they recommend is appropriate in every situation. Accounting simply provides a certain type of information and the tools needed to evaluate it. The advice provided by accountants should not be used in isolation, although it often provides useful perspectives regarding the financial consequences of a particular course of action.

Remember that many indigenous, ethnic, and rural peoples are distinct and different from the mainstream clients commonly encountered in business. As a result, accountants might have difficulty effectively serving and responding to those idiosyncratic groups. This potential lack of experience with such people and communities should not be forgotten or ignored.

Although both financial and managerial accounting focus upon monetary issues, other methods of evaluation exist that, transcending financial considerations are more robust, complicated, and complex. The Triple Bottom Line, for example, evaluates organizations and their behavior using the multiple standards of (1) financial profit, (2) social concerns, and (3) ecological responsibility. Although controversial and potentially difficult to evaluate, broader and more far-reaching tools such as these are currently expanding the way in which strategies and tactics are assessed. Many indigenous, ethnic, and rural peoples will find such tools to be a useful means of supplementing accounting in ways that are relevant to their communities. Initially, we will discuss some mainstream basics before turning to these trends and options.

Double entry bookkeeping

A basic foundation of modern accounting recognizes that every financial action has two distinct, interrelated, and opposite impacts. This method goes back hundreds of years to Italy (see Lee 1977).

If, for example, I pay a bill (1) the amount of money I have on hand is reduced while (2) my debts are lessened by the same amount. As a result, my financial situation remains in balance. In double entry bookkeeping, all financial activities are dealt with using this systematic, two-step/two-account approach. Unless a clerical mistake is made, the two sides of the equation will always remain in balance. Happily, modern accounting software prevents simple mathematical mistakes.

The key formulation of accounting is typically presented as:

Assets = Liabilities + Equity

In this presentation, "Assets" are everything that is owned by the individual or the organization, "Liabilities" are the total obligations or debts, and "Equity" is whatever is left over (i.e. what the owner possesses "free and clear" after all the debts have been taken into account). When double entry bookkeeping is used, a particular transaction impacts both the Assets and the Liabilities/Equity sides of the equation, keeping them in balance.

Although this method of double entry bookkeeping accounting is systematic, in some situations it might inadvertently misrepresent the actual value of an asset. If a factory is acquired and its value is depreciated by 10 percent of the purchase price every year, in ten years, the value of the factory "on the books" would be $0.00. In reality, of course, if the factory has been maintained in a responsible manner, it would continue to have a significant value although naïve double entry bookkeeping would not recognize this worth. Of course, the accounting profession has responded to these possibilities with the development and utilization of more accurate methods of appraisal such as "fair value methods" (see Arya and Reinstein 2010); nonetheless, examples such as this demonstrate the possibility of imprecision.

The opposite is also true. An obsolete piece of equipment might have a $100,000 value "on the books" even though the true worth might be $0.00 (or a minimal scrap value). Once again some form of fair valuation can be of service under such circumstances. Nonetheless, accounting systems are not perfect and human judgement is often useful when actual evaluations and decisions are made.

In double entry bookkeeping, all financial activities are initially entered in the "Ledger" which is an ongoing diary of financial exchanges that are recorded approximately when they occur. These transactions are eventually reconciled in what is called a "trial balance" in which the entries in the Ledger (that are recorded in the order in which they occurred) are placed into their appropriate categories and reconciled. This systematic and better organized record is used to create a number of important financial documents.

Although the theoretic and practitioner underpinning of this method is simple, the actual application can be very complex because in most cases many different accounts exist in ways that can be bewildering and confusing. The key to understanding, however, is to remember that the two sides of the equation are kept in balance. It is also useful to remember (as we saw above) that financial accounting, even when done correctly and honestly, might not reflect the true value of assets.

The information created by double entry bookkeeping is used for various branches of accounting, such as financial and managerial accounting. Each is discussed below.

Financial accounting

As we saw above, bookkeeping is simply keeping a financial diary of the organization, creating a Trial Balance, and presenting data in a systematic manner that accountants can use to analyze financial affairs. Thus, bookkeeping and related activities create the raw material needed to analyze data and present it in useful and trustworthy formats.

Financial accounting summarizes and analyzes the financial transactions that bookkeepers have recorded (see Harrison et al. 2013 or other basic textbooks for full details regarding this section). Part of this process involves creating a variety of documents that provide information in a systematic manner as required by outsiders. A bank, for example, might need information regarding the financial strength of an organization before making a loan. Other stakeholders might have their own reasons for evaluating an organization's financial position and request records and information in order to do so.

If outsiders did not trust the information provided by accountants, a crisis in business and finance would result because people would hesitate to invest in a business or extend credit if they had no way to objectively assess the risks of doing so. The resulting distrust and caution would discourage economic activity and all would suffer. As a result, accounting is highly regulated in order to build trust and, thereby, encourage commerce and other financial activities. Bookkeepers merely record facts; accountants provide trustworthy information that others use to make decisions.

As a result of this importance, financial accountants must adhere to local, country-wide, and international accounting standards that provide guidelines, standards, conventions, and rules that are mandated and must be followed.

Representative financial statements

In order to present accounting data in a meaningful and easily understood fashion, a number of financial documents have become standardized (and are typically demanded when organizations are being evaluated from a financial perspective. Three of these keystone documents are the Balance Sheet, The Profit–Loss Statement, and the Cash Flow Statement. Other specialized documents also exist. These three documents will be briefly discussed in order to foster a better understanding of financial accounting and the services it provides.

Balance sheet

As mentioned in the section on bookkeeping (above), a key equation in accounting is:

Assets = Liabilities (Obligations due to others) + Equity (Ownership)

In this equation, "assets" (known as credits) are everything that the organization possesses, "Liabilities" (known as "debits") are debts and obligations, along with "Equity": whatever is left over (i.e. the residual value after all debts and obligations have been taken into account). A very simple Balance Sheet is presented in Table 8.1.

In most cases, of course, the balance sheet is much more complicated than this because a wide range of categories typically exist in each Debit and Credit category. Nonetheless, this basic format is used and presented as an equation in perfect balance.

The balance sheet provides a variety of useful information including the amount of equity and debt that exists. The balance sheet can also provide information regarding how much of an investment is needed to gain a certain level of profits. If two companies both earn $50,000 a year, one might require a $500,000 investment and another might only need $250,000. If all other factors are equal, earning the same amount using a smaller investment is preferable.

On the other hand, in order to earn $50,000 using a $250,000 investment might require borrowing a large sum of money that must be paid back according to a mandated schedule. In case of an economic downturn, a high

Table 8.1 Balance sheet

TRIBAL MANAGEMENT COMPANY For the Period Ended December 31, 20XX			
Current assets		**Current liabilities**	
Cash	$1,000	Current bills due	$2,000
Receivables	$4,000	Wages owed	$1,000
Fixed assets		**Long-term liabilities**	
Vehicle	$5,000	Mortgage	$14,000
Building	$20,000	**Equity**	$13,000
Total assets	$30,000	**Total liability/equity**	$30,000

debt load can be disastrous if these payments cannot be made. Thus, generating profits using other people's money might be attractive during good times, but doing so comes at a risk if an economic downturn unexpectedly arises. Accountants can provide insights on issues such as this, but the final decision regarding what to do rests with the individual or the organization and is based on its strategies, goals, priorities, and needs.

Profit–loss statement

The profit and loss statement provides information regarding whether the organization is making money or not and what factors contribute most significantly to its financial situation. In its most basic presentation, the profit and loss statement can be presented as

Total Revenue − Total Costs = Amount of Profit or Loss.

Presented in this very basic manner, however, is not very useful because doing so does not adequately describe what is going on financially and what can be done to change the status quo for the better. These issues, of course, are of prime importance to those who evaluate organizations or make strategic decisions regarding them.

Costs, for example, can be fixed or variable. Fixed costs must be paid no matter how much work an organization completes over a particular period of time. Thus, if a new factory is bought and the payments on the loan are $10,000 a month, that amount must be paid no matter how much product is produced and sold. An old, inefficient factory, in contrast, might be paid for and have no loan to service. Thus, fixed costs will be lower if the old factory is kept making the organization less vulnerable in case of economic reversals.

Variable costs, in contrast, are the additional expenses that are required to produce one additional unit. Thus, in the old factory the variable cost per item might be $10.00 per unit while in the new, more efficient, factory the variable cost might be $7.50. It is easy to see that investing in a new factory might be a good idea if you knew the production would be high and stay at that level for a long time.

On the other hand, if sales go down sharply for an extended period of time, the organization might have trouble servicing the loan required to buy the new factory. If such an event is likely, keeping the old facility and continuing to pay higher variable costs per unit might be a good idea.

Profit and Loss Statements typically start with a report of total revenues. The total cost of goods sold is subtracted to calculate what is known as the Gross Margin. Thus:

Total Revenues − Total Costs of Goods Sold = Gross Margin.

If, for example, the merchandise for a store is bought for $200,000 and sold for $300,000, a gross margin of $100,000 would exist.

This, however, is not the total picture, because in order to sell the goods, a store must be operated, employees hired, bills paid, and so forth. When these costs are factored in, the Operating Margin is calculated. This can be formulated as:

Gross Margin − Operating Costs = Operating Margin.

Having stated the Operating Margin, all the other costs (such as Taxes and so forth) can be calculated and subtracted from the Operating Margin. This results in the actual profit or loss and presented in the following equation:

Operating Margin − Other Expenses = Profit or Loss.

The information provided by these calculations can be quite valuable when evaluating an organization. Let's say, for example, that a company is losing $10,000 a year. Looking at the profit and loss statement, we find that this situation results from the fact that the cost of goods sold is higher than the revenue generated from selling it. Thus, the Gross Margin would be unattractive. Unless we have a good plan for reducing costs and/or increasing prices, buying this company will not be a good idea.

A second company losing $10,000 a year might generate a good Gross Margin but be unprofitable because of the high fixed costs of servicing a mortgage. If the loan can be refinanced at a lower rate, the operating costs might be reduced to a level where the company becomes profitable. A careful examination of the profit and loss statement can often reveal vital insights that can be used to evaluate options. Both creditors and investors are very interested in this type of information. See Table 8.2 for a simple example of a Profit–loss statement.

Table 8.2 Profit–loss statement

TRIBAL MANAGEMENT COMPANY
For the Period Ended December 31, 20XX

Item	Monetary value	Percentage
Revenues	$300,000	100
Cost of goods	$240,000	80
GROSS MARGIN	$60,000	20
Operating expenses	$30,000	10
OPERATING MARGIN	$30,000	10
Other	$00	0
NET INCOME	$30,000	10

The profit–loss statement, therefore, provides valuable information regarding profitability (or the lack of it) as well as factors that contribute to this situation. Both investors and creditors can profit from the information presented. Organizations typically need to provide information such as this when they seek to do business with others, borrow money, ask for credit, and so forth.

The cash flow statement

Let's say that a "Cash and Carry" lumber company pays cash for all of it inventory when received. At closing time, the employees are paid for their day's work. All other expenses are immediately paid in a similar manner.

People come to the store, buy building supplies, and immediately pay in cash. If $1,000 worth of goods is sold during a day, at closing time $1,000 will be in the cash register, minus anything paid out for additional inventory, for wages, and so forth. Everything operates on a strictly cash basis. When such situations exist, accounting is straightforward, simple, and easy to understand.

In reality, of course, most businesses do not operate in this fashion. They buy and sell on credit. This means that the actual money on hand at any particular time does not fully reflect the organization's financial situation because obligations and assets (such as accounts payable and receivable) also need to be considered. Taking them into account is especially important when sales are immediately calculated as "profit" even though the money has not been received.

During the 1980s, for example, numerous savings and loan organizations got into the bad habit of granting risky loans and keeping them on the books as lucrative assets when, in fact, the debtors were defaulting. As a result of this situation, these institutions appeared to be healthy and profitable when, in reality, they were weak and vulnerable. In the long run, many of these negligent organizations failed. Suddenly, accountants and business practitioners became interested in the actual flow of money in and out of organizations, not merely projections of profit based on some other measure, such as sales.

In a cash flow statement, the monies coming in and going out of an organization are analyzed and placed into various categories such as "Operating Activities," "Financial Activities," and "Investing Activities." Each is briefly discussed below.

Operating activities refers to cash that (1) goes out or (2) comes into the organization as a direct result of the normal operation of the business. Cash going out refers to any money paid that involves normal business operations. Cash inflows refers to any money received for merchandise, services provided, and so forth.

This information can be very useful in understanding the health of the organization and how it conducts business. A company's income statement, for example, might indicate high sales and a growing profit margin. A look at the cash flow statement, however, might reveal that relatively little cash is actually coming in from these sales and/or that the amount of cash received is becoming lower and lower. Why is this true? Perhaps, an unacceptably large number of customers are not paying and these accounts are becoming uncollectable even though they are still "on the books" as profitable assets.

Or let's say that the owner who has put a company up for sale boasts of an ever-growing profit margin. A high price might be asked for the company as a result of this enviable growth in sales. But the accountants note that recently the percentage of cash coming in from sales is significantly decreasing. What is happening?

Maybe the owner is generating high sales by extending credit to risky customers. By doing so, the profitability of the firm appears to be higher because sales have increased. Increased sales are used to justify a high asking price for the business.

After the business is sold at a premium because the projections of profit have been inflated in this manner, the buyer learns that many of these accounts receivable will not be paid and must be "written off." As a result, the buyer suffers a "double whammy": the purchase price was too high and the amount of money generated from accounts receivable is less than anticipated. Paying attention to cash flows can be very important and provide important clues that should not be ignored.

Financing activities refers to the money that comes in or out of an organization due to activities involving finance. Cash can come in from those who invest in a business or extend loans. Generally, outflows are the result of paying various types of short- and long-term debt. In addition, a corporation might pay dividends as well as acquiring shares of its own stock.

Studying these financing activities can often provide useful information. A corporation that pays a large amount to service loans, for example, might be vulnerable in case of an economic downturn. A corporation that pays the same amount in dividends to stockholders, on the other hand, will not be as vulnerable because the organization is not obligated to pay dividends and can withhold them in lean times.

On the other hand, if borrowing money can be done cheaply, the organization might be more profitable if it uses borrowed money to finance its operations. The goal of using debt might be to minimize the amount of outstanding stock in order to give shareholders a greater return on their investment. Accountants should not dictate what should be done, but they can explain the implications of specific decisions and actions.

The last category of the Cash Flow Statement is **Investment activities** which represent (1) financial investments (such as buying stocks and bonds issued by other companies and (2) acquiring productive assets (such as factories and equipment) that represent the organization investing in itself. Cash inflows include money that derives from these financial investments (such as dividends from stocks that are owned) as well as the cash derived from the sale of productive assets. The proceeds from the sale of productive assets (such as equipment), furthermore, constitute an additional influx of money from investment activities.

Outputs include the cash required to pay for these assets. By studying cash flows, important information can be gathered. An accountant might be concerned, for example, because the amount of cash held by an organization is becoming smaller and smaller. A careful look, however, might reveal that a lot of money has been spent on new equipment. Thus, the company is investing in itself. This fact might satisfy the accountant that the company is in good financial shape even though the amount of available cash is decreasing. If the amount of cash was dwindling and there appeared to be no good reason for this change, the accountant might continue to be concerned. Table 8.3 provides an example of a sample Cash Flow Statement.

This example shows a decrease in the amount of cash and an increase in equipment as well as interest charges that built up before full payment for the new piece of equipment had been made. The cash flow statement does not indicate a decrease in cash due to unprofitable operations. In fact, operating activities resulted in an increase in cash.

When investing in (or doing business with) an organization, getting clear information about its financial health is vital. When others do business with an organization, they will also demand this information. As a result, providing and/or using the facts provided by financial accountants and the statements

Table 8.3 Cash flow statement

TRIBAL MANAGEMENT COMPANY		
For the Period Ended December 31, 20XX		
Operating activities		
	Inflows (sales)	$100,000
	Outflows (expenses)	$90,000
	Change	$10,000
Investing activities		
	Inflows (sell investment)	$10,000
	Outflows (bought equipment)	$30,000
	Change	($20,000)
Financing activities		
	Inflows	0
	Outflows (Interest on new equipment)	$500
	Change	($500)
Net change		($10,500)

they provide is inevitable. By knowing the data that needs to be provided and why it is important, strategies can be developed that will lead to the creation of financial statements that satisfy investors and creditors.

The discussions above presented complex procedures in a very simplified manner. Because accounting is complicated, seeking the advice of a skilled professional accountant is strongly recommended. I hope, however, that this overview provides insights regarding what financial accounting is and what it does.

Managerial accounting

Bookkeeping involves keeping a chronological financial history that is reconciled into categories in order to create a trial balance. Based on this summarizing document, financial accountants perform a variety of services including the construction of a number of documents and statements that offer insights regarding the health of the organization and indications regarding how the organization pursues its mission. This information is typically used by outsiders who seek to gain a better understanding of organizations and their financial health.

The information provided by financial accountants is also employed by a wide array of subfields within accounting. Thus, auditors inspect the books to be sure that no carelessness, wrong doing, embezzling, or fraud has occurred. Tax accountings help organizations to plan financial activities and strategies that minimize tax obligations as well as making sure that no tax laws or rules are broken or ignored. A variety of other subfields exist.

Managerial accounting is a subfield that is involved with analyzing accounting data and presenting it in ways that helps the managerial team make appropriate and effective decisions (see Oliver and Horngren (2010) or other managerial accounting texts for fuller details). The style of work and the goal of managerial accounting is distinct in this way.

In financial accounting, somewhat rigid and mandated methods are used. The goal is to provide unambiguous and uniform information that outsiders can understand. Financial accounting looks towards the past and analyzes decisions and actions after they have occurred.

The work of managerial accounting, in contrast, is not dictated by obligatory rules and regulations. The goal is to gather, inspect, and present information in any way that best serves those inside the organization who will use it strategically.

While financial accounting reflects upon the past, managerial accounting is forward looking and helps people made decisions involving the future. The goal extends beyond providing outsiders with useful information. Just, the opposite; managerial accountants create information and evaluations that are kept secret in order to maintain a competitive advantage.

A commonly accepted definition of the field is: "Management accounting is a profession that involves partnering in management decision making, devising planning and performance management systems, and providing expertise in financial reporting and control to assist management in the formulation and implementation of an organization's strategy" (Institute of Management Accountants 2008). In order to do so, managerial accountants work in a number of areas including strategic planning, evaluating performance, assessing risks, and so forth.

Accounting data is used in various ways. Thus, information about who pays their bills on time and who does not is an example of accounting data. The billing addressees of customers provide information regarding where current customers are located. If managerial accountants systematize this knowledge and present it to management in an organized manner, the leadership team might be better able to make strategic decisions. Many more complex examples of presenting decision makers with useful information exist. By manipulating various forms of financial accounting data, managerial accountants seek to developing insights that are useful during the decision-making process.

Thus, where financial accounting records and information are reworked in ways that facilitate the decision-making process, managerial accountants are probably at work. Nonetheless, care needs to be exercised when using their services and the recommendations of other consultants. Ultimately, those who provide advice possess great power over the decision-making process because the way in which facts are presented can covertly suggest certain responses or solutions. Thus, managerial accountants should take great care to provide insights in a way that facilitates decisions that reflect clients and their desires, needs, and vulnerabilities. doing so, however, can be difficult if these advisors intuitively believe they possess the best solution to the problems faced and if they fail to take the uniqueness of the client into account.

When actionable advice is provided outside of a relevant context, inappropriate decisions can easily be made. Indigenous, ethnic, and rural clients need to keep this potential in mind. If managerial accountants are not culturally competent, they might provide advice that is poorly suited to the client and never realize they are doing so.

In the 1980s, the criticism was made that managerial accounting had not evolved very much in the previous 50 years and, as it result, it was increasingly out of touch regarding the ways in which business was actually being conducted. The complaints became so loud that "Statement 4 of the Accounting Education Change Commission" urged practitioners and scholars to focus upon actual business practices, not academic paradigms or truisms (Accounting Education Change Commission 1993). These suggestions ultimately led to significant changes in managerial accounting.

The implications of these actions are clear. Managerial accounting should reflect the actual needs and practices of people and their organizations by responding to what clients actually do and what they want to accomplish. They should not merely offer all their patrons the same generic advice based on ivory tower musings.

The distinctiveness of specific types of people and organizations ought to be acknowledged whenever indigenous, ethnic, and rural peoples embrace concerns and priorities that are distinct from those of mainstream people and organizations. Because of these differences, managerial accounting needs to adjust accordingly. Both clients and the managerial accountants who provide services to them need to be aware of this reality. It is hoped that all in the profession will develop the insights needed to most effectively serve indigenous, ethnic, and rural clients by responding to their unique needs. In the meantime, clients may need to be cautious regarding the advice provided by managerial accounting.

The need for alternatives

As should be obvious from the above discussions, conventional accounting is a method of analysis that uses money and financial considerations as the means by which choices and options are evaluated and decisions are made. Benefits arise from doing so. Conventional accounting, for example, concentrates upon one specific and unambiguous measure (money). It does so, in part, in order to avoid "comparing apples and oranges" in a quest for objective comparisons and judgments. As a result, discussing and considering alternatives in a systematic and detached manner is facilitated.

Such evenhanded systems of decision making (accounting in this case), however, might create a false feeling of impartiality and objectivity by dealing with qualitative feelings in a quantitative manner. Significant problems and inaccuracies potentially exist when the quantitative and objective measure of money is used to depict subjective and qualitative feeling and emotions.

Conventional accounting, for example, tends to reduce non-monetary phenomena to an artificial cash value and force calculations and judgements to be made based on such criteria. According to this technique, pain and suffering (as well as happiness and joy) are reduced to a cash value. This sort of equating unavoidably impacts the decision-making process, possibly in ways that are not appropriate. Consider, for example, the apparent reasoning of the strategic thinkers and/or managerial accountants who examined the options regarding the Ford Pinto, a defective and dangerous automobile.

The Ford Pinto (along with the Lynx, a Mercury version of the same basic vehicle) was a 1970s sub-compact car designed to provide basic transportation at a reasonable price. Soon after its introduction, The National Highway Traffic Safety Administration received a rash of complaints that the Pinto was prone to burst into flames after rear-end collisions.

Investigative journalism appearing in *Mother Jones Magazine* (Dowie 1977) ultimately provided evidence that Ford was long aware of this hazardous flaw. Even more damningly, the magazine suggested that Ford failed to take corrective action because strategic planners or managerial accountants concluded that paying off the law suits of those who were injured or killed would be cheaper than fixing the problem. Although the so-called *Ford Pinto Memo* was provocative, it was ruled to be inadmissible at a civil trail regarding damages by an injured party (Strobel 1980). Nonetheless, the Pinto example underscores that under some circumstances, a managerial accounting style of calculation might focus so much upon money that other, more important, considerations are ignored.

This extreme example demonstrates that not all decisions should be based upon monetary and financial considerations. If the accusations against Ford are correct, its actions were clearly wrong and immoral. Other choices that are overly reliant upon financial considerations, however, might be equally inappropriate even if those who advocate them are attempting to do the right thing, but are blinded by the tools they use. Can the pain and social disruption be triggered by economic development be mitigated solely by monetary solutions?

If a choice generates maximum profits, for example, but triggers hurtful changes within the community, will managerial accounting be able to adequately take these costs into account when decisions are made? It has been my experience that even good and well-meaning people can possess blindspots in this regard, resulting in hurtful and ill-advised decisions.

When strategies and tactics focus exclusively upon money, unfortunately, the long-term health of communities and the feelings of its members can easily be overlooked. Where this potential exists, a broader and more robust yardstick of evaluation is clearly needed. This is true even if the evaluation is complicated and the categories used for assessment are vague or imprecise. As a result of this reality and its implications, circumstances exist where conventional accounting needs to be replaced, or at least supplemented, with broader and more evenhanded tools of evaluation.

The Triple Bottom Line

The Triple Bottom Line is a means of evaluating options from multiple perspectives. The quest to do so is not new and the Triple Bottom Line merely is one way of doing so. In the late nineteenth and early twentieth centuries, for example, Patrick Geddes, spoke of the three concepts of "folk, work, place" as a means of weighing options and calculating results. Geddes, you may recall, was a prominent social planner who sought to mix social change with cultural and architectural preservation in a nurturing and empowering manner.

In this regard, Geddes observes: "… Planning … to be successful … must be folk planning. This means that its task is not to coerce people … against … [their] wishes…. Instead its task is to find the right [solutions for] people" (Geddes 1947: 22). In a similar fashion, the Triple Bottom Line is made up of (1) Social/Cultural, (2) Environmental/Ecological and (3) Economic/Profit Centers that are presented as "People, Planet, and Profit." The model is an artifact of the current era in which profit-making is envisioned within the context of simultaneously dealing with pollution, encouraging sustainability, and reducing waste while addressing cultural issues.

Popularized by John Elkington (1999), this paradigm of appraisal and action views economic choices from multiple contexts, not merely with a reference to the financial considerations addressed by conventional accounting. Andrew Savitz (2006), for example, defines the Triple Bottom Line as a method that measures the impact of businesses and organizations upon the world with an emphasis upon profitability, environmental impacts, and so forth.

This multiple vision is often used as a means of focusing upon the balanced stewardship of natural resources in ways that expand beyond merely reaping short-term profits. Thus, although the Triple Bottom Line is designed to consider human and cultural issues, it is often utilized by those who are primarily interested in ecological sustainability.

Measures of evaluation

When using conventional accounting as the tool of evaluation, calculations are relatively simple because a universal measure (money value) is the basis of analysis and comparison. Reducing everything to a "dollars and cents" worth, unfortunately, can mask significant differences that need to be acknowledged and addressed.

In reality, of course, accurately reducing everything to some monetary value is impossible. As was discussed above, however, doing so is a common practice of conventional accounting and, on occasion, this technique is even used within a Triple Bottom Line context.

The case can be made that focusing upon the complexity of life outweighs the convenience of using arbitrary financial measures that imperfectly depict costs and benefits. As indicated by the Pinto example, employing universal financial measures can be the catalyst for horrific and appalling results. Gaining an accurate understanding of the true situation and the costs triggered by it should be the goal, even if doing so is difficult and unwieldy.

One technique that can be used to do so involves breaking the basic pillars of the Triple Bottom Line down to its component parts and dealing with each in distinctive and discrete ways. This provides a useful and actionable alternative to employing generic measures, such as financial and monetary measures.

To demonstrate this method, examples of doing so are provided to demonstrate how indigenous, ethnic, and rural peoples can use Triple Bottom Line types of calculations (and other similarly robust methods) to portray goals, vulnerabilities, and strategies. To do so, each component of the Triple Bottom Line is expanded and strategically analyzed in a relevant manner. These suggested categories are representative and are not presented as complete or "carved in granite," but merely offered as examples. Each community can benefit from developing its own Triple Bottom Line yardsticks.

People: The people component focuses upon human issues, including individuals, groups, societies, the cultural heritage, and so forth. Environmental/ecological evaluations desires, vulnerabilities and self-determinism are among the issues addressed and considered.

Unfortunately, when plans, goals, and strategies are developed, the needs, rights, and wants of people can easily get lost in the shuffle. Decision makers, for example, might conclude that some sort of cultural evolution (such as so-called "globalization") is inevitably moving in a particular direction. Based on such projections, evaluators may conclude that the ways in which people respond and what they hold dear is passé or doomed, causing their value and significance to be ignored or discounted. These opinions can impact decisions.

Many ethnocentric people, furthermore, are convinced that they and their way of life possess the "right" answers or solutions and that their actions should be emulated by others. This kind of attitude, of course, can easily inhibit an evenhanded evaluation of the situation under evaluation. And, of course, in the quest for profits, some self-centered individuals might concentrate upon the bottom line and short-term profits to such a degree that other considerations blur and fade.

Such potentials are very real and they can impact the analytic and decision-making processes. Three questions regarding a particular course of action that can be asked include (1) Are people empowered? (2) Will culture and community be disrupted?, and (3) Will the balance of power shift? These are representative issues and not meant to be exhaustive. Each is discussed.

Are people empowered? Increasingly, indigenous, ethnic, and rural peoples demand that they are able to control their own destiny in appropriate ways. In an earlier era of social Darwinism, the case was made that those in the developed regions should take the leadership role and that hinterland populations would benefit from taking their advice. Today, the tables are turned and these peoples are asserting the right to make decisions regarding their lives. Insuring this ability is increasingly viewed as a criteria of good and equitable social planning.

Is the community or culture disrupted? Economic and social development triggers changes. Although some results are typically beneficial, others can be traumatic and disruptive. Anticipating and mitigating such hurtful side effects is increasingly recognized as an important component of social policy.

Will the balance of power shift? When social and economic changes arise, power shifts tend to be inevitable. These transformations typically trigger a host of costs and benefits. The benefits received and the prices paid as a result of this reconfiguration, however, are likely to impact some groups more than others. Often, for example, an elite and well-connected minority within the community will prosper while others tend to suffer and lose ground. The implications of this possibility needs to be acknowledged and addressed. Table 8.4 portrays these issues.

Thus, the "people component" of the Triple Bottom Line is complex. It clearly includes a cultural component that goes beyond mere physical well-being. Indigenous, ethnic, and rural peoples need to clearly articulate this fact when considering and negotiating options.

Planet: Ecological sustainability has emerged as a key issue in the modern world. Indeed, many people who embrace the Triple Bottom Line do so in order to address environmental concerns. Nevertheless, the issue is complicated by the fact that strategies for dealing with "planet" issues may or may not work towards the specific wellbeing of indigenous, ethnic, and rural peoples. Three topics that need to be considered include (1) Macro vs micro issues, (2) Environment and way of life, and (3) Is the decision truly sustainable both culturally and ecologically?

Macro vs. micro issues: Macro ecological evaluations are concerned with the world in general. If a choice tends to benefit the planet as a whole (or not inflict damage), it will pass the macro test of appropriateness. Although this sort of global perspectives is valuable, many indigenous, ethnic, and rural peoples are also concerned with how choices will affect the specific place where they live.

Thus, a decision can be justified on global grounds but be hurtful and disruptive to the local environment, causing grievous suffering. Due to the nature of the tradeoffs that are considered, both macro and micro issues need to be addressed when decisions are made. Globally centered decision

Table 8.4 People

Issue	Analysis
Are people empowered?	People seek self-determinism and control over their lives. Methods for evaluating options need to consider the degree to which their goals are achieved or frustrated.
Culture/ community disrupted?	Many economic and social options can lead to cultural and social disruption and negative side effects. These issues need to addressed.
Power shifts?	Decisions may result in power shifts within the community. Are these potential changes and their implications acknowledged and mitigated?

DISCUSSION
People, both individuals and communities, are impacted by economic and social decisions. Conventional accounting is often ill-suited to deal with these impacts. Methods, such as the Triple Bottom Line, are better able to factor in these considerations.

makers and plans, unfortunately, might not adequately focus upon local concerns.

Environment and the way of life: Many indigenous, ethnic, and rural peoples possess cultures and ways of life that are intimately connected with the particular environment in which they live. When this is true, the cultural survival of the people is intimately linked to the health and preservation of the environment. People who practice subsistence hunting and fishing, for example, must have available hunting and fishing areas in order for their culture and way of life to survive. Although outsiders might look as the environment as a resource to be harvested (possibly through disruptive extractive activities), local people might view the same asset as the venue that is needed to facilitate a way of life. These different visions and their implications need to be recognized.

Is the solution sustainable? Cultural and social sustainability should be balanced in a meaningful and equitable manner. Most indigenous, ethnic, and rural peoples want to preserve at least some aspects of their traditional way of life. Developing ways to achieve this goal is vitally important.

These considerations can be expanded. I hope that communities, envisioning who they are and what they want, will do so. In the meantime, such issues are portrayed in Table 8.5.

Table 8.5 Planet

Issue	Analysis
Macro vs. micro	Much Triple Bottom Line thought evaluates sustainability from a global or macro perspective. When doing so, the impact upon the local community can be overlooked or deemphasized. Communities often need to focus upon the impact of change upon their local environment by focusing upon micro, not macro, issues.
Social aspects	Many people possess a way of life that is intimately connected to the specific environment in which they live. As a result, changes in the environment will trigger profound social and cultural transformations, many of them possibly hurtful. These potentials need to be recognized.
Sustainability	Does the suggested strategy lead to ecological and social sustainability?

DISCUSSION
Many people possess a way of life that is intimately connected to the environment. Under such circumstances, this dependence needs to be considered when possible ecological changes are considered. Thus, both social and ecological sustainability needs to be addressed.

Many who embrace the Triple Bottom Line are primarily concerned with ecological or environmental sustainability. Although doing so is legitimate, cultural and social sustainability is equally important. That issue can be addressed by a broader application of the model.

Profit: The final component of the Triple Bottom Line is profits. This however is a complicated topic that needs to be addressed in a broad and multi-dimensional manner. Three issues that need to be addressed include (1) who profits, (2) the method of distribution, and (3) the impact upon the community.

Who profits? Who will ultimately profit is a key issue, On the one hand, will local people or outsiders gain the majority of the profits? Will this situation weaken or strengthen the community? What arrangement is most equitable? What arrangement will lead to the greatest degree of sustainability?

The method of distribution: How much profits will outsiders receive? How much profit will local people receive? How will the local profits be distributed? If the recipient group is a tribe, for example, will the proceeds go directly to individual tribal members or will they go to the tribe as an entity? What are the pros and cons of the option that is selected?

The impact upon the community: Profits and their distribution can exert significant impacts upon the community. In addition, certain unanticipated costs often exert a cost upon some people while not significantly affecting others. What are the expected impacts, both beneficial and hurtful? How can benefits be enhanced and deficits mitigated? How can costs be spread throughout the community in an equitable manner? What efforts have been taken to ensure the distribution is equitable? Table 8.6 presents these issues in graphic form.

Profits and their distribution, therefore, are important issues that deserve considerable thought. Arrangements need to take into account both costs and benefits and should be well established in order to resolve disagreements that might occur at a later date.

In conclusion, methods such as the Triple Bottom Line, can be presented and employed in ways that are flexible and able to deal with the concerns of indigenous, ethnic, and rural peoples. Doing so is crucial if these tools are to serve communities and not merely reflect mainstream guidelines and priorities. A sample method of doing so was presented as an example regarding how to accomplish this goal. Each community, however, will benefit by constructing its own means of using such tools that are tailored to local needs. By doing so, local peoples will be better able to articulate their concerns and develop actionable solutions to the unique problems they face.

Concluding statement

This chapter has focused upon methods for evaluating future options and past performances. The discussion began with an overview of mainstream accounting that is based upon money and finance. This discussion sets the

Table 8.6 Profit

Issue	Analysis
Who profits?	Who will benefit from profits? To what degree will outsiders profit? When local people profit, will the proceeds primarily benefit a particular group or will they be spread throughout the community?
Distribution method	What is the particular method of distribution of profits? What will be the timing? How will profits be dispersed? Will a steady flow of profits exist or will "boom and bust" cycles result in social disruptions?
Impact upon community	Will certain unrecognized costs exist? If so, who will be forced to accept them? How will the community, specific segments, and individuals be impacted by these costs. Will possibly unrecognized and uncompensated costs be thrust upon some groups or individuals in an inequitable manner?

DISCUSSION

Dealing with profits can be complicated and trigger a host of costs and benefits. Not only should the amount of profits going to outsiders be monitored, the ways in which internal profits impact the community need to be considered.

---

stage for considering more complex, robust, but less exact techniques such as the Triple Bottom Line.

Initially, we considered bookkeeping which involves creating a financial diary of the organization and using monetary records to present this information in a systematic manner (known as the Trial Balance). Accountants manipulate the work of bookkeepers for specific purposes.

Financial accounting provides an historic analysis of the organization that outsiders routinely consult in order to make decisions regarding lending money, extending credit, and so forth.

Managerial accounting, in contrast, manipulates accounting records in forward looking ways, not to understand the past. The products of this branch of the profession tends to be used by the management team in order to make more effective decisions. Managerial accountants provide proprietary information that is typically kept secret because it can provide a strategic advantage.

Although accounting is an invaluable tool, it is solely concerned with money and financial issues. Other considerations are ignored or reduced to an arbitrary cash value. Alternatives such at the Triple Bottom Line expand the analysis by considering two variables in addition to money. One is the impact upon people; the other is the environmental or ecological ramifications. Although reconciling money with these other items can be difficult, such methods are more robust than conventional accounting and are increasingly employed.

When indigenous, ethnic, and rural people are involved, the way People, Place, and Profits are analyzed might need to be tailored to suit the communities being examined. By doing so, more effective evaluation can result.

Relevant terms

Accounting: Creating and analyzing financial records.

Balance Sheet: A statement outlining assets, liabilities, and equity.

Bookkeeping: The process of keeping and reconciling financial records that are analyzed and manipulated by accountants.

Cash Flow Statement: A financial statement that indicates the amount of money coming in and out of the organization and the nature of various funds.

Elkington, John: A leader in the Triple Bottom Line movement.

Financial Accounting: Keeping financial records that provide an analysis of day-to-day dealings and the financial health of the organization. Much of the information is designed to be shared with others.

Financing Activities: Actions that involve acquiring and/or managing the financial resources needed for a business or organization to operate.

"Folk, work, place": Typology formulated by Patrick Geddes in the late nineteenth/early twentieth centuries that is similar to the Triple Bottom Line.

GAAP: Generally Accepted Accounting Principles.

Geddes, Patrick: Late nineteenth-/early twentieth-century social planner whose work parallels the Triple Bottom Line.

IFRS: International Financial Reporting Standards.

Investment Activities: Actions such as acquiring productive assets, investing in other assets, disposing of valuable assets, and so forth.

Macro: Concerned with broad social and economic forces that transcend the organization and its influence.

Managerial Accounting: Manipulating accounting and financial information in order to assist decision making.

Micro: Concerned with distinct organizations and their influence.

Operating Activities: Actions that result from the normal operation of a business or organization.

People: The social and cultural component of the Triple Bottom Line.

Planet: The ecological or environmental component of the Triple Bottom Line.

Profits: A component of the Triple Bottom Line that is concerned with profits.

Profit–Loss Statement: An accounting statement that outlines profits and losses and what, in particular, contributed to them.

Sustainability: The ability of a system to continue indefinitely. A major focus of the Triple Bottom Line.

Triple Bottom Line: A mode of economic analysis that adds human and environmental dimensions in order to expand beyond conventional accounting and its focus upon money and financial issues.

Discussion questions

1   Compare bookkeeping and accounting. What does bookkeeping do? What does it not do? What are its benefits? What are its limitations?
2   Discuss financial accounting. Discuss the basic tasks performed. Who uses the information provided by financial accountants? Why is this information important?
3   What is managerial accounting? Who uses the information gained? Is the format more highly or less structured than financial accounting? Why?
4   Discuss the Triple Bottom Line as an alternative to conventional accounting. What are the benefits of using it? What are the deficits or limitations of using it?
5   Why might the Triple Bottom Line need to be tailored in order to deal with specific groups of people? Discuss this from a strategic point of view.

References

Accounting Education Change Commission (1993). *"Positions and Issues"*. Issues Statement Number 4: Improving the Early Employment Experience of Accountants. Sarasota, FL: American Accounting Association.

Alali, F. and Cao, L. (2010). "International Financial Reporting Standards – Credible and Reliable? An Overview." *Advances in Accounting: Incorporating Advances in International Accounting* 26(1), 79–86.

Arya, A. and Reinstein, A. (2010). Recent Developments in Fair Value Accounting. *The CPA Journal* (August), 20–29.

Dowie, Mark (1977). "Pinto Madness." *Mother Jones.* September/October.

Elkington, John (1999). *Cannibals with Forks: The Triple Bottom Line of 21st Century Business* (Montgomery AL: Capstone Publishing).

Geddes, Patrick (1947). "Report on the Towns in the Madras Presidency, 1915, Madura," in Tyrwhitt, J. *Patrick Geddes in India* (London: Lund Humphries).

Harrison, Walter T., Horngren, Charles T. and Thomas, William (2013). *Financial Accounting*, 9th edition (Upper Saddle River, NJ: Prentice Hall).

Institute of Management Accountants (2008). *Definition of Management Accounting.* Retrieved from: www.imanet.org/?ssopc=1.

Lee, Geoffrey A. (1977). "The Coming of Age of Double Entry: The Giovanni Farolfi Ledger of 1299–1300." *Accounting Historians Journal* 4(2), 79–95.

Meeks, Geoff, and Swann, G. M. Peter, (2009). "Accounting Standards and the Economics of Standards." *Accounting and Business Research* (39)3, 191–210.

Oliver, M. Suzanne and Horngren, Charles (2010). *Managerial Accounting* (Upper Saddle NJ: Prentice Hall).

Savitz, Andrew (2006). *The Triple Bottom Line* (San Francisco: Jossey-Bass).

Strobel, Lee Patrick (1980). *Reckless Homicide? Ford's Pinto Trial* (South Bend, Indiana: And Books).

Part III

Providing service

Chapter 9

Internal service

Learning objectives

Many economic development specialists suggest that indigenous, ethnic, and, rural people need to accept the advice and guidance of informed outsiders when decisions are made. Although advice is useful, however, people are often able to fruitfully decide for themselves. Thus, internal service can frequently be locally directed. In this chapter, models of outside vs. internal control and decision making are juxtaposed.

Specific learning objectives include:

1   Be aware that outsiders often seek to control indigenous, ethnic and rural peoples.
2   Understand self-determinism at a local level.
3   Appreciate the bottom up methods of the Tupelo Model.
4   Understand the emerging field of "tribal management."
5   Consider Postmodern Public administration theory as a tool that local leaders can use to justify providing internal services to themselves.

Introduction

The next two chapters analyze how communities can provide service in equitable and effective ways. This discussion (Chapter 9) concentrates upon people helping themselves and their communities. Doing so is envisioned as "internal service." After dealing with these important locally inspired tasks, Chapter 10 deals with providing service to others and benefiting from the resulting exchange. This is referred to as "external service." Although these two types of service can (and should) coexist in a positive symbiosis, conflict between them is possible and sometimes inevitable.

Although internal service involves people helping themselves, questions may arise regarding who should take a leadership role when strategies and tactics are forged. Outsiders have often asserted that local people lack the experience and the ability to do so; as a result of this void, the suggestion is sometimes made that others should take the leadership role.

This chapter begins with an analysis of paradigms that question the ability of indigenous, ethnic, and rural people to make productive choices regarding their futures. By reviewing these perspectives, the insights and perspectives needed to critique and challenge such ideas are presented.

Having offered this analysis, specific strategies for providing internal service are evaluated. The ultimate goal of this discussion is to encourage people to make wise and independent decisions regarding their futures.

A legacy of chauvinism

Communities should take steps to assure that their needs are satisfied. But who should take the leadership role in directing these efforts? Since ancient times, outsiders have routinely suggested that indigenous, ethnic, and rural peoples are poorly equipped to make key decisions regarding their lives. These tasks, their logic argues, should be reserved for outsiders who possess superior skills and insights.

Consider the ancient Greeks who asserted that they were superior to other peoples (who were lumped together and dismissed as lowly barbarians). Plato, the revered philosopher and social architect, encouraged the Greek elite to systematically strip away the essence of local cultures in order to help them become "civilized."

Look closely, however, and you will see that in spite of such chauvinistic strategies, many Greeks apparently felt respect for these "wretched savages." Consider, for example, *The Dying Gaul*, a famous statue that depicts a barbarian warrior brought down by a fatal sword wound. Awaiting inevitable death, the dying combatant lies on the ground, holding himself up with one arm, as life slowly fades. But inconsistent with Greek ideology, he is not portrayed as coarse and vulgar. The sympathetic artist presents a handsome and noble man holding his head up high until the bitter end. My art historian friends tell me that this sort of depiction, in direct conflict with the prevailing Greek chauvinism of those times, acknowledges respect for the alien and accepts him as an equal. Apparently, the artist and the audience had a more complex view of non-Greeks than the opinions held by the xenophobic elites.

Or look at the story of *Ruth* in the *Old Testament*, the sacred literature of Jews and Christians. According to the account, Ruth is tainted because she is not of Jewish descent. Like the doomed barbarian, however, she possesses a nobility that chauvinism and prejudice overlook. Living an exemplary life in spite of her ethnic and religious outsiderness, Ruth emerges as a founder of the linage that leads to King David, and eventually to Jesus Christ. Thus, David and Jesus (heroic leaders of the faiths) spring from loathed gentile roots. The message of *Ruth* is clear, many outsiders are worthy and can make profound contributions. Dismissing them and their significance is morally wrong and blindly stupid.

Jumping to the nineteenth century, Rudyard Kipling, with equally chauvinistic tendencies, portrayed the British Empire as inherently superior to the rabble of the earth. He invented the term "the "white man's burden" and, consistent with it, depicted indigenous, ethnic, and rural peoples as inferior and in need of guidance that white colonialists offered.

In spite of Kipling's elitist tendencies, he also wrote the poem "Gunda Din" about a local porter for the British colonial army in India who is treated with disrespect by his white "superiors." In a life and death battle, however, this indigenous peon, performs far beyond the call of duty and saved the narrator, giving up his life in the process. After these noble actions, the narrator observes:

> Tho' I've belted you an' flayed you,
> By livin' Gawd that made you,
> You're a better man than I am, Gunga Din!

Kipling's message is clear: even elitists and chauvinists can gain respect for others. Thus, in a long tradition ranging as far back as the ancient Greeks and moving forward, feelings of superiority stand side by side with an acknowledgement of equality and dignity.

In all of these examples, dominant forces justify their power and position even though more egalitarian alternatives exists. Thus, although outside elites often assert superiority over others, a more humane alternative inevitably challenges that notion: that intellectual and moral battle continues to this day.

Non-racist chauvinism

Phraseology such as "the white man's burden" and assertions of racial superiority have become distasteful. Officially, most people in the developed world repudiate racial and ethnic prejudice. As a result, discussions of superiority have been transformed in ways that emphasize broad cultural and technological "progress," not genetic or tribal traits. Doing so has led to more "politically correct" ways to argue that indigenous, ethnic, and rural peoples lack the tools needed to control their destiny.

Here we will briefly review a number of rationales that justify outsiders dominating the decision-making process of indigenous, ethnic, and rural peoples. They include (1) unilineal evolutionary theories, (2) structural models, (3) globalization, and (4) the "tragedy of the commons" model. The list is not exhaustive and is presented as representative of perspectives that are commonly encountered. Some of these perspectives may be "officially" recognized as passé while stubbornly retaining a degree of currency and influence. Each suggests, in its own way, that local people are ill equipped to control their own destinies.

Unilineal evolutionary models

At least since the 1870s and the publication of Lewis Henry Morgan's *Ancient Society* (1877), universal models of cultural evolution have been popular even if their accuracy has been constantly a point of contention (see my *Rethinking Business Anthropology* 2013). Paradigms such as these are usually referred to "unilineal evolutionary theories" because they envision one line of cultural progress, evolution, and adaption that universally impacts all peoples and cultures.

In the 1950s, Walter Rostow popularized an influential unilineal model of development that, although dated, is both influential and representative. Rostow assumes that technology and progress create a particular flow of cultural evolution that can be harnessed to encourage productive and predictable economic development.

Rostow's professional life goes back to the Marshall Plan of the late 1940s when he helped regions of Europe rebuild after having been devastated by World War II. His efforts emphasized bolstering private enterprise in ways that were designed to subdue the Soviet ambitions of the early Cold War era.

With his Marshall Plan experiences behind him, Rostow began to focus upon the developing world in an era when the West and the Soviet Union were struggling to win the allegiance of the non-aligned countries of the post-colonial era. This mission was very different from helping industrialized and developed people rebuild after their physical infrastructures had been destroyed. The developing regions, in contrast, lacked both the "brick and mortar" foundations of modern life as well as populations that were prepared to effectively use them.

Rostow depicts this more complex process of economic intervention and transformation in terms of a series of evolutionary stages that begins with the dominance of traditional cultures and culminates with a modern consumer-oriented society.

As the process begins, Rostow pictures the existence of a *traditional society* that is backward, haunted by superstition, paralyzed by the past, and so forth. The norms and attitudes that are necessary for economic development are completely lacking. Before the cycle of progress and development can begin, certain *preconditions for takeoff*, such as secular education, investment capital, the beginnings of a managerial or entrepreneurial class, and so forth are required. Rostow believes that these prerequisites must be introduced by outsiders. Once in place, substantial obstacles and limitations remain, but a platform to build upon begins to take shape.

Rostow envisions that as local people begin to recognize the benefits of development, the grip of the old ways weakens as mainstream thought and action exert an increasingly powerful influence. During this "*takeoff*" some small "entry level" industries are typically established. As this process continues and deepens, it eventually blends into the *drive to maturity* in which growth in the early "entry level" industries levels off with future growth taking place in other more complex and lucrative industries. The resulting economic activity causes the standard of living to rise. Poverty, adversity, and sacrifice are reduced. Optimism and a belief in progress grows. The transition is complete when an era of *mass consumption* arises that offers people a way of life that is comparable to that of the developed West. In a manner reminiscent of Maslow's hierarchy, the focus of mankind moves from squalid and pathetic survival to gaining status and achieving personal goals. The Rostow model is portrayed in graphic form in Table 9.1.

In the final analysis, unilineal evolutionary models, such as Rostow's, often assert that indigenous, ethnic, and rural peoples are largely incapable to controlling their own destiny because they lack knowledge, skill, and perspective.

Table 9.1 The Rostow Cycle

Phase	Analysis
Traditional society	Traditional societies lack the ability to take advantage of economic opportunities. They rely upon fate or luck, not effort and ingenuity. The people are superstitious, fatalistic, non-scientific, and ill-equipped for economic development.
Preconditions	Certain preconditions for takeoff must exist before development begins, including adequate educational opportunities, the availability of investment capital, a managerial class, and so forth. "Outsiders" tend to provide these preconditions.
Takeoff	The power of tradition begins to weaken. Mainstream thought and action attract positive attention. Small "entry level" industries build confidence, hone the skills of future business leaders, and demonstrate the power of modern alternatives to tradition.
Drive to maturity	The successes of the initial takeoff multiply and build upon each other in powerful and synergistic ways leading to growth, optimism, opportunity, and a higher standard of living.
Mass consumption	Over time, development grows to a point where the quality of life experienced by the people parallel the developed world. The struggle for mere survival is replaced by a focus upon personal interests, skills, and goals.

DISCUSSION
Rostow understands that this process is slow and variations exist. Nonetheless, he views his evolutionary model as a template of economic development that is encouraged and directed by informed outsiders.

After stating this observation, the assertion is made that by accepting the advice of the developed world, these communities can transcend their "backwardness" and progress. There is nothing inherently "racist" in this model and nothing about it shows prejudice against any particular group. Nonetheless, (a) local people are discredited, and (b) a justification for overriding their opinions and wishes is presented.

Certainly, unilineal models have value, but they potentially skew thinking in counterproductive ways that underestimate the abilities of local people to make sound and appropriate decisions. This oversight can ignore the fact that local people may possess a reservoir of tradition, heritage, and knowledge that might provide superior insights and judgments within their own world. The potential value of this local knowledge and insights should not be forgotten.

Structural models

In addition to theories of lineal evolution, such as Rostow's, structural change models emphasize that developing regions and peoples are composed of competing economic sectors such as (a) subsistence/rural, and (b) industrial/urban. Of these two, the industrial/urban is viewed as most productive even though it is often held back by the dominance of supposedly unproductive subsistence activities that, the model asserts, squander the resources and potentials of society. The theory is advanced that this problem can be overcome if the emphasis upon subsistence is reduced in order to free up labor and other resources in order to nurture the more fruitful urban and industrial sectors. Doing so can be accomplished through the establishment of a cash economy, encouraging wage labor, jump-starting industrialization, and introducing urban life on a larger scale. By embracing these changes, the social and economic foundations of society can be restructured in ways that serve as a catalyst for industrialization and urbanization.

One example of this mode of thinking is the "Dual-Sector Model" developed by Arthur Lewis (a Nobel Prize winner) that views people pursuing subsistence activities as a reservoir of underutilized "surplus labor" that should be redeployed to accomplish other, more productive, tasks. In other words, Lewis argues that subsistence activities squander resources that should be used in more fruitful ways. By employing these assets in a more productive industrialized manner, the economy can grow using minimal additional inputs and resources.

Lewis, like Rostow, tends to covertly assume that indigenous, ethnic, and rural peoples are ill equipped to control their own destiny and/or to make key decisions regarding their future. The model assumes that these populations and communities are linked to traditional practices (such as subsistence) that are a drag on the economy. By discarding their passé heritage, however, people can overcome poverty and underdevelopment. In order to make this powerful transition, relying upon outside leadership can be useful. An overview of the Lewis model is presented in Table 9.2.

Although the Lewis model appears to be straightforward, certain key questions need to be asked. First, "Is the subsistence way of life really inefficient?" Subsistence farming, for example, typically demands minimal labor, freeing up people for other activities except during a few labor-intensive periods. Subsistence farming, furthermore, requires minimal cash outlays for equipment and fertilizer. People in a subsistence economy are able to live in their own homes in rural settings instead of relocating to urban areas and paying rent in order to be available for wage labor. Although people living a subsistence lifestyle may not have much money, they typically do not need a large supply of cash because they produce most of what they consume.

In today's world, furthermore, few people live in a wholly subsistence economy. Subsistence is practiced as part of a "mixed economy" in which significant subsistence activities are supplemented with some cash-generating labor or projects. In this way, people live in their rural homes, pay no rent, are close to the land, and produce much of what they use while earning some money for items that subsistence activities cannot provide.

While living in Belize, for example, I visited Maya farmers in the Toledo District who lived primarily in a subsistence manner while growing a limited amount of organic cacao as a cash crop. Additional money was earned when men performed casual labor as opportunities presented themselves while

Table 9.2 Arthur Lewis Dual-Sector Model

Issue	Analysis
Subsistence	Subsistence is viewed as inefficient. The assertion is often made that an over-reliance upon these activities can inhibit economic growth.
Urban/industrial	Urban life and industrial (non-subsistence) production can lead to economic growth, greater opportunities, and a higher standard of living.
Tactic of development	Subsistence activities tie up assets. Redeploying these assets away from subsistence and towards industrialization can generate economic growth.
Net result	More efficient means of production use the same assets to provide a greater payoff to society. Economic growth and a better life for all are the expected results.

DISCUSSION
The assertion can easily be made that (a) those who follow a subsistence way of life are ill equipped to make the transition to urbanism and industrialization, and (b) progress can best be achieved when informed outsiders take a leadership role in planning and transforming society.

women created souvenirs for the tourist trade. These Maya also collectively owned and managed a restaurant and a craft store. They appeared to be living happy and healthy lives, especially when compared to many of the urban dwellers who were marooned in the slums of Belize City, the nation's urban center.

The Belize example challenges the assertion that subsistence efforts have little value and should be replaced with urban and industrial activities. In reality, subsistence provides these Belizean Maya with a good life that is sustainable. In addition, many people prefer rural subsistence life and do not want to trade it for an urban and industrial existence.

A side issue is that urban life and industrialization typically require a greater reliance upon a cash economy and wage labor. As a result, by focusing on financial statistics, the value of subsistence might be underestimated.

Let's say, for example, that a family gives up a subsistence lifestyle in which $20,000 worth of benefits are earned in order to go to town and work for $15,000 in wages; doing so creates a $5,000 shortfall. (This evaluation of subsistence activities considers, for example, the cost of housing that is saved by living in a rural area, lowered or eliminated transportation costs, the full replacement value of items created by subsistence, and so forth). Nevertheless, some analysts who gather statistics might credit the economy with $15,000 growth because no formal records of these subsistence activities were kept and, therefore, the evaluation calculates that nothing was lost when the transition to urban/industrial life was made. Their calculation will be a $15,000 gain although in reality a $5,000 loss occurred.

Remember, structural models tend to place a low value upon subsistence activities. In reality, however, subsistence activities often provide significant benefits while reducing expenses that require cash. In the hypothetical case discussed above, when subsistence activities were abandoned, the economy actually shrunk by $5,000 as the family lost 25 percent of its "buying power." This reality, however, is likely to be clouded and unrecognized when evaluated using mainstream yardsticks of evaluation.

These possibilities need to be addressed. When making decisions, the true value of subsistence activities needs to be considered and acknowledged. If calculations do not reflect the true value of subsistence activities, economic planners might advocate strategies that are inappropriate and counterproductive. When local communities and their leaders are considering their options, such potentials for miscalculation should not be forgotten.

The Lewis model, like Rostow's is over 50 years old. Nonetheless, Lewis' logic crystalizes a common belief that (a) developing people need to overcome their traditions, heritage, and established ways of life, and (b) people will enjoy a better standard of living through urbanization and industrialization. Challenging Lewis' contentions, our discussion recognizes that traditional activities such as subsistence farming might be productive and efficient even if some "mainstream" methods of economic evaluation suggest otherwise. People, furthermore, might prefer this lifestyle and benefit by pursuing it.

When projections and evaluations are offered by consultants and other outsiders, be sure to recognize the full economic value of non-urban and non-industrial activities that must be abandoned if these options are embraced. At the same time, consider the full range of tradeoffs that must occur if urban and industrial options are chosen. When making evaluations consider both economic and non-economic impacts. Even if economic benefits are projected to increase, will embracing an option require other costs (such as sacrificing a valued lifestyle or giving up a degree of independence and/or sustainability)? These potential sacrifices should be considered when calculating the full costs and benefits of an option.

Globalization and cultural convergence

Contemporary views of economic development often focus upon the premise that technological changes, cheaper transportation costs, advances in mass communication, economic interdependence, and so forth are creating an unprecedented degree of worldwide cultural homogeneity. As a result of these trends towards uniformity, growing cultural convergence can arise in areas such as shared fashions, universal opportunities, emerging similarities in tastes, similar media exposure, universal technical products, and so forth. This process is often portrayed as an inevitable fact of modern life.

These tendencies, in turn, are triggering important strategic changes in many organizations. Historically, the preferred tactic was to adjust products, services, and ways of doing business in order to cater to local demands. Today, the strategy is apt to involve offering a universal product or service, keeping prices down, and forcing customers to accept the uniform product that is offered. Global strategies (such as those proposed by Theodore Levitt), for example, advocate riding what is viewed as inevitable cultural convergence by ignoring local variation and catering to humanity as one big homogeneous target market.

Levitt asserts that the resulting "one product strategy" will reduce operating costs, lead to lower prices, and force people, worldwide, to accept the same products and services. He feels that this process, writ large, is destined to create a process of ever-increasing cultural convergence that will take on a life of its own and further eliminate pockets of cultural and economic variation.

A corollary of this point of view is that catering to local needs, preferences, and tastes will become increasingly unnecessary and eventually emerge as counterproductive. As a result, Levitt urges decision makers to embrace the future by ignoring differences in the belief that these variations face extinction and are ceasing to be relevant variables. The essence of the global/cultural convergence model is presented in Table 9.3.

When dealing with advisors and outsiders, indigenous, ethnic, and rural people should determine the degree to which their partners and counterparts

Table 9.3 The global/cultural convergence model

Issue	Analysis
Cultural convergence	A trend in which technology, enhanced levels of communication, uniform products etc. profoundly reduce worldwide cultural variation.
Globalization	A strategy that focuses upon the similarities between people worldwide and ignores remaining areas of cultural distinctiveness.
Strategic implications	By focusing upon cultural convergence and forging strategic plans around it, attempts are made to exploit trends toward increased homogeneity.
Cultural distinctiveness	Although pockets of cultural distinctiveness might continue, they are vestigial remains destined for oblivion. Strategies should not center on such fading traits.

DISCUSSION
The basic assumption of the global approach is that cultural variation is inevitably doomed. As a result, strategies need to center upon an anticipated future that will be characterized by increased cultural homogeneity.

embrace this global perspective. Global strategies are likely to ignore cultural variations on the assumption that they do not lead to a productive course of action. People embracing this global orientation might seek to cushion the pain of change and loss as traditions fade, but they will not attempt to prevent what they view as inevitable.

An alternative view (often held by many indigenous, ethnic, and rural peoples) insists that although their cultures will be forced to change and adapt, they and their distinctiveness can (and preferably will) survive. These people believe that the goal should be for communities to adapt in unique and relevant ways to inevitable change.

Indigenous, ethnic, and rural peoples need to decide what path they will take when seeking ways to provide internal service to their communities. They also need to remember that the future is not carved in one particular mold typified by theories such as cultural convergence and globalization. Universal and inevitable change can walk side-by-side with cultural preservation and adaption.

The tragedy of the commons and outside domination

Earlier in this book, we discussed Garrett Hardin's perspectives regarding collectively owned/managed resources as discussed in his "The Tragedy of the Commons" (1968) Hardin's model includes a powerful suggestion that local people might not be able to effectively help themselves because individual self-interest is likely to thwart sustainability. In that discussion, those views were rethought.

At first glance, Hardin's work can be read as an enlightened plea for ecological responsibility. Within its appeals for sustainability, however, is a provocative justification for taking decision-making responsibilities and authority away from local people. The model defends doing so on the pretext that the collective use of resources is likely to lead to ecological degradation or destruction. To forestall this tragedy, giving leadership authority to others can be justified.

In particular, when assets are collectively managed, Hardin suggests that rational self-interest can encourage people to abuse these resources in order to maximize individual short-term benefits. This hurtful potential can be mitigated by outside intervention. One option for doing so is to eliminate collective ownership and management of resources so that the individual owner is motivated to wisely utilize the resource in ways that insure it survival though wise shepherding, preservation, and sustainability. Another option is for the government or some other outside authority to issue strict guidelines that prevent destructive practices that individual self-interest would otherwise encourage. In both cases, these solutions rely upon external decision making replacing local choice. In essence, interlopers are given the role of protecting the people from themselves.

Local people need to remember that although Hardin's argument appears to represent enlightened sustainability and ecology, it simultaneously justifies taking power away from the local community. Whenever the Tragedy of the Commons (or similar arguments) is raised, indigenous, ethnic, and rural people need to determine if this rationale justifies usurping local authority. An overview of the Tragedy of the Commons model is presented in Table 9.4.

Table 9.4 The tragedy of outside leadership

Issue	Analysis
Basic premise	When assets are collectively used and managed, a cycle of degradation and destruction inevitably arises.
Cause of problem	Individual self-interest will prompt people to maximize their benefits in ways that contributed to the destruction of the asset that is collectively managed.
Remedy	Decision makers and managers capable of eliminating or mitigating the problems of degradation are needed.
Mechanisms	Outside leadership or private-ownership methods that ensure ecologically sound and sustainable solutions.

DISCUSSION
Local people can be viewed as incapable of acting in their long-term benefit. This perceived problem can be mitigated by outside controls or by a system of ownership that encourages rational sustainability.

Table 9.5 Paradigms compared

Paradigm	Analysis
Unilineal	There is one basic flow of cultural evolution that impacts all people. Outside experts are best able to help people deal with these transitions.
Structural	Subsistence is relatively non-productive and should be replaced by industrialization and urbanization. Outside experts can help communities respond to these challenges.
Globalization	Cultural convergence is increasing the similarities between people. The old ways are passé; knowledgeable outsiders can best help people to make inevitable transitions.
Tragedy of the Commons	Collective ownership and management can lead to ecological destruction. Outsiders can provide more appropriate strategies and responses.

DISCUSSION
Although local communities want to control their own destiny, a wide variety of rationales suggest that they are ill equipped to do so. Indigenous, ethnic, and rural people need to be aware of these points of view and how to counter them.

As we saw earlier, the notion that collective ownership/usage is inevitably linked to the destruction of the resource can be challenged. Nonetheless, the justification for outside control presented by the Tragedy of the Commons model may need to be addressed. The greater issue, of course, is the suggestion that private ownership and outside control should be used to help protect indigenous, ethnic, and rural people from themselves. Challenging such assertions may be needed in order to defend local self-determinism.

Thus, a variety of theories and paradigms exist that argue that outsiders need to control local decisions. These orientations provide a justification for eliminating self-determination on the grounds that doing so is the key to sustainable economic development. The representative sample of approaches discussed above is compared and contrasted in Table 9.5.

In essence, each of these models can be used to justify taking power, the decision-making authority, and self-determinism away from people. As a result, they can potentially inhibit people from choosing strategies of internal service that are meaningful to them. The full implications of these points of view need to be understood as well as techniques for challenging the conclusions and policy implications that can be drawn from them.

Community alternatives

As emphasized above, the assertion is sometimes made that indigenous, ethnic, and rural people lack the ability to make appropriate decisions regarding their world and their futures. When such conclusions are drawn, outsiders might seek decision-making authority on behalf of such people. Doing so potentially denies these people the opportunity to control their own destiny and practice self-determinism. This can interfere with the ability of people to choose how to provide internal service to their communities.

An important trend, however, appears to be moving in the other direction because many peoples are demanding the ability to control their lives. This movement is taking place in diverse places including North America, New Zealand, and among the Maya of Central America. It is facilitated, on many occasions, by informed leaders and advisors.

The Mosuo, an ethnic minority of China, is an example of an indigenous people who seek greater control over their lives. Two rival groups have arisen to facilitate economic development for the people and their region. One was founded by a governmental employee and appears to advocate outside leadership and advice. The other (the Lugu Lake Mosuo Cultural Development Association) is more reflective of local, indigenous thought and leadership, although outsiders such as Western anthropologists provide some advice. The association affirms:

> Any non-Mosuo who are involved serve in an advisory/supportive position, to help the Mosuo accomplish those goals. Anyone seeking to come in and tell the Mosuo what they should do, or to run their own projects, will not be included in our work.
> (Lugu Lake Mosuo Cultural Development Association)

The association also seeks dignity and respect insisting: "[The Mosuo will never be presented] as a poor, pitiful people.... They have already accomplished much on their own, despite meager resources and significant obstacles" (ibid.). The association seeks to control its own destiny, even in a changing world, observing:

> ... change is inevitable and unstoppable. It's going to happen.... In this regard, there are two main possibilities:
>
> (1) The Mosuo could simply be overwhelmed by the "outside" world, and within 50 years we may see the complete demise of their culture ...
> (2) The Mosuo will change, but still retain unique aspects of their own culture ... although it will change, much of the Mosuo culture will

also be preserved ... the second option is by far the better of the two.

(Ibid.)

Thus, the Mosuo have two organizations to choose from. One looks to outsiders for inspiration and advice while the other is much more locally controlled. Throughout the world, this later approach is gaining support from indigenous, ethnic, and rural people.

Focusing upon the needs, wants, and priorities of local people can occur in a number of ways. Two representative approaches include (a) what has been called the Tupelo model of economic development and (b) the tactics of an emerging strategic science often called "tribal management." Each is discussed below.

The Tupelo Model

Economic development specialists sometimes suggest that outsiders are best equipped to develop and implement strategic plans on behalf of indigenous, ethnic, and rural peoples. Doing so may provide advantages especially when specialized knowledge is required. An overreliance upon others, however, might be costly in the long run if, in the process, local people fail to develop the skills and abilities that they need to control their own destiny.

The "Tupelo Model," developed by Vaughn Grisham (1999a, 1999b) and Rob Gurwitt (and advocated by rural leadership and development organizations, such as the Brushy Folk Institute that serves Appalachian people, provides one way of developing local managerial and decision-making abilities. The technique can be graphically presented in the form of a pyramid in which the foundation levels create an underpinning upon which more advanced abilities are built.

According to the Tupelo Model, the most basic tactic of helping communities to develop economically and socially should be upgrading the skills and abilities of local people. This is done in the belief that true economic development starts with providing local people with the tools needed to succeed.

After members of the local community capture these abilities, they can be groomed to embrace useful leadership roles, reducing the need for outsiders. Once local leaders with the appropriate skills are in place, they can serve as a catalyst leading to further local progress and self-determinism (such as organizational and community development). With these improvements in place, true economic development emerges.

Thus, this cumulative process builds upon the enhanced abilities of individuals that, in turn, transforms community resources and institutions in positive ways. Doing so is a powerful alternative to relying upon outside leadership without a conscious and systematic plan to transfer skills and authority to local people. Enhancing the abilities of local people and growing community-based institutions benefits the community in lasting ways that serve all.

An old cliché of economic development observes that if you give people food, you feed them for a day, but if you teach them to farm you feed them forever. The long-term benefits of doing so occur because local talent is developed and channeled in productive ways. The Tupelo Model can also be viewed from this perspective.

Believing that true progress and prosperity depend upon and are linked to the growth of local leadership, the value of reducing a reliance upon outsiders becomes obvious. The Tupelo Model is the antithesis of top-down leadership methods that are staffed by outsiders. Although outside experts might produce optimum short-term strategies and although they have a role to play for ad hoc purposes, relying upon them does little to enhance local skills and capabilities.

Being locally centered, the Tupelo Model can help indigenous, ethnic, and rural people improve their skills and strengthen their communities. The long-term goal is to implement a multi-step process that leads to the growth of local skills and allows for the gradual reduction in the need for outside leadership. This is true even when expatriate experts may be needed for ad hoc purposes. Graphically portrayed, the Tupelo Model is presented in Figure 9.1.

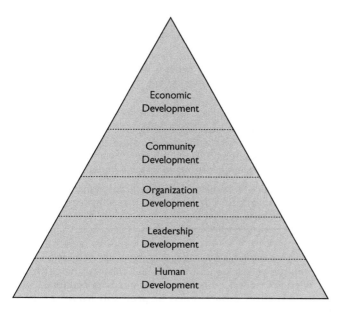

Figure 9.1 The Tupelo Model.

Although the indigenous, ethnic, and rural leaders I have worked with do not indicate an awareness of the Tupelo Model, many of them appear to have independently invented its basic orientation and applied it to their goals, strategies, and orientations.

Outside, intrusive organizations, in contrast, might seek to maintain a fairly tight control over leadership, decision making, and so forth. And they might have legitimate short-term reasons for doing so. This approach, however, can prevent local individuals and communities from developing expertise, skills, and decision-making abilities. In tabular form, the Tupelo is portrayed in Table 9.6.

The Tupelo Model provides a way to understand and explain why many communities prefer local leadership. By acknowledging that indigenous, ethnic, and rural peoples have their own values, goals, and challenges, local communities can cease to be viewed as vestigial remains destined for speedy and inevitable extinction. This perspective can lead to a better understanding of insights and perspectives that can help local people respond in strong and appropriate ways.

Table 9.6 The Tupelo Model

Issue	Analysis
Strategy	The goal of the Tupelo Model is to build the managerial and professional skills of the community in order to encourage true economic development.
Tradeoffs	Short-term benefits and profits may be sacrificed if extensive training is provided to local people and if they are placed in positions where outsiders could be more effective.
Benefits	By receiving training and positions of authority, community members gain skills and experience. Although in the short term they might not be as effective as outsiders, the resulting inefficiencies are viewed as a cost of training that has long-term benefits.
Process	Help people develop skills. Facilitate individual leadership and organization development that enhances the community as a whole.

DISCUSSION
True economic development begins by increasing the skills of local people and allowing these abilities to trickle up through and enhance the entire community. Thus, outside leadership and control is not true economic development because although resources may be profitably harvested, local abilities are not enhanced.

Tribal management

In recent years, a new discipline has emerged that is increasingly known as "tribal management." Its goal is to help indigenous, ethnic, and rural peoples make wise decisions regarding their social and economic development. Although this movement is often identified with American Indians, Alaska Natives, the Maori of New Zealand, and so forth, Ray Barnhardt (a cross cultural and Alaska Native specialist at the University of Alaska at Fairbanks) has told me that in many ways the emerging field appears to have been influenced by the early work of Appalachian Studies.

The Appalachian people, of course, are an ethnic group residing in the mountainous regions of the Southeastern United States who descend from Scots/Irish settlers of the eighteenth century. Thus, these people are not indigenous. Nonetheless, the Appalachians are recognized as distinct both by themselves and by outsiders. They are a unique ethnic group with their own traditions (some of which, including their music, are revered and influential).

Early in my career, I taught Appalachian Studies at Alice Lloyd College, a small college founded in the early twentieth to provide educational and economic opportunities to the rugged mountainous regions that was home to the Hatfields and McCoys. More recently, I taught tribal management at Ilisavgik College in Barrow, Alaska (the only tribal college in the state); in this role, I provided managerial training seminars to those who lived in the small villages that are scattered over the North Slope.

Key to my vision of tribal management is the fact that the goals, needs, opportunities, and risks faced by indigenous, ethnic, and rural peoples tend to be very different from those of many mainstream people. Unfortunately, consultants, advisors, and teachers serving these groups have often failed to adequately adjust their services to the local communities being served.

Because business thinking often seeks to develop generic strategies and tactics, these advisors are likely to favor universal methods and modes of analysis that lump indigenous, ethnic, and rural people with everybody else.

My perspectives are the opposite. I believe that specific peoples are both distinct and capable of deciding what is right for themselves. The proper course for mainstream people might not be the best path for all. Do not forget that when people make their own idiosyncratic decisions, doing so does not inevitably result from shallow thinking.

When serving as an advisor, I certainly want the people I work with to understand the full implications of their actions and I want them to consider the potential results of the decisions they make. I, on the other hand, do not attempt to force decisions in ways that fit my vision instead of theirs.

On occasion, some goals of indigenous people might appear as nonsensical to outsiders. As an example, the Pebble Mine project in Alaska has sought for years to gain access to monumental copper and gold reserves located in Southwest Alaska. If the mine ever goes into operation, the local people will gain generous rewards. And yet, the project has met with dogged opposition. Why? Because many of the Alaska Natives who live in the region prefer salmon fishing and a subsistence lifestyle that the mine potentially threatens. Those negotiating on behalf of the mining consortium, no doubt, have trouble understanding why a relatively poor population shuns affluence in order to live a precarious and strenuous life of hunting and fishing. But that is what many of the people prefer. And, it appears, the local Alaska Native communities of the region make this decision with full awareness of the sacrifices that are involved in keeping the mine out. Thus, rational and informed people can make decisions and hold priorities that differ from those of the mainstream. These people have a right to fight to control their destiny, just like anybody else. Their logic is not necessarily flawed just because it is different.

I remember a conversation about proposed oil drilling activities that took place in Point Hope (an Inupiaq village on the Bering Sea of Alaska). The people of Point Hope wanted to stop these actions because they worried that oil exploration might damage or frighten the wildlife that the community depended upon for subsistence. Maybe the polar bears, seals, and walruses would be scared away by drilling activities. Perhaps the whales will shun the region if large oil rigs and ships ply the waters. "What will happen to us then," the people wanted to know. Many of these people were more concerned about hunting and fishing than with the money that the oil industry would bring.

Tribal management typically helps people to recognize and articulate what they want in order to develop a clear and strategic course of action (see Walle 2009). Local people might find it difficult to effectively communicate with outsiders when policies, strategies, and tactics are being discussed. Tribal management might help to develop these skills.

Many indigenous, ethnic, and rural people are concerned because they live in fragile environments where intrusive economic development projects might undercut the ability of the people to maintain their way of life. On many occasions, "economic development" involves extractive industries that disrupt the land and cart away resources that are then reworked by others who earn the majority of the profits.

"What are the pitfalls of an opportunity?," I often asked. "How will a project affect the environment and your community?" I admitted to those I worked with that I didn't always know the answers, but reminded them that these were questions that needed to be considered.

Thus, indigenous, ethnic, and rural people need to consider the implications of their actions. Strategies such as the Tupelo Model seek to enhance the communities by developing local talent as the foundation of true economic development. Initiatives such as tribal management also seek to develop local skills and enhance the ability to view opportunities from the perspective of the community, not the agendas or perceptions of outsiders.

Doing so can help local people better understand their options and control their destiny.

Both the Tupelo Model and the emerging discipline of tribal management are primarily concerned with providing internal service to the community and its members. Providing service to others is viewed as a tactic that serves local people, their culture, and society. With these issues in mind, the role of public administration will be discussed.

Tailored public administration

Earlier in this book, public administration was discussed as a series of theories and practices that organizations, such as governments, use when establishing policies and strategies. In particular, we saw a tension that exists between those who advocate universal methods of public service that focus upon efficiency (not values and norms) vs. more moral and thoughtful alternatives (such as the New Public Administration) that requires practitioners to employ judgment and ethical standards when carrying out their assigned tasks. This later view emphasizes that there is no universal "right way" to pursue public service because circumstances, conditions, subjective principles, and social customs must be taken into account.

Those who are involved in providing internal service to their communities must deal with evaluation and choice within a particular context. Those who advocate subjective judgment and concentrate upon cultural distinctiveness often embrace perspectives that are in line with what has come to be called "postmodern public administration." As in many other disciplines, post-modernism and post-structuralism in public administration has emerged as an alternative to "scientific" methods that look for universal answers; the analytic alternatives offered are nested in the specific situation. In recent years, a number of useful overviews of postmodern public administration have become available including (Miller 2002) as well as discussions regarding post-modernism within the social sciences in general (Rosenau 1992; Hollinger 1994).

In layman's terms, modernism involves a belief in "progress" and the possibility of discovering, developing, or inventing the one best way of doing things. Earlier in this chapter we discussed the work of Walter Rostow who embraced an evolutionary theory that provided universal advice regarding how to overcome "backwardness" in order to benefit from the advantages of modern life. Those who embrace a postmodern perspective, in contrast, question if generic or universal options are truly (and always) superior. As an alternative, the postmodern approach looks at the distinctiveness of people and insists upon viewing them within a relevant context and on their own terms. Thus, "good solutions" are viewed as uniquely tailored and suited to circumstances. When doing so, universal yardsticks of evaluation preferred by modernists are no longer applicable.

This emerging paradigm is similar to a number of earlier precedents. Thus, a powerful rejoinder to the eighteenth century's optimistic belief of the perfection and standardization of human institutions was Romantic Nationalism that viewed culture, law, social conventions, and so forth locally and not with reference to universal criteria or modes of evaluation. A classic example of doing so is the rejection of the Napoleonic Code of law by people of non-French origin who complained it was culturally incompatible.

Becoming a force in the second half of the twentieth century, however, postmodern and post-structural approaches to public administration are directly inspired by existentialism that focuses upon specific peoples and individuals, not universal tendencies created by human nature or overarching cultural traditions. Existentialism, of course, stems from a rejection of Fredrick Hegel's celebration of the collective culture by focusing upon individuals or smaller groups that stand apart from the dominant majority.

In such a spirit, postmodern public administration looks at specific cases within a relevant context. Universal and modern recommendations are not touted as tactics that should be emulated by all. Such postmodern methods of analysis can be of value when evaluating how to best serve entities (such as indigenous, ethnic, and rural groups) that stand apart from the mainstream and harbor atypical priorities, goals, and visions.

King (2005) recalls the early days of postmodern public administration when the budding movement was pitted against entrenched scientifically oriented scholars, theorists, and practitioners who dominated the field. Those were heady and exciting days, she recalls. King goes on to set up the dichotomy between the modern-looking establishment and the emerging postmodern movement with reference to what she calls "Large T Truth" vs. "small t truth." Large T Truth refers to a paradigm in which the assumption is made that certain universal Truths exist that can be discovered and universally applied. The mainstream of the discipline focused upon such paradigms. Small t truth embraced by the postmodern alternative, in contrast, looks at specific situations and determines what is "true" from that non-universal vantage point. Small t analysis became the province of postmodern public administration because it can more effectively deal with local circumstances and what is right and effective within that particular and non-universal context.

Postmodern public administration, as a recognizable entity, goes back at least to 1978 with the establishment of the Public Administration Theory Network (that has come to be commonly called PAT-NET). Growth was rapid with a large contingent emerging that began holding annual conferences in the late 1980s. The organization publishes the *Journal of Administrative Theory and Praxis*. In recent years a growing number of international scholars has become involved, especially from Europe and Australia.

Within the context of this chapter, postmodern perspectives can help provide insights regarding how people should provide internal service to each other. When dealing with indigenous, ethnic, and rural people, doing so can become confusing because organizations that are technically private might be de facto public in nature. An example of this is the impact of the Alaska Native Claims Settlement Act that provided resources to Native Alaskans in return for the rescinding of certain rights and privileges. These funds were not given directly to tribes because the United States government mandated that this compensation be channeled through profit-making corporations with tribal members holding shares of stock. Thus, although private in charter, these organizations possessed a degree of publicness. Under these circumstances, those who manage these private corporations can benefit from the counsel provided by public administration theories. As the postmodern approach emphasizes, when evaluations and recommendations are made, focusing upon particular circumstances is important.

Relevant aspects of postmodern public administration are provided in Table 9.7.

By viewing postmodern public administration with reference to the Tupelo Model and tribal management, a variety of parallels and connections emerge. All three view people from a local or individual perspective. Each, in its own way, recommends strategies and tactics that resonate from distinctiveness and, as a result, underplay universal patterns or solutions. As a result, they can be envisioned as interconnected as is portrayed in Table 9.8.

Table 9.7 Postmodern public administration

Issue	Analysis
Influences	Postmodern public administration is influenced by existential thought that centers upon the situation of individuals and circumscribed groups. It is an alternative to collective and universal methods of analysis.
Focus	The distinctiveness of specific peoples or circumstances. Forging analyses and recommendations that reflect this variation and non-universality.
Provides alternative to	Mainstream modernism that often seeks universal solutions and/or the one best way of doing things.
Value	Provides a means of looking at people on their own terms and not with reference to alien paradigms or universal models that might be inappropriate.

DISCUSSION
Historically, public administration has sought universally superior methods and tactics. The postmodern alternative focuses upon viewing people on their own terms with reference to their distinctiveness. By doing so the inappropriate application of universal solutions can be avoided.

Table 9.8 Integrating the models

Issue	Analysis
Tupelo Model	Centers upon the need to focus upon individual circumstances in order to develop plans of economic development that are distinct and community centered. The goal is to build local skills and institutions, not merely generate short term profit.
Tribal management	Helping distinctive peoples to develop methods of organization, control, and decision making in ways that are culturally compatible and appropriate. By doing so, universal solutions are downplayed in favor of local alternatives.
Postmodern public administration	Viewing public organizations and policies from within a specific cultural or situational focus, not with reference to universal rules or methods.
Integration	All of these methods converge in ways that are centered upon the local community and strategies that serve it in unique ways

DISCUSSION
A common thread of economic development seeks methods that are appropriate. Mainstream methods often attempt to provide indigenous, ethnic, and rural peoples with universal tools. By doing so, the attempt is made to most effectively serve the local group by providing state of the art methods. An alternatives is to look at the group first and craft solution around it and its unique nature and needs.

The need, therefore, exists for indigenous, ethnic, and rural peoples to devise ways to provide internal services to their communities. When planning to do so, issues of leadership invariably emerge. Historically, the case has been made that because outsiders possess the leadership, managerial expertise, and skills needed to foster productive change and adaption, they should be placed in positions of authority.

Increasingly, an alternative vision has focused upon the ability of local people to forge their own solutions and to decide what criteria of development and change are relevant to them.

Discussion and conclusion

A tendency exists among some leaders and decision makers to assume that outside experts possess superior knowledge and insights that should dominate decisions regarding indigenous, ethnic, and rural peoples. These orientations go back to ancient times and can still be seen in a variety of contemporary approaches that continue to exert an influence today.

Although outside experts may have superior ad hoc tools that are of value in specific situations, local people often possess a clear and sophisticated understanding of what they want. When decisions are being made regarding how to provide service to the local community, this potential (and the self-determinism it fosters) should be recognized. In this regard, tools provided by methods such as the Tupelo Model and tribal management emphasize the value of developing and using local talent in order to serve the community in ways that are directed by and tailored to unique needs and preferences.

The Tupelo Model and tribal management merge nicely with postmodern theories of public administration that emphasize that policies and strategies should reflect local needs, desires, and traditions, and do not merely attempt to reflect some universal standard that is viewed as modern and inherently superior.

By keeping these locally centered perspectives in mind, indigenous, ethnic, and rural peoples (as well as those who provide counsel to them) can develop perspectives that serve people on their own terms. Due to the significance of cultural differences, these perspectives can be invaluable.

Internal service involves actions that serve the local community and do so in ad hoc ways. Although people might need to be advised regarding the full implications of the choices and options before them, they are often well equipped to make these decisions as well as operationalizing them in relevant and tailored ways.

Relevant terms

Cultural convergence: The theory that technology, rapid travel, the internet, and so forth are reducing worldwide cultural variation.

Drive to maturity: A continuation and deepening of the Takeoff stage of the Rostow model which is characterized by economic growth, optimism and a rising standard of living.

Dual-Sector Model: A model of development advocated by Arthur Lewis that compares two sectors of the economy: the "subsistence/rural" and the "industrial/urban." Lewis indicates that by shifting resources towards the industrial sector economies can most effectively develop.

Globalization: A strategy that focuses upon increasing similarities between people and attempts to ignore cultural distinctiveness.

Industrialization/urbanization: According to the Dual-Sector Model, the favored means of production/social organization that should replace the subsistence way of life.

Internal service: Helping the community to help itself on its own terms without strategically focusing upon others to benefit the community.

Lewis, Arthur: The economic development specialist who developed the Dual-Sector Model that juxtaposes industrialization/urbanization vs. subsistence/rural.

Mass consumption: In Rostow's model, the culmination of the development process in which people enjoy a life on a par with the developed West.

PAT-NET: An influential organization that advocates postmodern public administration.

Postmodern public administration: The branch of public administration that attempts to analyze options within a particular context instead of proposing methods that are viewed as inherently superior and universal in nature.

Preconditions for takeoff: A phase of the Rostow Model that outlines conditions (including educational opportunities and the beginnings of a managerial class and so forth) that must exist before economic development can begin.

Public administration: A discipline dedicated to helping civil servants (and those acting in that capacity) to most effectively accomplish their goals.

Rostow, Walter: An economic development theorist who advocated a unilineal theory of economic development that was very popular in the middle of the twentieth century.

Structural models: Models of development that focus upon the structure of the society and culture and suggest that industrial/urban structures are most effective.

Subsistence/rural: According to the Dual-Sector Model, a relatively ineffective means of production that should be replaced by industrialization/urbanization.

Takeoff: A phase in the Rostow model in which initial progress is made including the establishment of enterprises, the maturity of a managerial class, and a greater acceptance of the potentials of development.

Traditional society: A phase in the Rostow model that occurs before economic development takes place. Rostow depicts it as backward and in need of being replaced.

Tragedy of the Commons: A model developed by Garrett Hardin that indicates that collectively managed resources are typically degraded or destroyed by individuals pursuing self-interest. It can be used to argue that local people should be denied self-determinism in order to prevent these tragedies.

Tribal management: A discipline that seeks to establish appropriate managerial and strategic thought that reflects the needs and priorities of indigenous, ethnic, and rural people.

Tupelo Model: A model of economic development that focuses upon enhancing the skills and abilities of local people and views human development as the key to true economic development.

Unilineal evolution: A theory that asserts that all people are proceeding through the same evolutionary stages, although some are backward people are doing so more slowly. They need the help of the developed world to reach their potential.

White man's burden: A concept articulated by Rudyard Kipling that asserts that the White and developed West is obligated to help underdeveloped people gain the advantages of technology and civilization.

References

Grisham, Vaughn (1999a). *Hand in Hand: Community Development in Tupelo* (Aspen CO: Aspen Institute).

Grisham, Vaughn (1999b). *Tupelo: The Evolution of a Community* (Dayton OH: Kettering Institute).

Hardin, Garrett (1968). "The Tragedy of the Commons." *Science*, 162, 1243–1248.

Hollinger, R. (1994). *Postmodernism and the Social Sciences. A Thematic Approach* (London: Sage).

King, Cheryl S. (2005). "Postmodern Public Administration in the Shadow of Post Modernism." *Administrative Theory and Praxis*, 27, 517–532.

Luga Lake Mosou Cultural Development Association (2011). Retrieved March 15, 2011 from: http://mosuoproject.org/.

Miller, H. T. (2002). *Postmodern Public Policy* (Albany NY: State University of New York Press).

Morgan, Lewis Henry (1877). *Ancient Society* (New York: Henry Holt).

Rosenau, P. M. (1992). *Post-Modernism and the Social Sciences. Insights, Inroads and Intrusions* (Princeton NJ: Princeton University Press).

Walle, Alf H. (2009). "Pro-Choice [Tribal Management]." *Cultural Survival Quarterly* 33(1), 22–31.

Walle, Alf H. (2013). *Rethinking Business Anthropology: Cultural Strategies in Marketing and Management* (Sheffield: Greenleaf).

Chapter 10

External service

Learning objectives

Gaining benefits through serving others typically involves marketing. When viewed from neoclassical perspectives, marketing is viewed as rational and universal. This approach can easily overlook specifics including hurtful side effects. Non-neoclassical models of marketing can better portray other implications and influences. The sub-discipline of macromarketing, furthermore, expands beyond the neoclassical paradigm by addressing marketing's full ramifications. Indigenous, ethnic, and rural peoples can benefit from such expanded and evenhanded views. Specific objectives of this chapter include:

1   Understanding that marketing typically involves serving others in order to benefit as a result.
2   Being aware of non-neoclassical alternative paradigms of marketing and their relevance.
3   Recognizing beneficial aspects of non-neoclassical alternatives to marketing.
4   Appreciating the broader focus of macromarketing.
5   Envisioning how communities can serve others in order to achieve their goals.

Introduction

The last chapter discussed how indigenous, ethnic, and rural people can serve themselves and their communities. That conversation began by discussing justifications that advocate outsiders taking control on the grounds that local leaders are apt to be ineffective. That assertion was tempered by reminding the reader that self-determination can benefit local communities and people. Postmodern public administration provided additional tools and clues regarding equity and parity.

In addition to overtly advancing their own specific agendas, people can profit by serving others and benefiting as a result. That process is usually referred to as "marketing." That is the topic of this chapter.

The importance of serving others (via marketing or other methods) varies from situation to situation. Where a subsistence way of life dominates, serving others might be relatively less important than the alternative of independently satisfying needs. Some sort of "mixed economy" usually exists where some items are produced locally while others are gained through exchange with others. A sliding scale can be envisioned involving different levels of barter, cash/labor, self-reliant subsistence, and so forth. On one end of the continuum, almost total subsistence dominates; on the other extreme, a strict cash economy is present.

Interdependence

Although complete subsistence probably does not exist anywhere in the world, a partial reliance upon it survives in many places. Ecological conditions, opportunities to trade, and so forth influence the degree of independence.

An explanation for the propensity to trade is modeled by the economic principle of "advantage." Some desired goods and services, of course, are more efficiently and cheaply produced in certain places. Where this is true, surpluses can be more cheaply produced and successfully traded. Doing so can benefit all; local people have something to sell while trading partners have access to items that would otherwise be unavailable or be able to acquire to them at reduced prices.

In his seminal *Wealth of Nations*, Adam Smith observes: "If a foreign country can supply us with a commodity cheaper than we ourselves can make it, better buy it" (Smith 1776). This observation gave rise to the principle of "absolute advantage" (that exists when an individual, region, company, country, and so forth) creates products or services more cheaply than competitors. Even though Smith was focusing upon only one variable (labor) his ideas have been expanded to deal with other components of production. Central America, for example, has an absolute advantage in producing bananas over Vermont. Vermont, however, has an absolute advantage when it comes to producing maple syrup.

In the early nineteenth century, David Ricardo built upon Smith's work to create his theory of "comparative advantage" that observes that if various trading partners are each capable of creating two products, one producer might be able to produce one of them more efficiently. When this situation exists, it will export that product and export the other. All the trading partners can benefit as a result. The resulting advantage provides a rationale for abandoning local subsistence.

Of course, specific circumstances may cause people to act contrary to such strategies. A community, for example, might sacrifice the benefits of efficiency in order to develop or maintain local production capabilities. Some communities might be willing to sacrifice short term profits and efficiencies in order to facilitate local people gaining professional experience and job skills.

Benefiting through specialization often exists in subsistence economies. Alaska, for example, possesses a wide variety of ecological niches that provide specific resources (such as food and raw materials). Regional products, however, are varied and their harvest times are scattered throughout the year. As a result, the people in one region often enjoy a surplus of particular resources which are scarce elsewhere. Methods of redistribution known as "Potlatches" arose in which local surpluses are provided to those in need.

Consider an Alaska Native village near the water that enjoys a bountiful supply of salmon during the summer. At harvest time, the people produce much more smoked fish than they consume. Historically, these people invariably hosted redistribution mechanisms known as "potlatches" and gave food to those living further inland (with little access to salmon) who were probably experiencing a scarcity of food around the time the salmon were harvested. The potlatch system provides a mechanism for sharing resources that otherwise would go to waste.

Potlatches resemble a community-wide party open to outsiders that is typified by conspicuous consumption and gift giving, intertwined with festivities and entertainment. A more practical result is that hungry people gain the resources needed to survive while local people simultaneously disposed of their excessive surpluses.

The needy recipients who receive the salmon, furthermore, might live in areas that are adjacent to the annual caribou migration. During the hunting season, these people would gain an unneeded surplus of caribou meat, hides, and antlers. It would now be their turn to host a potlatch and invite the salmon gatherers to attend. As a result of this system, resources harvested in different regions benefit all. In Chapter 2, we discussed substantive methods of economic organization that are based on tradition, sentiment, and feelings of obligation (not upon calculation and rational attempts to benefit through an exchange). The potlatch system is a classic example of such substantive activities.

Today, overt and systematic methods and practices of business are increasingly commonplace and dominant. In this environment, serving others tends to be envisioned in terms of marketing that typically involves rationally serving others in order to self-consciously seek benefits.

Marketing as a strategic focus

As indicated in the potlatch example above, useful and productive exchanges can be facilitated using substantive methods that are centered upon tradition and sentiment. Under these circumstances, costs and benefits are not calculated in an ad hoc manner. Such methods of distribution are increasingly being replaced with an eye towards calculating a maximum return at a minimum price. As mentioned in Chapter 2, marketing is a strategic method of gaining benefits by providing goods and services to others. Doing so reflects neoclassical economic tactics of rationally determining what goods and services are offered in order to benefit.

As usually envisioned, marketing involves anticipating and satisfying the needs, desires, and goals of those being served in order to earn a profit (or some surrogate measure of profit in the case of a not for profit organization) and/or to achieve other goals. The tactic of benefiting through serving others is codified by the "marketing concept" that emphasizes that the only reason for an organization to exist is to help its customers or clients. This truism has become a ubiquitous slogan that justifies the field.

The controllable variables marketers strategically manipulate are envisioned in terms of four categories labelled "Product," "Place," "Promotion," and "Price"; since each starts with "P," this approach has come to be known as the "4 Ps of Marketing Management."

The **product** is what the client or customer gets. Some products are tangible and physical while, others are intangible (such as providing advice, information, or entertainment). Products tend to be envisioned with the customers' demands in mind and manipulated in order to better serve and please them.

Although this strategy has its merits, members of indigenous, ethnic, or rural communities need to remember that producing and marketing certain sorts of products might exert a harmful impact. If the product is "logs," forests must be cut down. What are the long-term costs and implications of destroying the forest? Should this consequence be factored into the decision-making process? Thus, concentrating upon the needs and desires of outsiders can overshadow important issues that need to be addressed internally. (Later discussions in this chapter deal with such concerns). Initially, the other controllable variables are discussed below, leading to an evaluation of Marketing Management which analyzes the full impact of these variables operating in tandem.

Price policies have a dual role: (1) providing a reward for helping others, and (2) strategically encouraging or discouraging customers. Pricing structures are often used to control demand. If a community can only comfortably serve a certain number of tourists, for example, the price might be adjusted to keep the number of visitors at that level. Of course, prices must be set in order to ensure profitability. Prices, furthermore, can respond very quickly to circumstances and, therefore, adjusting them might offer a "quick fix" or be part of an ongoing seasonal strategy.

Place: Where will the product be sold and made available? If cultural products (such as crafts and performances) are being marketed, location can be an important consideration. Thus, the local community itself might choose to provide goods and services at another venue for reasons of privacy and so forth. What are the implications of each option? How can the needs of all stakeholders be most effectively accommodated? These options should be evaluated with likely side effects in mind, not merely short-term profits.

Promotion typically refers to various types of communication that are intended to encourage patronage. In modern business practice, promotion is usually envisioned as "integrated marketing communications" that include the synergistic effects of advertising, personal selling, public relations, and "sales promotion" and so on.

On many occasions, promotional strategies designed to attract customers and patrons might prove hurtful to the host community or its members. People who buying art objects and crafts, for example, often want to meet the artist. Because bona fide traditional craftspeople are often not available, some clever marketers have hired others (who may be craftspeople themselves or merely actors) to pose as the craftsperson. Doing so can exert hurtful impacts: one acknowledged basket maker, for example, observed: "It hurts when somebody else puts their name on your baskets" (NEA 1986).

Marketing Management involves tactically or strategically combining all of the controllable variables of marketing in a systematic manner that synergistically reinforces the sales pitch in ways that are more powerful and compelling than if these variables were employed without reference to one another.

In summary, the contemporary marketing profession typically views its mission as (1) choosing a target market and coming to understand what it wants, followed by (2) manipulating the available controllable variables in order to cater to the demands of that sought-after market. This process is the essence of contemporary marketing (see Table 10.1).

Table 10.1 The 4 Ps of Marketing Management

Variable	Analysis
Product	The good or service being offered to a target market(s).
Price	The charge for a good or service (taking profits and strategies into account).
Place	The location or venue where the product can be bought or consumed.
Promotion	Communication designed to reinforce the marketing strategy.
Marketing Management	Combining the controllable variables in order to cater to a target market(s).

DISCUSSION
Modern marketing reflects the neoclassical model of using rational thought to achieve personal gain. It does so by anticipating customers' needs and adjusting to them. Useful in many ways, the focus upon customer demands can draw attention away from the needs, wants, of those who provide goods and services.

Contemporary marketing, therefore, views itself as a strategic science that (1) tends to focus upon the needs of specific external groups by (2) adjusting the organization's controllable variables in order to satisfy these clients and customers.

Although doing so can orient the organization in strategic ways, it can easily ignore or deemphasize the impact of a course of action upon the local community.

Although contemporary marketing and other neoclassical business tactics are valuable tools, care needs to be employed to ensure that hurtful side effects and counterproductive side effects do not cancel out or overshadow sought after benefits. An opportunity, for example, might provide profits but be disruptive to individuals or the community, alter relationships in negative and/or unpredictable ways, damage the environment, and so forth. Or, perhaps, a particular plan might prevent local people from developing skills or gaining future opportunities. When they exist, costs and sacrifices such as these need to be addressed and mitigated when plans are made and implemented.

A key point to remember is that the full implications of a decision need to be measured and addressed. Neoclassical business models primarily seek to serve others in order to gain benefits that tend to be calculated purely in terms of cash. This rational approach assumes buyers and sellers are fully aware of the implications of doing so. On many occasions, unfortunately, these conditions do not exist and harmful consequences can slip in as a result.

Beyond neoclassical marketing management

Although contemporary marketing methods tend to reflect the neoclassical model, other paradigms expand beyond it. Before the neoclassical model came to dominate marketing in the 1960s, these alternatives exerted a strong influence and provided a more balanced view of marketing and what it does. If revitalized, these vintage models can be of significant value to indigenous, ethnic, and rural peoples.

In spite of being ignored due to the onslaught of neoclassical thought, their significance has not been totally forgotten. Sheth and Garrett, for example, observe: "these classical schools of marketing thought have an abundance of intriguing and potentially valuable concepts that need to be rediscovered and revitalized" (1986: 241). Indigenous, ethnic, and rural people, for example, can use these tools to more effectively and robustly understand the full implications of serving a wider range of stakeholders than merely patrons and clients. Three such methods are functionalism, institutionalism, and the commodity approach.

The functional method: When marketing was first emerging as a distinct business discipline, it embraced a functional approach (Fullbrook 1940: 229–237). By doing so, it looked beyond actual marketing activities in order to focus upon the underlying purposes or functions that these activities sought to accomplish. Although currently overshadowed by neoclassical models, Walle points out that the functional method can and should be rehabilitated and given a significant role in the decision-making process (Walle 2000). Serving indigenous, ethnic, and rural people is one example of this potential.

The functional method breaks marketing activities down into sub-tasks that must be performed when customers and clients are being served. Instead of concentrating merely upon customers, (as neoclassical models tend to do), the functional method looks at the full array of marketing activities, how and why they occur, who is served, and what is accomplished.

In the last edition of his influential marketing textbook, Paul Converse (1965) breaks functionalism within marketing into an array of tasks including transitions of ownership, the physical movement of the product, facilitating possession, and so forth. According to this method, marketing management is presented as just another of several needed and inevitable functions (Converse et al. 1965: 127–128). In neoclassical models of marketing, in contrast, marketing management is the keystone activity that underlies all marketing thought and action.

The key point is that marketing involves a wide variety of functions that must take place. Although the customer is ultimately served, the needs of a broad range of non-customers (including the local community and its members) are addressed. Paying attention to such considerations is vital because if these functions are not performed, the ability to effectively serve may be compromised. The functional method provides a way of envisioning the full requirements and ramifications of pursuing a particular marketing strategy and does so in ways that extend to a wide range of stakeholders, not merely customers and clients.

Consider, for example, the function of physical movement within cultural tourism. One option would be to take the visitors to where the indigenous people are located. Doing so might be costly, disruptive to the local community, and an unattractive option for many visitors. On the other hand, visitors would gain a real-life glimpse into the lives of those being showcased.

An alternative might be to take members of the culture to a comfortable and convenient location where the visitors are located. Doing so might be cheaper and more appealing to many tourists. This arrangement, however, might alienate some of those providing services as well as delivering a rather shallow portrayal of the people being exhibited. In addition, the benefits to the community might be limited to the small minority of performers who are actively involved and not involve a wider range of participants. Thus, the function of transportation can involve complicated choices that need to be considered with reference to multiple stakeholders, not merely those who buy services.

Functional analysis, furthermore, allows neoclassical marketing management activities to be segregated into a separate section of the analysis; in

Converse's listing, for example, marketing management is viewed as a distinct and discrete activity. When employing the contemporary marketing management paradigm, in contrast, a customer focus is envisioned as an overarching orientation that is the underpinning of all marketing activities. When enmeshed in this way, marketing management cannot be easily untangled from other functions.

This neoclassical "customer is king" mentality, therefore, may not be totally appropriate when strategies and tactics that best serve local communities are forged. The functional approach, in contrast, is able to deal with these important needs, priorities, and vulnerabilities in ways that equitably serve both communities and customers.

Marketing institutions: The institutional approach identifies certain types of institutions that are involved in marketing as well as discussing their nature, needs, strengths, vulnerabilities, and other relevant variables. By identifying similarities in specific types of institutions and their typical responses, generalizations are developed that can increase effectiveness.

In 1936, for example, marketing pioneer Paul Converse observed:

> The institutional approach leads to a consideration of the various types of middlemen or agencies involved in marketing. It shows how they operate, their place in the marketing system, their importance, the functions they perform, and the commodities they handle.
>
> (1936: 135)

In the 1939 edition of *Principles of Marketing* by Harold Maynard, Walter Weidler, and Theodore Beckman paid significant attention to a variety of different marketing institutions. In order to simplify the analysis, they first present general categories, such as the "Retail System" and "Wholesaling." These broad groupings were then broken down into smaller groups along with discussions on how to effectively serve them.

The institutional approach remained distinctive as late as the mid-1960s (Converse et al. 1965: 144–161), but was eventually absorbed in neoclassical marketing management, although it continues to covertly exist in courses such as "Introduction to Retailing."

A focus upon institutions, however, can be revitalized and adapted by envisioning peoples, cultures, traditions, and communities as "institutions" that need to be acknowledged when marketing arrangements are developed. By rehabilitating this classic paradigm of marketing, the distinct goals and vulnerabilities of host communities and cultures can be more effectively addressed.

Examples of specific types of cultural institutions might include "subsistence economies," "rural communities with a 'mixed economy'" "wage-earning," and so on. By envisioning these categories and how they typically respond, a generalized institutional approach can be developed for dealing with a wide variety of indigenous, ethnic, and rural peoples. This can result in an analysis of how cultural institutions are impacted (in both positive and negative ways) by a particular marketing strategy or tactic. Such modeling has great value when a host community and its business partners seek viable and equitable strategies of economic development.

Most broadly, then, the institutional approach looks at the characteristics of different types of organizations that might include host communities, outside partners, specific types of economic activities, and so forth. When considering marketing strategies, host communities should consider the various institutions with which they may become involved and the possible impact of relationships with them. By doing so, more advantageous and equitable strategies can be developed.

The commodity approach: Not only are various institutions involved in the marketing process, a number of different products or commodities are sold in distinct ways. Many of these commodities can be placed in certain categories based upon their similarities. A classic discussion of this process is provided by Paul Converse who observes: "Marketing may be studied by taking up various commodities.... The study of each commodity would involve a discussion of the necessary functions or services and the middlemen or institutions concerned" (Converse 1936: 141). This approach can be very useful because instead of providing generic advice, it offers a better understanding of precisely what is being marketed, its characteristics, and how the nature of the product might impact the marketing process. Nonetheless, this approach has its drawbacks. Thus: "This method may become tedious with its long descriptions and unless care is taken, it may involve much repetition of material. But many commodities involve the same functions and methods [so patterns can be perceived]" (Converse 1936: 141). Because dealing with a large number of different commodities may result in wasted time and bore students, the method is largely ignored in the classroom.

Nonetheless, developing strategies that are tailored to the situation is a practical activity, not an academic exercise. Doing so has a significant role in the process of creating and implementing unique plans for particular host communities. Viewed from this perspective, the value of examining specific commodities and how they can best be marketed is a valuable task.

A key point to remember is that the nature of the commodity can dictate the type of marketing strategy that will be most effective. It is a fact of life, for example, that fresh food spoils. Thus, fresh food must get to the ultimate consumer quickly. The perishable nature of the commodity, not the philosophy of business or the demands of customers, determines how this fragile commodity is bought and sold.

Functionalism, institutionalism, and the commodity approach, therefore, usefully supplement the prevailing neoclassical approach of marketing that focuses almost entirely upon serving others. Although these three tools have largely been ignored in recent decades, each has a significant role to play

Table 10.2 Alternative paradigms of marketing

Issue	Analysis
Functional	A method of marketing analysis that focuses upon the actual function of various marketing related activities and how they contribute to the marketing effort.
Institutional	An analysis of the various types of institutions that are involved in marketing, their characteristics, needs, and how they tend to respond.
Commodity	A study of various items and commodities that are sold and how marketing needs to be adjusted to the characteristics of these products and services.

DISCUSSION
A variety of marketing paradigms exist that expand beyond the neoclassical marketing management model. These models add robustness and flexibility. In addition, they provide useful and informative supplements to neoclassical 4Ps marketing management.

when indigenous, ethnic, and rural peoples envision their options, plan economic development strategies, and negotiate with outsiders regarding their futures. These benefits are outlined in Table 10.2.

After 1960, modern marketing management and its neoclassical underpinnings came to dominate marketing thought and practice. This transformation, unfortunately, resulted in abandoning a number of perspectives that were of great explanative and practical value. These tools are of especial potential value when dealing with issues that are not adequately addressed by neoclassical models including the challenges facing many indigenous, ethnic, and rural peoples.

Macromarketing

The alternative methods mentioned above demonstrate the complexity of marketing and the wide variety of issues that should be considered when decisions are made. Chief among them is the fact that marketing involves more than merely the relationships between buyers and sellers operating in some sort of an economic vacuum. The field of macromarketing deals with this reality.

In a nutshell, macromarketing involves looking at the full implications of marketing, not merely relationships between patrons and clients and benefits that accrue to them. While 4Ps Marketing Management focuses upon those overtly involved in a marketing relationship, macromarketing looks at the full implications of an option, including unintended and unwanted side effects as well as how people can be affected by marketing decisions that they are not involved with.

Some communities, for example, might become more involved with a cash economy. What are the full implications when new marketing arrangements shift or alter the preexisting relationships between people? When visiting a Miao community in the Hunan Province of China, for example, I noted that many of the people continued to be involved with traditional subsistence activities. I saw people planting rice in the age-old manner. In addition, to this traditional economic behavior, some members of the community earn money by serving tourists. Thus, a cash economy based on tourism increasingly supplements but does not completely replace the old way of life. How will these changes ripple through the community and its economy? Who will win and who will lose? How traumatic will these shifts be? How can negative repercussions be mitigated?

Macromarketing is able to deal with the implications of these changes and anticipate side effects in ways that usefully and strategically extend beyond neoclassical marketing management and its micro focus upon patron and clients. Doing so can be invaluable where economic and marketing changes potentially trigger side effects that might have far-reaching consequences.

The term "commodification," furthermore, is often used to discuss processes that can occur when something that has a broad value or purpose is reduced in people's minds to merely its short-term cash (or other) value. Thus, if people begin to sell aspects of their cultural heritage the possibility exists that its role as a money-making activity might transform the ways in which some members of the community view their heritage. Will doing so simultaneously transform the way people who harbor and maintain these traditions?

Such a tendency might have unfortunate consequences because cultural and artistic activities often possess powerful roles, purposes, and meanings that transcend economic considerations. How can these sacred and community centered roles be maintained when they are simultaneously involved in money-earning activities involving outsiders? Because macromarketing looks at the full impacts of a marketing relationship, it can consider questions such as these, anticipate possible issues that might arise, and suggest ways to mitigate them.

The impact of marketing upon cultural traditions is an issue of concern to macromarketing. Thus, Belk and Groves (1999) discuss how aboriginal Australian art has different meanings and implications for different people and stakeholders, ranging from members of the indigenous community to outsiders. Belk and Groves find striking shifts "in the meanings and uses of these artworks, and it is concluded that the success of Australian Aboriginal art is a mixed blessing with both positive and negative consequences" (1999: 20).

When strategies are being forged, furthermore, it is a good idea to think in terms of the local "carrying capacity" (i.e. how much economic activity can be pursued before sustainability is sacrificed?). If the carrying capacity is exceeded for an extended period of time, the environment and the community will suffer and the wellbeing of the people might be placed in jeopardy. Once again, macro considerations have an important role to play in helping indigenous, ethnic, and rural peoples understand and respond to economic development opportunities and challenges.

All of these examples are unified by the fact that marketing exerts profound and multidimensional impacts that often need to be considered but can easily be ignored. Recognizing the broader impact of marketing upon society, macromarketing acknowledges that economic intervention often impacts the larger, macro world in significant ways. Macromarketing is concerned with equitably considering the needs of the community and devising ways to enhance the quality of life of its people. It goes without saying that many indigenous, ethnic, and rural peoples need to contemplate these issues.

As far back as the 1970s, Charles Slater affirmed that marketing should not be viewed in isolation. He, for example observed: "… marketing is a part of the whole social process system rather than only a function within each firm or institution" (Slater and Jenkins 1979: 374).

From the beginning, macromarketing has employed some form of systems theory analysis; Slater noted, for example, that "the common thread … was the systems concept of putting marketing in the context of both the firm and society" (Slater 1977: 1).

The systems theory approach in marketing goes back at least to the late 1950s/early 1960s when marketing pioneer Wroe Alderson began to model the marketing system and its impacts in a holistic manner. Alderson was influenced by the general systems theory model provided by his friend Kenneth Boulding (1956) who envisioned an array of increasingly complex paradigms that can be used to model behavior in terms of interrelationships between the various parts of a system. Some elementary paradigms (such as the "clockwork model") depict actions as completely predictable, static, and/or exhibiting pre-ordained and inevitable responses. More sophisticated and dynamic systems theory models, in contrast, transcend that relatively simple style of analysis and are better able to deal with change and transformations.

More recently, Layton (2007) argues that the study of marketing systems should play a crucial role, even though doing so can be accomplished in a number of different ways. He feels that a systems approach places core macromarketing ideas in a meaningful context and provides a mechanism that helps the field to be integrated with a variety of different disciplines.

Systems theory approaches view the elements of culture/society (including marketing relationships) in terms of how they fit into the greater social, ecological, and technological context, contribute to it, and, perhaps, function as agents of change. Systems analyses can also anticipate how marketing impacts people who are not involved in a marketing relationship. In the 1960s, George Fisk (1967) wrote an introductory marketing text with a systems theory orientation. Unfortunately, it was published just as neoclassical marketing management was coming to dominate and, as a result, it didn't have the impact it otherwise would have made. Nevertheless, his work provides useful clues regarding how marketing can be envisioned from a systems theory orientation.

Such an analysis can be vital because in many situations, some people might receive no benefits from marketing efforts even though they experience negative consequences. This reality raises both practical and ethical considerations that transcend the customer orientation that is embraced by conventional marketing thinking. Because such issues are often of significant importance to indigenous, ethnic, and rural peoples, macromarketing has a great contribution to make.

Extractive industries, for example, might reduce the productiveness of the ecosystem. Subsistence hunters and gatherers who do not directly benefit from these extractive economic activities might suffer if the land becomes less fruitful as a result. Where such changes are pronounced, these people will be forced to pay a price while receiving no benefits. Other people, however, might prosper as a result of these involuntary sacrifices forced on marginal groups. In other words, marketing does not merely involve those who are actively involved (such as buyers and sellers). A systems analysis can be used to seek a more accurate projection of the true costs and benefits as well as determining who benefits and who suffers.

As macromarketing developed, it built upon Alderson's systems theory approach in order to map and address the full impact of marketing strategies. By 1982, the new field of macromarketing was consciously defined by George Fisk as dealing with:

1   Impacts and consequences of society on marketing and actions (marketing externalities),
2   The impact and consequences of society on marketing systems and actions (social sanctions), and
3   The understanding of marketing systems in their aggregate dimensions (macro-systems analysis).

The term "marketing externalities" refers to everything which is outside of the buyer/seller relationship involving the organization and its customers. As just discussed above, many groups not involved in marketing might be forced to deal with its hurtful consequences. As a result, the influences upon those who are outside of a marketing relationship need to be acknowledged.

The typical rebuttal for such demands is the assertion that economic development aids the entire community and, therefore, the benefits "trickle down" to everybody. Nevertheless, some people might benefit at the expense of others; such potentials need to be considered. The possibility that some segments of the local population may benefit from economic development while others must absorb the costs should be a matter of concern for indigenous, ethnic, and rural peoples.

Thus, externality issues and how change effects different people in disproportionate ways are legitimate concerns. Macromarketing is able to deal with these issues in an evenhanded manner that is relevant to the host community, and can be used to suggest strategies for mitigating these costs.

Current macromarketing researchers, for example, are recognizing that multiple varieties of subsistence economies exist that include nature-based, nonprofit-based, market-based, and hybrid. This research also identifies a range of marketing institutions that serve these economies including those within the community and cross community arrangements. (Banbury et al. 2015) This growing stream of research demonstrates that macromarketers have significant contributions to make when indigenous, ethnic, and rural people develop strategies regarding equitable economic policies and strategies.

Responsible marketing

A relevant consideration involves social and ecological responsibility. A classic article that deals with these issues is George Fisk's "Criteria for a Theory of Responsible Consumption" (1973) which concentrates upon the fact that catering to consumers often possesses hurtful and negative implications. The majority of Fisk's discussion involves strategies that cater to consumer demands for convenience and how they can accelerate the levels of pollution and waste. People who are not involved in the buying, selling, and consumption processes may be forced to bear the costs of these economic choices while receiving few or no benefits. Thus, "no deposit-no return" beer bottles might please the consumer but spoil the beach for others.

This basic chain of thought can be expanded beyond issues of conservation and pollution in order to deal with the stress inflicted upon people who do not benefit from marketing but face its negative consequences. Inequities of this sort are often particularly pronounced in rural areas where indigenous, ethnic, and rural minorities reside.

Since 1973 when Fisk wrote his seminal article and 1983 when he provided a definition of macromarketing, the core ideas embedded in the field have been refined, but they remain essentially intact. In particular, the systems theory model has been integrated into the field. Two useful articles in this regard are Donald Dixon's "Macromarketing: A Social Systems Perspective" (1984) and William Meade and Robert Nason's "Toward a Unified Theory of Macromarketing: A Systems Theory Approach" (1991). The approaches introduced in these articles suggest ways in which host communities can model the impact of economic activities from a macro perspective.

Macromarketing, therefore, is able to usefully transcend the micro-oriented buyer/seller orientation in ways that consider the wellbeing of all impacted stakeholders. The systems theory model provides the field with a means of addressing the wide range of impacts that marketing and consumption may exert upon the host community. An overview of the macromarketing model is provided in Table 10.3.

In many ways, the macromarketing movement preserves the essence of the classic functional, institutional, and commodity approaches to marketing and integrates them using the techniques of systems theory. While these orientations are often overlooked by those who embrace a micro or neoclassical orientation, they offer useful tools to indigenous, ethnic, and rural communities.

Thus, neoclassical micromarketing and modern macromarketing are both valuable tools. They, however, address different concerns and focus upon their own universe of discourse. These attributes are compared and juxtaposed in Table 10.4

Both micromarketing and macromarketing, therefore, are legitimate and needed. Neither orientation should overshadow the other. Unfortunately, in

Table 10.3 Macromarketing: an overview

Issue	Focus	Ethical concerns	Stakeholders
Externalities	Impacts that extend beyond customers and those who serve them.	Acknowledging impacts besides benefits to customers and organizations serving them.	Considering externalities facilitates an ability to deal with various groups besides customers.
Impacts	Marketing has multiple impacts. Unintended and unanticipated consequences may impact those who are beyond a patron–client relationship.	The marketing process exerts diverse impacts. Assessing and mitigating them as necessary is the ethical course of action.	Marketing impacts a wide variety of stakeholders besides those directly involved.
Systems theory	Systems theory deals with relationships between the parts of a larger whole.	Holistic models facilitate developing an ethical focus involving multiple stakeholders.	Systems theory can model complex responses by focusing on interconnections.

DISCUSSION
Macromarketing expands beyond neoclassical marketing management that is concerned with the relationships between patrons and clients. Macro perspectives consider how other groups and the environment are effected by a marketing agenda and it can be used to develop ways to mitigate negative ramifications.

Table 10.4 Micromarketing and macromarketing compared

Issue	Micromarketing	Macromarketing
Focus	The micro patron–client relationship between an organization and its customers.	The broader implications of marketing. Not limited to the patron–client relationship.
Unique perspective	Organizations exist to serve clients. The entire organization should revolve around clients.	Marketing exists within the larger environment and exerts a variety of influences. These implications should be addressed.
Breadth of field	Choosing a lucrative target market and then strategically manipulating the product or service to please it.	A broad systems theory analysis, in addition to marketing management needs to be employed.
Significance	Since communities need the support of a target market, catering to it in strategic ways is important.	Communities have specific needs. A macromarketing perspective is best able to deal with these complexities.
Relevance	Micromarketing/ marketing management emphasizes the needs of those who are involved in the buying/selling relationship.	Macromarketing considers the needs of a wide array of stakeholders, not merely customers and businesses that serve them.

DISCUSSION
Both micromarketing and macromarketing make valuable contributions. Macromarketing is best able to anticipate and deal with side-issues and influences beyond the patron–client relationship that might need to be addressed.

many economic development projects, the primary decision makers embrace a micromarketing orientation. This is true even in an environment where more robust models such as the Triple Bottom Line are increasingly powerful.

Concluding statement

The name of this chapter is "External Service" which emphasizes that marketing typically involves serving others. Although doing so is a usual and much needed tactic, the needs of local people and the community should also be considered. Host communities seeking economic development typically deal with mainstream business leaders who embrace a micromarketing perspective that focuses primarily upon serving customers. These decision makers tend to think in terms of catering to the demands of target markets and adjusting the goods and services that are provided accordingly.

This micro approach is ill-equipped to deal with the needs of other stakeholders, such as host communities. In addition, it is not designed to evaluate the full costs that the host community (and especially those who are beyond the patron–client relationship) must pay. As a result, analysis stemming from micromarketing may not accurately assess the true costs and benefits experienced by a local community, its culture, and its people.

Increasingly, host communities demand arrangements that go beyond a customer-centered focus. In order to do so, the unique needs, assets, desires and vulnerabilities of indigenous, ethnic, and rural people must be factored into the equation. The functional, institutional, and commodity paradigms are useful in such contexts. When strengthened via systems theory, macromarketing can serve this role in an even more effective manner.

It is important to emphasize that many decision makers and practitioners do not think in terms of a macromarketing perspective. Nevertheless, such people are probably somewhat familiar with this basic approach. As a result, indigenous, ethnic, and rural peoples can use the macromarketing model to explain their positions and goals when negotiating with members of the business community. Because macromarketing provides a useful way for host communities to articulate their concerns, it has a valuable role to play when strategies are discussed and articulated.

Relevant terms

4 Ps of Management Marketing: A paradigm of marketing that (1) chooses a target market, and (2) manipulates the controllable variables of marketing in order to please it.

Absolute advantage: One producer has the ability to produce a product cheaper or more efficiently than another producer.

Commodity approach: A paradigm of marketing that focuses on the nature of the commodity being sold and how its characteristics influence the marketing process.

Comparative advantage: Even if two or more competitors can produce a good or service at a similar cost, an advantage that arises from other issues (such as other products that can be produced using the same resources.

Functional method: A paradigm of marketing that centers upon the various functions that must be dealt with in order for successful marketing to take place.

Institutional approach: A paradigm of marketing that examines the needs and behaviors of institutions that are involved in the marketing process.

Macromarketing: Looking at the full implications of marketing, not merely the relationships between buyers and sellers.

Marketing: The process by which users, consumers, etc. are encouraged or discouraged to use/acquire, etc. a good or service.

Marketing Management: The process of manipulating the various controllable variables of marketing in order to influence sales, consumption habits, and so forth.

Place: A controllable variable of marketing that deals with location or distribution.

Price: A controllable variable of marketing that deals with what sacrifice the buyer/consumer must experience in order to acquire a good or service.

Product: The actual good or service being marketed as envisioned as a controllable variable.

Promotion: The controllable variable of marketing that is concerned with communication with relevant stakeholders, often customers or users.

Responsible marketing: Being aware of the full and often negative implications of marketing and acting in way to control or mitigate these hurtful potentials.

Systems theory: Looking at behavior from within a context in which one action is likely to trigger other changes and actions.

Discussion questions

1   Conventional marketing management selects a target market and devised ways to please it. Mention important variables that are not addressed by this approach. Why might they be of importance to indigenous, ethnic, and rural peoples?

2   Discuss the 4 Ps of Marketing Management as an extension of neoclassical economic theory and practice. What are the benefits of doing so? What are the drawbacks?

3   Before the dominance of the neoclassical 4 Ps of Marketing Management, a number of other paradigms of marketing existed. We discussed three. What are they and how does each transcend the 4 Ps of Marketing Management in useful ways?

4   How is macromarketing distinctive from micromarketing? Why might a macro approach be especially useful to indigenous, ethnic, and rural peoples?

5   Envision how communities can devise equitable and sustainable ways to help themselves by serving others. Discuss various tradeoffs that might be required and how they can be justified.

References

Banbury, Catherine, Herkenhoff, Linda, and Subrahmanyan, Saroja (2015). "Understanding Different Types of Subsistence Economies: The Case of the Batwa of Buhoma, Uganda." *Journal of Macromarketing*, June, 35, 243–256.

Belk, Russell W. and Groves, Ronald (1999). "Marketing and the Multiple Meanings of Australian Aboriginal Art." *Journal of Macromarketing*, June, 19(1), 20–33.

Boulding, Kenneth (1956). "General Systems Theory: The Skeleton of Science." *Management Science*, 2(3), 197–208.

Converse, Paul (1936). *Elements of Marketing* (Upper Saddle River, NJ USA: Prentice Hall).

Converse, Paul, Huegy, Harvey Wilborn and Mitchell, Robert Victor (1965). *The Elements of Marketing*, 7th edition (New York: Prentice Hall).

Dixon, Donald (1984). "Macromarketing: A Social Systems Approach." *Journal Of Macromarketing* (Fall), 4–17.

Fisk, George (1967). *Marketing Systems: An Introductory Analysis* (New York: Harper and Row).

Fullbrook, E. S. (1940). "The Functional Concept in Marketing." *Journal of Marketing*, 4, 229–237.

Layton, Roger, A. (2007). "Marketing Systems – A Core Macromarketing Concept." *Journal of Macromarketing*, September, 27(3), 227–242.

Maynard, Harold (1939). *Principles of Marketing* (New York: Ronald Press Company).

Meade, William and Nason, Robert. (1991). "Towards a Unified Theory of Macromarketing: A Systems Theory Approach." *Journal of Macromarketing*, 11(2), 172–182.

NEA Folk Arts Program (1986). Meeting on Crafts and Public Funding Program, White Paper, July.

Sheth, Jagdish and Garrett, Dennis E. (1986). *Marketing Theory: Classic and Contemporary Readings* (South Western Publishing Co).

Slater, Charles C. (1977). "Introduction." In Distributive processes from a societal perspective: The proceedings of the macro-marketing seminar, ed. Charles C. Slater, 1–5 (Boulder, CO: Business Research Division, Graduate School of Business Administration, University of Colorado at Boulder).

Slater, Charles C. and Jenkins, Dorothy (1979). "Systems Approach to Comparative 'Macromarketing'" in Fisk, George and Nason, Robert (eds) *Macro-Marketing: New Steps In The Learning Curve* (Boulder CO: Graduate School of Business).

Smith, Adam (1776). *An Inquiry into the Nature and Causes of the Wealth of Nations* (London: W. Strahan).

Walle, Alf H. (2000). *Rethinking Marketing: Strategic Thought and Exotic Visions* (Westport, Connecticut USA: Quorum Books).

Chapter 11

Vulnerabilities and responses

Learning objectives

The traumatic nature of change and the need for its mitigation are addressed with specific reference to indigenous cultures, ethnic groups, and traditional communities. Hurtful potentials are discussed with reference to the concept of anomie in which socially acceptable goals can no longer be achieved in socially acceptable ways. This concept provides a means of dealing with the pain and dysfunction that often accompanies economic development. This discussion is augmented with an introduction to the concepts of "tyranny of the majority" in which people's needs are denied after being outvoted. Perspectives, such as the "concurrent majority," demonstrate how minorities can protect their rights. Specific goals of the chapter include:

1　Appreciating the impact of change and how it can trigger dysfunction and pain.
2　Perceiving how anomie (an inability to achieve socially acceptable goals in socially acceptable ways) can be a disruptive force and/or lead to positive cultural adjustments.
3　Exploring both dysfunctional and functional ways of responding to social change and anomie.
4　Discussing the concepts of the tyranny of the majority and the concurrent majority with reference to the plight of indigenous, ethnic, and rural peoples.
5　Understanding the theory and methods of the concurrent majority and how it can be used to advance the rights of indigenous, ethnic, and peoples.

Introduction

A basic theme of this entire book is that economic and/or social development or change, especially when envisioned and implemented by outsiders, is apt to inflict hurtful side effects, many of which might be initially unanticipated.

These problems tend to be correlated with an accompanying decline of the local culture, its heritage, and its traditions.

Once social and economic transformations are introduced, controlling and mitigating them can be difficult, if not impossible. A positive means of governing and dealing with these hurtful possibilities involves anticipating the full implications of a proposed course of action and developing strategies and tactics that alleviate harmful and destructive implications, ideally before they arise. This capstone chapter provides clues regarding how to do so.

Change, stress, and pain

Social scientists and psychologists routinely observe that people are often adversely affected by cultural, social, economic, and technological change. Hurtful responses of this variety are particularly common during periods when indigenous, ethnic, or rural cultures and peoples are exposed to rapid and unexpected transformations caused by massive and unprecedented contact with powerful outside forces. In other words, "minorities" (envisioned here as those lacking power and control) often suffer due to contact with "majorities" during phases of social and economic adjustment. The end result can be significant psychological dysfunctions.

Discussing these pressures from within the mainstream world, Romanov, Appelberg, Honkasalo, and Koskenvuo (1996) report that people who experienced a significant conflict at work during the previous five years are more likely to be diagnosed with a psychiatric problem than those who did not. Apparently significant stress in dealings with other people can have detrimental ramifications.

The average person who experiences difficulties on the job, however, is still a member of a viable and intact culture or society. Presumably, the way of life experienced by these individuals continues at least somewhat normally and, in the process, it provides comfort and grounding to those who experience loss, hardship, and negativity. When away from work, furthermore, such sufferers enjoy a respite from their adverse working conditions by participating in the larger community. Even when these comforting intervals are available, however, mental illness and its pain increase.

The relative comfort provided by cultural stability can be juxtaposed with the opposite situation where the entire culture, heritage, and traditions of a people are under attack, weakened, rendered passé, or even destroyed. If people within a viable and functioning culture are adversely affected merely by "on the job" pressures, those whose entire heritage, traditions, and culture are stripped away are likely to be even more vulnerable to adverse psychological response.

For many years, social scientists and advocates for indigenous, ethnic, and rural peoples have understood that change has hurtful potentials that need to be proactively addressed. The necessity to do so is particularly important when a people's way of life has been quickly transformed, weakened, or destroyed by some unanticipated, uncontrolled, and/or unmitigated onslaught. The actions of some "majority" (however defined) are typical catalysts for maladies of this sort.

Consider the case of Ishi, the lone survivor of a California tribe who was dubbed the "Last Savage" by the media and became a tourist attraction as well as the subject of anthropological research in the early twentieth century (Kroeber 1964).

Many Native American thinkers point to the treatment of Ishi as a classic example of oppressive exploitation in which outsiders first destroyed the man's way of life and then went on to turn him into a commodity to be studied and gawked at. Although such conclusions are understandable, the story and message of Ishi is much more complex than that. It is chronicled by Theodora Kroeber in *Ishi: The Last of his Tribe* (1964) which explores the relationship between her husband (anthropologist Alfred Louis Kroeber) and Ishi as each man comforted the other.

Theodora observes that around the time that Ishi stumbled into the modern world, starving and alone, Kroeber had suffered his own grievous loss. His first wife had died before her time and, as a result, Kroeber was thrown into a profound and disabling depression. Possessing great knowledge of the indigenous people of California, however, Kroeber was called in to help calm this unruly "wild man" that had unexpectedly appeared. Kroeber found a grief-stricken soul who had lost everything, not just a wife. Ishi's world was completely gone and everyone and everything that was important to him was dead. Nothing remained. Ultimately, Kroeber realized that suffering over a lost wife was relatively insignificant when compared to the agony of a victim whose entire social universe had quickly and irreversibly become extinct. In the process of helping Ishi adjust and cope, the grieving widower learned to deal with his own pain and put it in perspective. Both men found salvation by helping each other.

Fittingly, Ishi spent his remaining years recording and documenting the details of his old ways of life, ensuring its survival in some form even though it had become extinct as a living society and culture.

The point of these observations is that Kroeber came to recognize the profound pain people feel when their heritage is stripped away. Although Ishi provides an extreme example of such anguish, this type of cultural and social loss is very common among Indigenous, ethnic, and rural peoples who are confronted by the mainstream world. This pain should be recognized as well as the potential for dysfunction stemming from it.

A classic discussion regarding this discomfort is presented by G. N. Appell who observes that a strong and robust cultural heritage can help mitigate the impacts of traumatic change. Appell reminds us that "A society undergoing change ... has a right to access its cultural traditions, its language and its social history" (Appell 1977: 14) because these cultural assets can help temper the pain and disorientation caused by what he calls the social separation syndrome which "involves role conflict and ambiguity, threat to one's self esteem, and an impaired social identity."

Discussing this social and psychological threat, Appell continues:

> Social bereavement arising from social change seems to follow a developmental sequence similar to personal bereavement.... There is first a period of denial as numbness accompanied by anxiety, fear, and feelings of threat to one's identity. This is succeeded by a phase of frustrated searching for the lost world or individual, hoping for a reversal and then bitter pining and unrelieved sense of pain.... Following this is a period of depression and apathy.... Finally there is the phase of reorganization when the bereaved begins to build new plans and assumptions about the world.
>
> (1977: 14)

Although some of the details of Appell's vintage observations might be dated or metaphoric, the gist of his message continues to resonate clearly. Cultures are powerful coping devises that provide grounding, practical tools, comfort, and a sense of identity. They offer solutions to the problems that people face as well as presenting suggestions regarding how to think, act, and respond. If these tools are undercut, rendered passé, or destroyed, a void can emerge causing people to lack the tools needed to live in a socially and psychologically healthy fashion.

Although this vulnerability is real, it does not inevitably condemn small-scale societies to extinction. In a classic observation, for example, David Maybury-Lewis reminds us that "There is no natural or historic law that militates against small societies. There are only political choices" (1977 58). Thus, the demise of indigenous, ethnic, and rural cultures is not unavoidable even if popular paradigms of evolution and extinction reflect the world view (and perhaps the priorities) of many advocates of economic development and change.

Anomie: the disruption of change

In the late nineteenth century, French anthropologist/sociologist, Émile Durkheim demonstrated that change can trigger unhappiness and despair that is correlated with a growing suicide rate (Durkheim 1984 [1893]). He did so with reference to what he called "anomie" which refers to tensions and alienation triggered by significant alterations in the daily life experienced by people. This pioneering social scientist clearly recognized that unmitigated social change can produce dysfunctional, harmful, and counterproductive behavior.

Durkheim envisioned anomie as an inconsistency between (1) the standards of socially acceptable behavior and the goals embraced by a social group, and (2) the realities that actually exist. When the inconsistency between the two is great, the rules of society begin to deteriorate or break down creating a chaotic and unpredictable environment capable of launching hurtful responses.

In the 1940s and 1950s, Robert Merton (1957) expanded Durkheim's concept of anomie, arguing that the norms of society provide individuals with (1) goals to which they should aspire, on the one hand, and (2) conventional methods for achieving these objectives, on the other. Merton understood that over time, the social structure (or the socio-economic milieu in which a community exists) may change to such a degree that its members are no longer able to attain sanctioned and honored achievements in the traditionally acceptable manner. Under such conditions, the predisposition for deviant and/or dysfunctional behavior tends to increase.

Social and economic development projects involving indigenous, ethnic, and rural peoples can easily create conditions that give rise to anomie. The ways in which people respond under these conditions, however, vary with some alternatives being more productive and positive than others. Merton provides a typology of responses to anomie that includes (1) Conformity, (2) Innovation, (3) Ritualization, (4) Retreatism, and (5) Rebellion (Merton 1957). They can be described as conformity, innovation, ritualization, retreatism, and rebellion.

Conformity is the situation in which people continue to embrace the goals of the society and seek to achieve them in the traditional socially acceptable way. Conformers continue to respond the way they did before the pressures causing anomie were present. Conformity is a conservative response and it preserves traditional relationships between people. Conformity, however, can inhibit the ability to adjust to new conditions.

Innovation is a situation where people embrace the goals of society but attempt to achieve them using new methods that might not be socially acceptable. Mainstream sociologists often characterize these methods as resorting to illegal and antisocial behavior. Among indigenous, ethnic, and rural people, however, innovation might include responses that while violating traditional norms or expectations result in productive adaptation. If so, embracing productive, but taboo, behaviors as legitimate methods for achieving socially acceptable goals might be a positive response.

Ritualization is a situation where the person acts according to the norms of society but loses track of the goals to be achieved. In this case, people begin to act in a rote manner using tradition as a guide with little focus upon the costs vs. the benefits of doing so. This type of response is not strategic and is not likely to be productive. When people follow the old ways merely as an end in itself, the ability to respond in a productive and beneficial manner is reduced.

Retreatism is a situation where the person rejects both the cultural goals and the institutionalized methods for achieving them. Although people might reject the status quo, they do not necessarily embrace any positive or beneficial alternative. The potential for dysfunctional responses, such as alcohol abuse, increases. While under the influence of alcohol or drugs, for example, the victim might be temporarily distracted from the plight faced, but fail to respond in an effective manner.

Rebellion is a situation where the person (1) rejects both the goals that society provides and the traditional means of achieving them while (2) simultaneously embracing substitutes that take their place. Under such circumstances, the break with the old ways is profound and complete. Massive changes of thought and attitude take place when the old ways are discarded and new alternatives embraced. Chaos might result. Different factions might arise in conflict with one another. The situation created by widespread rebellion can be particularly painful to those who hold on to tradition and/or fear change.

Anomie, therefore, can spawn a wide variety of responses that are directly related to how individuals and the community deal with the pressures faced. These alternatives are compared in Table 11.1.

Table 11.1 Responses to anomie

Response	Description	Analysis
Conformity	The traditions of the culture are preserved. People and the community continue to be motivated and act as in the past.	The community and its culture is stable, but strategically responding to circumstances is minimal. Little positive adaptation.
Innovation	Although the goals of society remain intact, people embrace new methods of achieving them.	Although maintaining the goals of the community, the means of achieving them evolves to reflect new circumstances.
Ritualization	People continue to act according to the old conventions of behavior although doing so has little ad hoc value.	Although the ways of the past continue to be embraced, strategically responding to new conditions is insignificant.
Retreatism	People withdraw and abandon the old ways, but do not embrace a new alternative.	Psychologically, people are cut off from their heritage. Dysfunctional responses are likely.
Rebellion	New goals and new codes of behavior are embraced.	People replace both the traditional goals and the strategies that are used to achieve them.

DISCUSSION

When indigenous, ethnic, and rural people confront change and anomie, a number of possible responses exist. The way people respond can have far-reaching consequences for the health of the people and their strategic responses, both individually and collectively.

In conclusion, the concept of anomie deals with the tensions caused by social change and it can be used to describe various ways in which people cope with the disruptive pressures facing them. In recent decades, various refinements, such as *strain theory*, have been developed that focus upon how and why people behave in deviant ways. Although such theories are often used to depict criminal and antisocial behavior and its causes, they can also be used to model any significant change in behavior, good or bad, that people embrace when facing stress and doubt. On many occasions, anomie and similar responses are disruptive and painful to indigenous, ethnic, and rural peoples.

Representative examples of dysfunction

On some occasions, people exhibit rather bizarre beliefs and actions when confronted with the pain and stress caused by unmitigated social or economic change. Two such examples are the ghost dance (Mooney 1896; Kehoe 1989) and the "cargo cult" (Harris 1974; Inglis 1957; Worsley 1957).

The Ghost Dance was a religious movement among Native Americans that was influential in the late nineteenth century. The most prominent leader was a visionary named Wovoka who intertwined aspects of local traditions with a new religion. Some of his recommendations involved living in a more productive, moral, and harmonious manner. These suggestions can be viewed as positive and productive aspects of the movement.

Other predictions and recommendations made by the ghost dance, however, were counterproductive and hurtful. Wovoka, for example, taught that if a certain dance was properly performed, the dead ancestors would come back to life, herds of buffalo would return, the white intruders would go away, and the old way of life would be restored. None of these projections, unfortunately, reflected reality. Acting according to them was a tragically counterproductive strategy.

Some devotees were even convinced that if they wore "ghost shirts" they could not be killed by the guns of the white man and, therefore, victory was assured. Believers, furthermore, affirmed that Wovoka was able to perform miracles such as healing the sick. The emerging ghost dance movement and religion appealed to many indigenous people who had suffered grievously due to reservation life, sickness, cultural decline, and governmental policies that sought to undercut the local Native American heritage. Sadly, ghost dance activities led to the massacre at Wounded Knee, the last major bloodbath of the Indian Wars.

Viewed from the perspective of anomie, the ghost dance can be viewed as an example of conformity in which the traditions of the culture were largely preserved and embraced, albeit in an unproductive manner. People were encouraged to look to the past, ignore reality, and act accordingly. Unfortunately, by doing so the actual circumstances being faced were not addressed in any meaningful manner. The result was disastrous.

The cargo cult, usually associated with Melanesia, involves people whose lives were hurtfully transformed and disrupted by social and economic change associated with outside contact in the early twentieth century. Apparently, these reactions to circumstance were attempts by indigenous people to reassert control over their lives in a world that was being irrevocably changed in ways that undermined the old economic system and way of life, leaving the local people in a precarious and bewildering situation.

The responses to these hurtful circumstances are well known. When intrusive foreigners began to gain a foothold in the Melanesia, members of the indigenous community noted that these powerful outsiders built airports and harbors and then waited for airplanes and ships to arrive with great wealth. Apparently, the local people, becoming desperate and jealous, wanted their share of the cargo. One ploy they used was to build phony airports in the misguided belief that by doing so they could magically attract their own supernatural airplanes and gain affluence as a result.

Although such responses are typically associated with some charismatic leader, a common explanation is that these cargo cults are responses to sorrow, fear, and anxiety caused by rapid and uncontrolled change. Although such strategies might be associated ignorance and, superstition coupled with a lack of familiarity with modern economics and technology, desperation, hopelessness and disappointment seem to have been the most important catalysts.

Viewed from the perspective of anomie, the cargo cults appear as innovative and/or rebellious responses to anomie. Devotees of the cult, for example, embraced new ways to achieve goals (luring cargo-carrying planes by building bogus airports) even though other aspects of the society might have remained intact. This behavior might also be reflective of rebellion in which new goals (a desire for Western goods brought by planes) was accompanied by new economic strategies. In any event, a major adjustment (although counterproductive) took place. It was precipitated by profound tensions in the culture and economy caused by rapid outside contact.

The basic point is that a strong potential exists for people to make poor decisions when they are faced with outside intervention that causes a hurtful disruption in the traditional way of life. The theory of anomie can be used to model these changes. With this in mind, the ghost dance and the cargo cult is compared in Table 11.2.

Although the ghost dance and cargo cults point to damaging and ineffective reactions, other responses by local communities demonstrate that some indigenous, ethnic, and rural peoples have charted a more productive path. A key perspective of this book is that even if people are thrust into the modern world and forced to experience profound changes, the destruction of their culture and way of life is not inevitable. Cultures and their members, in contrast, might respond in positive and constructive ways that maintain their unique character and distinctiveness. As a result, positive and beneficial

Table 11.2 The ghost dance and cargo cult compared

Issue	Ghost dance	Cargo cult
Trigger	Cultural stress. Economic reversals.	Cultural stress. Economic reversals.
Response	A belief in a magical return of ancestors, the old ways, and personal invincibility.	A misguided copying of the techniques used by outsiders who threatened the traditional way of life.
Impact	Suicidal behavior. Reliance upon magic.	Counterproductive economic strategies.

DISCUSSION
The ghost dance and the cargo cult represent hurtful and unproductive responses to change, stress, and anxiety. If cultures are to successfully cope with change, they need to avoid alternatives such as these.

cultural revitalization may result. The example of the Iroquois Indians of New York State (USA)/Ontario (Canada) and the Yup'ik of Alaska (USA) are examples.

Positive adaptations

The Iroquois of New York State (USA) and the Province of Ontario (Canada) are impressive in many ways. In the eighteenth century they successfully manipulated the colonial forces of Britain and France, reaping significant benefits in the process. During the French and Indian War (1754–1763), known as the Seven Years War in Europe, the Iroquois strategically controlled the situation and enjoyed prosperity as a result. Once the French had been totally defeated and driven from North America, however, the Iroquois were "no longer able to play off the British and French against each other and [found themselves] surrounded by a circle of British forts" (Wallace 1970: 442). Because an alliance with the Iroquois was no longer needed, British generosity dwindled and economic suffering crept in.

When the Revolutionary War between Britain and their North American colonists began, the Iroquois again became embroiled in a conflict that was larger than their world. Realizing that the British valued the region merely for trading purposes while victorious colonialists would probably be tempted to migrate into Iroquois territory, most Iroquois sided with Britain. The decision was costly:

[During the war, the Iroquois homeland] was devastated by the John Sullivan [United States military commander] expedition in 1778, which in a three pronged offensive managed to burn the houses and the crops in almost every major Iroquois town. Many of the women and children, and the surviving warriors, took refuge at Fort Niagara with the British, who housed them in a refugee camp, inadequately clothed, inadequately fed, inadequately sheltered, and swept by disease. By the end of the war, despite their military successes, the Iroquois population had been cut approximately in half.

(Wallace 1970: 443)

After the war, the victorious United States, remembering that the Iroquois had been their enemy, showed them few favors. And, as the Iroquois had feared, White settlers were attracted to the area. By the turn of the nineteenth century the Iroquois were beaten in war, decimated by diseases brought by the Whites, and besieged by new economic rivals. The results of this unenviable situation included infighting, personal resignation, despair, and retreat. As is often the case under such circumstances, dysfunctional behavior (including alcoholism) became rampant.

Anthropologist, Anthony Wallace, an Iroquois specialist, points to the widespread dysfunction that arose, including violence, uncontrolled weeping and pining, fear of peers (as evidenced by accusations of witchcraft), social disunity, and, widespread alcoholism. Clinical depression was commonplace and Wallace observes that when people were sober, they were likely to be suicidal (1970: 196–201). With the culture and its people in total disarray, the Iroquois, as a viable culture, was headed towards extinction.

Within this milieu of cultural decline, Handsome Lake, a once respected indigenous leader, had fallen into hopeless alcoholism and his productive life appeared to be over. By the spring of 1799 he was "bedridden, reputedly … as a consequence of prolonged [alcoholism] (Wallace 1970: 445).

In June of that year:

> Handsome Lake collapsed [and] appeared to have died, but actually he was in a trance state and was experiencing the first of a series of visions in which messengers of the Creator instructed him in his own and his people's religious obligations.

(Wallace 1970: 445)

After recuperating, Handsome Lake dedicated his life to sobriety and to the restoration of Iroquois culture and society.

On the one hand, Handsome Lake encouraged his people to embrace their cultural traditions in innovative ways. The late eighteenth and early nineteenth century had devastated the Iroquois; their culture was in a state of complete disarray. Economically, the Iroquois could not effectively compete with the new settlers who entered the regions. Although embracing and championing Iroquois culture, Handsome Lake also recognized that Iroquois society needed to adjust to the emerging economic realities in order to rise again.

Iroquois men, for example, focused upon hunting and warfare and viewed farming as an unmanly and shameful profession that was left to women. When white settlers migrated into Iroquois territory, however, new methods of farming (that included men performing their share of the work) proved to be more efficient and productive. The success of these outsiders further undercut the Iroquois economy. Under these circumstances, Handsome Lake encouraged Iroquois men to take up farming and he urged them to perceive agriculture as a legitimate profession, not a source of shame or embarrassment. This change of attitude helped the Iroquois to rebound economically.

The response suggested by Handsome Lake is clearly an example of what Robert Merton describes as an innovative response to anomie in which the goals of society remain intact although people are provided with new methods for achieving them. While Merton often associated innovation with harmful and hurtful substitutes such as illegal activities, in this case innovation was a productive and legitimate rethinking of traditional sex roles. It allowed the Iroquois to adjust to emerging social and economic circumstances.

Handsome Lake, furthermore, forcefully denounced the disruptive and dysfunctional responses exhibited by his people. Drinking alcoholic beverages, in particular, was banned, along with promiscuous sexual behavior, the practice of witchcraft, and other troublesome habits that were undercutting the society and its people. Handsome Lake went on to insist that people acknowledge their past errors and refrain from similar misdeeds in the future.

From the perspective of anomie, Handsome Lake seems to have intuitively understood that many people had fallen into responses that resemble retreatism; they had abandoned the old ways but had not replaced them with any positive alternative. He demanded that people find a meaningful focus and began to combat social and individual degeneration.

Largely through Handsome Lake's example and message, the Iroquois people reversed their downward spiral of decline and re-emerged as a vital and viable culture. They continue as a powerful force today. This example emphasizes that indigenous, ethnic, and rural cultures can adapt to changing circumstances by tempering their traditions in productive and strategic ways. Cultures are powerful forces and as Appell indicated above, they often provide invaluable tools for both physical survival and psychological health. In addition, they are flexible and capable of innovation and change.

Approximately 175 years after Handsome Lake's achievements, Alaska Native Harold Napoleon provided another example of cultural renewal. Napoleon's *Yuuyaraq: The Way of Being Human* (1996) examines his indigenous people (the Yup'ik of southwestern Alaska), focusing upon the trauma and stress caused by contract with the outside world during the twentieth century. Napoleon chronicles the plight of a beaten and bewildered people who fell into disarray and dysfunction before beginning the process of healing and renewal.

Instead of being a scholar or professional researcher, Napoleon is an insightful layman who recovered from a personal battle with alcoholism.

Writing on a subjective and intuitive level, Napoleon discusses the horrible and traumatic events that undercut Yup'ik society (as well as the positive steps that can be taken to insure its renewal). Revealingly, these observations and recommendations independently duplicate the example and suggestions of Handsome Lake.

While not excusing or discounting his lapses and personal responsibilities, Napoleon focuses upon the destructive power of uncontrolled social and economic change and the alienation and disruption they can produce. He argues that social and individual dysfunction can best be overcome through cultural revitalization.

Napoleon points to the irony that profound decline among the Yup'ik was correlated and associated with economic progress and physical wellbeing The people had warm clothes, comfortable homes, and enough to eat. Famines were a thing of the past. Viewed from a material perspective, life was good. Nonetheless, the suffering was profound, alcoholism was rampant, and the suicide rate rose to epidemic proportions.

Napoleon explains these responses as the fruit of cultural destruction. He records that in the early twentieth century, disease had killed many of the elders who carried the traditions of Yup'ik culture. As a result, the survivors were denied their heritage and floundered emotionally as a result. Economically, moreover, the traditional subsistence lifestyle was rendered passé. This situation, of course, is largely similar to what Handsome Lake's Iroquois faced in the late eighteenth and early nineteenth centuries. The response, furthermore, was almost identical: dysfunctional behavior, mass suicide, despair, and passive resignation.

The solutions suggestions by the Iroquois and the Yup'ik, furthermore, are almost identical even though there is no evidence that Napoleon was aware of his predecessor. In both cases, cultural renewal and an embrace of the local heritage and traditions was urged. The rationale underlying these tactics is the belief that by nurturing and rebuilding cultural connections the people can heal from a painful past and a new and positive chapter in Yup'ik culture could begin.

Napoleon uses the theory of Post-Traumatic Stress Disorder as a metaphor to portray the painful process of stress, alienation, and dysfunction that long plagued his culture and people. Post-Traumatic Stress Disorder, of course, is a condition in which people develop dysfunctional patterns of response as a result of being exposed to danger, fear, stress, and so forth. Speaking with reference to this disorder, Napoleon argues that rapidly changing social and economic conditions caused unmitigated stress that, in turn, triggered dysfunctional responses and behaviors that almost destroyed the Yup'ik. This ongoing process proved to be a vicious circle because as the culture became weaker, it became less able to help people cope, leading to even more profound problems.

Discussed in terms of anomie, a pattern of retreatism emerged in which people abandoned their old ways, but did not replace them with new and powerful alternatives.

A key strength in Napoleon's account is that he is not a professional social scientist or psychologist. Indeed, his status as an insightful layman who is a member of his community gives his work added credibility. This analysis has special value because it independently verifies and reinforces the findings of researchers such as Merton and Appell while simultaneously paralleling the example of Handsome Lake.

The fact that pain and alienation may exist, of course, does not mean that people should be forced to preserve and live according to their traditions. Self-determinism should prevail. People, however, need to understand the full implications of their actions.

In this regard, Ormund Loomis has observed:

> Proposing ... efforts to stem ... inevitable change would be pointless. Further, in a free society, even expecting [organizations or] the government to slow ... [inevitable] progress would be wrong.... It is possible, however, to temper change so that it proceeds in accordance with the will of the people, and not in response to the pressures or faddish trends of insensitive public or private projects.
>
> (1983: 29)

Nevertheless, the cultural heritage and traditions of a people can be a source of strength and comfort. Rapid change, however, can undercut the ability of the culture to provide support to its people. When cultures are weakened, hurtful stress and psychological discomfort often arise (Salzman 2001; Walle 2004). Care needs to be taken to minimize this kind of negative and hurtful response.

Alternatives to anomie are essential and achievable. This possibility has been demonstrated by the Iroquois and the Yup'ik. The desires and rights of people deserve to be articulated in a straightforward manner that extends beyond a particular time and place; by doing so, useful tools and strategies can be developed. Many methods for doing so can be proposed. One example is the concept of what has been called the "concurrent majority" a political construct that was developed in the United States during the first half of the nineteenth century to protect the rights of minorities that are threatened by the will of the majority.

The tyranny of the majority

Empowering minorities (such as indigenous, ethnic, and rural peoples) to live as they see fit is profoundly important. The discussions of the Iroquois and the Yup'ik that were presented above dramatize this reality.

As also discussed, obstacles can arise if a dominant force prevents distinctive groups, such as indigenous, ethnic, and rural people, from following their preferred lifestyles. Denying people the right to self-determinism can be labeled the "tyranny of the majority." For present purposes, the term "majority" can be used to refer to being outvoted by a numerical superiority (such as in an election). Under certain circumstances, it can also refer to domination that results when others control a "majority" of some kind of power, such as economic or political clout, that is used as leverage.

The phrase goes back to the eighteenth century and was used by American political theorist John Adams in 1788. In the early nineteenth century, it was employed by Alexis de Tocqueville in his *Democracy in America* (1835). De Tocqueville, of course, was a liberal who favored democracy but was leery that unbridled majority rule could turn ugly, as it did during the French Revolution. The phrase and the concept it represents gained additional international attention in John Stuart Mill's, *On Liberty* (1859).

Indigenous, ethnic, and rural people often fear that dictates by the majority might be detrimental to them. Key questions arise when this possibility is considered. "To what degree does a raw majority have the right to control and veto the way of life and the economic activities of distinctive and established minorities?" Phrased in another manner, "Should minorities be able to practice self-determinism even when doing so violates principles that are held by the majority?" Many advocates for liberty and equity believe the answer to these questions should be "Yes."

Facing an economic or political "majority" can be equally challenging. Outsiders often possess specific agendas and strategically use them to their own advantage. As a result, local people might not be treated in a sensitive or equitable manner by those seeking to advance their own preferences.

These are complex issues. For justifiable and laudable reasons, many people (and the countries in which they reside) want to establish uniform standards that provide guidance in their territory (or even globally, as argued by proponents of universal human rights). Majority rule can help create these sought-after standards. On the other hand, if the dictates of the majority are strictly followed, the legitimate choices of minorities might be curtailed.

In the United States of America, this dichotomy has led to controversy and inconsistency. On some occasions, the United States demands that its indigenous people honor the demands of the majority. Thus, indigenous tribal courts are allowed to operate, but only if defendants are guaranteed all the rights granted by the United States (such as the ability to personally confront accusers and/or those who are witnesses against them). Thus, the rights of indigenous minorities, although acknowledged, are tempered by policies that are established by the majority which might conflict with local traditions.

In other circumstances, the will of minorities prevails over the preferences of the majority. Indigenous people of the United States, for example, are allowed to operate casinos and games of chance in states where the majority of the population has outlawed gambling. In such cases, the democratic decrees of the majority are overruled by the will of the minority. (The complex rationales for these conflicting policies are not discussed here because they are distinctly American. The point bring made is that ad hoc variation and inconsistency exist).

The Kurdish people of the Middle East present another example of majority vs. minority rights in conflict. The region of Kurdistan is a vast area in which the Kurds are in the majority. This region, however, is parceled out to a number of nations including Turkey, Syria, Iraq, and Iran. In each of these sovereign countries, the Kurds are a minority. Many Kurds complain that their inherent rights and needs are denied because of their minority status. In some countries, attempts are made to provide the Kurdish people with a degree of autonomy and home rule that takes their distinctiveness into account while simultaneously integrating these regions and their people into the countries where they reside. Even when such concessions are present, many Kurds believe that the only legitimate solution is for the various parts of Kurdistan to be united to form a new country.

By looking at these representative examples from North America and the Middle East, the potential problems and inequities associated with relying upon simple majority rule are showcased.

A method of response: the concurrent majority

Indigenous, ethnic, and rural people have an unexpected friend in nineteenth century American politician John C. Calhoun. Many will find this alliance to be ironic because Calhoun was a stalwart defender of a social and cultural elite that exploited racial and/or ethnic minorities (such as the nineteenth slave population of the United States).

In this regard, liberal American historian Richard Hofstadter (1948) observes:

> Not in the slightest was [Calhoun] concerned with minority rights as they are chiefly of interest to the modern liberal mind – the rights of dis-senters to express unorthodox opinions, of the individual conscience against the State, least of all of ethnic minorities.

This point is well taken, Calhoun was an apologist who supported slavery and the privileged classes that benefited from it.

In spite of championing an elite gentry who gained fortunes using slave labor, Calhoun was a political theorist who grappled with how to protect the rights of minorities even when outvoted. Although most progressive people today have little sympathy for the "minorities" that Calhoun defended, his logic and thinking, nevertheless, provide generic tactics that can be used to shield any group against the tyranny of the majority. The particular theory that Calhoun developed in this regard is usually called the "Concurrent Majority." It asserts that factions have a right to protect their interests even if outnumbered.

Calhoun's thinking arose in the early nineteenth century when strong tensions existed in the United States between the industrialized North and the agrarian South. The existence of slavery was a key issue, but not the only one (as demonstrated by arguments over tariffs which seemingly benefited the North at the expense of the South). Although Calhoun had initially favored a strong federal government, he gradually evolved into a stalwart defender of states' rights, and he sought to protect local, minority rights over the wishes of a collective majority.

Calhoun's fear that the minority might be downtrodden by the majority was not unreasonable, and he had seen the federal government unlawfully do so. On March 3, 1832, for example, the United States Supreme Court decided "Worcester vs. Georgia" a case that affirmed that the states (which reflect the will of the local majority) had no authority to meddle in the affairs of the American Indians (a minority) that resided in its territory. The case was brought to the Supreme Court by an individual who had been detained for breaking a Georgia law that interfered with the rights of indigenous people to have unregulated contact with whites.

The United States Supreme Court declared that these laws enacted by Georgia were null and void. Andrew Jackson, president of the United States at the time, however, disagreed and took no action. He is reputed to have said "[Chief] Justice Marshal has made his decision, now let's see him enforce it" (Boller and George 1989: 53). Since the court had no control over the military, Georgia was not forced to comply. In other words, the Jackson administration (voted into office by a white majority) denied a minority, composed of indigenous people, their legitimate rights in conscious disregard for the law.

Later in the same year, Calhoun and his state of South Carolina rebelled against President Jackson in what is called the Nullification Crisis. "Nullification" is the long-standing principle that if a federal law is illegal, the states may ignore it. At the end of the eighteenth century, the nullification argument had been employed by Thomas Jefferson and James Madison in their opposition of the Alien and Sedition Acts (as articulated in Thomas Jefferson's *Kentucky Resolution* and James Madison's *Virginia Resolution*). As a result of such precedence, South Carolina was in familiar territory when it sought relief by cancelling what it felt were illegitimate federal laws. On November 24, 1832, South Carolina passed a law nullifying the tariff within its territory and threatened to secede from the United States. President Jackson stood firm, declared that such action was treason, and threatened military intervention. Eventually a compromise was reached and the immediate crisis subsided. The underlying belief in nullification, however, remained among the Southern states, emerged as its rallying cry, and prepared the nation for Civil War.

The American Indian Removal Act of 1830 and the forced migrations of Eastern Indians to Oklahoma that it mandated is an even more blatant example of minority rights being denied by the federal government. Jackson's brutal enforcement, known as the Trail of Tears, is one of the greatest injustices in American history. These actions were an illegal, shameful, and a flagrant denial of the legitimate rights of a minority. Without doubt, Calhoun was well aware of these examples of the tyranny of the majority.

This was the environment in which Calhoun sought strategies for protecting the rights of minorities that were threatened by majority rule. In general, the term "concurrent majority" refers to methods which help a minority (however defined) to block the initiatives and desires of a majority even when outvoted. As might be expected, such remedies are popular among minorities who feel that, otherwise, they might not be treated with parity and equity.

As indicated above, in Calhoun's era, the agrarian cotton planters of the southeastern United States were outnumbered by the more populated Northern industrialists. In such an environment, Calhoun feared that the Northern majority would unjustly shift laws and economic policies (such as tariffs) to their advantage at the expense of the South. To avoid this possibility, Calhoun insisted that minorities must possess an ability to maintain their way of life, even when the majority is hostile to it. This basic reasoning continues to be a strong justification for the rights of minorities such as indigenous, ethnic, and rural peoples.

On many occasions, for example, indigenous peoples, such as the Maya of Belize, assert their traditional rights in ways that overtly contradict the will of the majority. They justify doing so by arguing that protecting these rights is a key to their survival as a people. Although minorities of this type are very different from the plantation owners who Calhoun defended, the situation they face is largely the same. Both opposed an eroding of the freedom to practice and enjoy their way of life. Calhoun developed the theory of the concurrent majority as a defense against the tyranny of the majority, and his logic is as strong today as when it was written in the early nineteenth century. Calhoun's writing, furthermore, is consistent with well-respected political theorists, including liberals such as John Stuart Mill who wrote the celebrated, *On Liberty* (1859).

When decisions are made purely with reference to majority rule, subgroups can emerge as losers in an inequitable power-grab that favors the numerical majority at the expense of minorities. Calhoun sought to control the tyranny of the majority through the creation of methods that protected minority rights. In this regard, Calhoun rhetorically asks, "How can those who are invested with the powers of government be prevented from employing them as the means of aggrandizing themselves instead of using them to protect and preserve society" (1851: 271–272). Because of this potential misuse of power, Calhoun argued that minorities must possess the ability to prevent their rights from being annulled and their wishes ignored.

These abilities can be justified by complaining that without them the will of the majority can be forced on minorities in hurtful and burdensome ways.

This potential is especially strong and oppressive if the minority is significantly distinct from the dominant majority (as is the case with indigenous, ethnic, and rural peoples).

Perhaps in a small and homogeneous community, simple majority rule might function effectively and equitably. As the population rises and divisions and differences between segments of the population expand, however, this ability is reduced. Recognizing this reality, Calhoun observes "the more extensive and populous the country, the more diversified the condition and pursuits of its population; and the richer, more luxurious, and dissimilar the people, the more difficult it is to equalize the action of the government" (1851: 273).

Under these conditions, Calhoun concludes that it becomes "more easy for one portion of the community to pervert its powers to oppress and plunder the other" (1851: 273). This, of course, is exactly the complaint that is made by many indigenous, ethnic, and rural people whose lands were invaded by outsiders seeking profits, land, or some other commodity.

Calhoun's basic point is that the mere will of a majority does not give it the right to destroy the way of life of a minority. Indigenous, ethnic, and rural people can use Calhoun's theory of the concurrent majority to affirm and protect rights that pure majority rule might undermine. Calhoun, furthermore, recognized that the greater the difference between people, the more likely that majority actions might prove inequitable to minorities. Under these circumstances, methods for transcending raw and naïve "majority rule" are likely to be needed.

Modern circumstances

Today a variety of situations that undercut indigenous, ethnic, and rural people can be identified along with a number of defenses against them. Three varieties include (1) Third World conditions where indigenous, ethnic, and rural people remain in a numerical majority, (2) Fourth World circumstances where patterns of outside immigration have made indigenous, ethnic, and rural people minorities in their own land, and (3) situations where a cultural enclave or minority segments of the population are outvoted or lose clout in some other manner.

Originally, the term "Third World" identified unaligned countries that the capitalistic and socialistic blocs vied to influence during the cold war. In the present discussion, however, the term refers to parts of the world where descendants of the pre-contact indigenous, ethnic, or rural peoples continue to be the majority. Throughout the colonial era, many of these groups were politically and/or economically dominated by outsiders, but demographically they continued to dominate. Few members of the "mother country" permanently migrated to these places, tended to live in expatriate compounds, and after a period of service most returned home.

After the end of the colonial era, these Third World populations have continued to maintain a numerical advantage even if economic and political realities have prevented them from enjoying full parity and equity. This dominance by outsiders can prove hurtful because, as Calhoun perceived, those who have power are likely to use it for their own advantage. In line with Calhoun's observation, dominant forces that have clout in Third World countries (such as profit-making corporations) tend to think and act in self-serving ways because they are created to generate profits. Although these organizations might obey the law, providing a maximum return to stockholders is their mandate. Because of this motivation, profit-making corporations can be expected to exploit the most lucrative legal options, even if doing so goes against the will of the local people.

Although the leaders of these outside organizations might attempt to be fair and equitable, a strong possibility exists that they do not adequately understand the people they are dealing with. In the chapters above, reference has been made to the fact that outsiders are likely to misjudge their indigenous, ethnic, and rural partners and counterparts. When such confusion arises, strangers are likely to embrace inappropriate strategies and tactics that work against the best interests of Third World peoples.

Remedies to such situations are consistent with the principle of the concurrent majority that defends the ability of people to control their destinies even if they are outvoted in some way (perhaps by the economic power of outsiders). As Calhoun emphasizes, protecting 'self-determinism' (he did not use the word, but this is what he is talking about) can be especially challenging when the outsiders who possess power are significantly different from those who are being controlled.

Third World countries, furthermore are often desperate to attract economic activities and, as a result, potential investors and partners frequently demand concessions as incentives. In order to comply in a quest to attract economic activity, the central government might be tempted to consider policies that conflict with the will and the wellbeing of specific groups. This is exactly the type of situation that concerned John C. Calhoun when he opposed economic policies that helped Northern manufacturing interests at the expense of the South.

Under these circumstances, care needs to be taken to ensure that all segments of the population are treated with equity and parity. The idea of a concurrent majority provides one method for doing so. In addition to the preferences of powerful outsiders, national policies must treat all stakeholders in a balanced manner that provides benefits to all and insists that everyone makes comparable sacrifices.

The term Fourth World (as used here), in contrast, refers to situations where patterns of immigration by outsiders has resulted in indigenous, ethnic, and rural peoples becoming minorities in their own homeland. This is the case in much of North America, Australia, New Zealand, and a number of other places. When this happens, the emerging majority installs its own legal and economic systems. The resulting transformations can easily work against the best interests of the indigenous, ethnic, and rural population because changing demographic patterns put them at a disadvantage. The classic defense under such circumstances is to argue that these people possess rights that predate the creation of the present regime and, therefore, do not depend upon a plurality of the current voters. Doing so is clearly in line with Calhoun's conception of the concurrent majority.

In the United States Supreme Court Case Worcester vs. Georgia (discussed above), for example, the decision concluded that when the United States was formed, it inherited the rights and privileges regarding the American Indians that had previously been established by Britain, the former regime. This legal principle pointed to a legal remedy that was more favorable to the indigenous people than the laws of Georgia. As a result, the older legal framework, more consistent with the principle of the concurrent majority, was embraced. The logic that American Indians of the United States are nations that should enjoy concurrent majority status continues to be based on this Supreme Court decision that harks back to rights and obligations established at an earlier era when Britain "controlled" North America as its colony.

To pursue this option, the history of the region in question needs to be searched for treaties, actions, or other indications that rights were granted at an earlier time. Having discovered such privileges, the argument is made that they have never been extinguished and, therefore, continue to be valid and enforceable, even if they have been inactive for a period of time.

This can be a good strategy (as demonstrated by the successes enjoyed by American Indians in the United States), but doing so is based upon the actions of others (such as earlier and probably defunct colonial regimes). Although this process can provide a good "paper trail" that demonstrates rights in ways that modern courts and governments recognize, good documentation does not always exist.

A defense that can be used in a wider range of circumstances is to argue that these people have rights that are based upon their cultural heritage which does not need to be validated by outsiders. In earlier chapters, the expansion of the definition of "indigenous" was discussed and the fact that certain rights accompany an indigenous status were mentioned. These rights do not need to be justified by the actions and agreements of others. The argument might be made that these rights are inherent, existed before the establishment of the current regime, and never died.

An indigenous people, for example, may have lived in a particular place for hundreds of years before the colonial era. Archaeological evidence, oral history, and so forth might verify this fact. Given this historic precedence, the people can claim the land based on rights that predates the authority of the sovereign nation that currently rules the territory. Doing so is a well-established method of validating claims. The discipline of ethnohistory, (that reconstructs the past using archaeological evidence, oral history, folklore, and historic/prehistoric knowledge) for example, was originally a practitioner-oriented profession that helped indigenous people to document their claim to rights. Doing so can be a powerful tool.

Under these circumstances, cultural minorities can be viewed as concurrent majorities possessing rights that predate the current government. If these rights can be established, a numerical majority might be prevented from asserting its will.

On other occasions, arbitrary circumstances might result in minorities losing rights and privileges. Perhaps an established cultural entity is outvoted by a homogenous and dominant majority. This has been the situation of the Kurds as discussed above. On other occasions, a coalition of various forces might team up in order to outvote a particular segment of the population. These may be viewed as examples of the tyranny of the majority.

Under these conditions, a solution might involve indigenous, ethnic and rural people working together. They can do so either nationally or internationally.

One of the most powerful strategies of the colonial era was to exploit the hostilities, rivalries, and tensions that many indigenous peoples feel against each other. Thus, in the French and Indian War, the Algonquin were allied with the French while the Iroquois fought with the British. As a result of bringing these local peoples into the fray, both indigenous groups were weakened while the colonial forces were required to sacrifice less.

The point is clear, if infighting is strong, others might gain leverage they would not otherwise possess. Although today's strategies might not involve actual warfare, exploiting rivalries might dilute and weaken the power and position of the indigenous community. This disabling potential can be overcome if former rivals replace competition with cooperation.

Although conflicts long existed among North America indigenous peoples, for example, many groups are collaborating in order to address issues of collective importance. This tendency has resulted in what are called "Intertribal Pow Wows" attended by various indigenous nations of the United States. Mutual respect is the norm. The primary goals include encouraging cooperation in forging collective strategies for advancing the cause of all tribes. Collaboration of this sort can be viewed as a grassroots movement that reflects the ideals of a concurrent majority.

Thus, indigenous, ethnic, and rural people possess a wide variety of techniques to protect their rights as concurrent majorities. The representative sample discussed is compared below in Table 11.3.

Thus, a variety of situations exist where people can attempt to assert their rights as concurrent majorities. Each situation is different and local people will need to determine what means of verifying rights works best for them. In any case, the argument needs to be made that these people have rights that can be used to challenge the will of the majority or those with strong powers that are based on economics or politics.

Table 11.3 Challenges and tactics

Variety	Description	Analysis
Third World	Indigenous, ethnic, or rural people remain in the numerical majority, but they lack economic, technological, and/or political power.	By building upon majority status, other limitations, such as economic and legal issues can be addressed in order to gain and maintain equity.
Fourth World	Due to immigration by outsiders, the indigenous, ethnic, and rural people who were once a majority have been reduced to a minority and have lost power as a result.	Although a former majority has become a minority, it might possess rights that predate the current situation. They might be used to asset concurrent majority status.
Outvoted enclave	A segment of the population that once enjoyed a degree of parity and equity has lost power due to majority rule.	Various factions and maneuvering might seek to undercut the rights of specific groups. The concept of the concurrent majority might be able to mitigate such attempts.

DISCUSSION
The concept of the concurrent majority can provide a valuable means for indigenous, ethnic, and rural people to protect their rights. By asserting that a minority has rights that transcend majority rule, people can better control their own destiny.

Plans and strategies

Pain and dysfunction are triggered by change. On many occasions, change cannot be controlled by local people. Some responses to pain and change are counterproductive such as the ghost dance and the cargo cult. Others are productive and can help people to adjust while maintaining their focus and heritage.

Many indigenous, ethnic, and rural people are concerned about what has been called the tyranny of the majority. One way to combat this threat is known as the theory of the concurrent majority. Although many remedies might be suggested, this technique was used as a representative example.

In any event, what is needed is a method that prevents minorities, especially indigenous, ethnic, and rural people from being overly dominated by more powerful outsiders. It is hoped that people adjusting to circumstances will recall that cultures and traditions (although vulnerable and fragile) are powerful and positive forces that help people cope in both "practical" and in psychological ways. As a result, careful protection and renewal can be vital. This book has suggested a number of ways to do so.

Relevant terms

Anomie: A situation where socially acceptable goals cannot be achieved in socially acceptable ways.

Calhoun, John C: Political theorist and practitioner who developed ways to protect minority rights from majority rule.

Cargo cult: A movement in Melanesia that involved a counterproductive response to anomie in which people believed that they would magically gain the abilities and assets of powerful outsiders.

Conformity: A response to anomie in which people continue to embrace the traditional socially acceptable goals and the socially acceptable means of achieving them.

Concurrent majority: According to John C. Calhoun, a situation where a minority is entitled to rights that cannot be denied by a simple popular vote.

Ethnohistory: Reconstructing the past using evidence such as folklore, oral history, and the archaeological record. Can be used in the quest to reestablish rights and privileges.

Fourth World: Situations were due to outside immigration; indigenous people have become a minority in their own land.

Ghost dance: A counterproductive response to anomie in which people believed that the old ways would magically reappear.

Handsome Lake: A Native American leader of the eighteenth and nineteenth centuries who helped his people adjust to changing times by adapting, while preserving, their cultural heritage.

Innovation: A response to anomie in which socially acceptable goals are maintained, but the means of achieving them change.

Ishi: A well-known individual whose cultural heritage was totally destroyed, causing great emotional pain.

Napoleon, Harold: A twentieth-century Native American leader who encouraged cultural revival and stability in order to stem dysfunction.

Rebellion: A response to anomie in which both the socially acceptable goals and the socially acceptable means of achieving them are replaced.

Retreatism: A response to anomie in which socially acceptable goals and methods of achieving them are rejected, but they are not replaced with alternatives.

Ritualization: A response to anomie in which the acceptable methods of achieving goals are maintained even though it is recognized that these goals are no longer effective.

Social bereavement: The sorrow and pain people feel when their cultural heritage is denied, undercut, or destroyed.

Social separation syndrome: Situation where alienation or a "disconnect" from the cultural heritage triggers dysfunction.

Third World: Situations where local ethnic groups remain in the majority in spite of outside interference and control.

Trail of Tears: The deporting and exiling of indigenous Native Americans in the 1830s by the will of the majority.

Worcester vs. Georgia: A court case in the United States that affirmed that a local majority cannot deny certain rights of an indigenous Native American minority.

Discussion questions

1   Discuss how change can trigger pain, How can this discomfort lead to social and personal dysfunction? Who should be responsible of mitigating such maladies? Why?

2   What is the basic concept of anomie and why might it be useful when discussing indigenous, ethnic, and rural people and their circumstances? Discuss the various responses to anomie listed by Robert Merton. How can anomie (an inability to achieve socially acceptable goals in socially acceptable ways) be a disruptive force as well at leading to useful cultural adjustments?

3   Explore both dysfunctional and functional ways of responding to social change and anomie that were provided as examples. Discuss whatever other examples come to mind. Do you think that being aware of both productive and nonproductive responses is useful? Why or why not?

4   The concept of the tyranny of the majority has existed at least since the eighteenth century. What is its basic premise and issue? Do you feel this concept is particularly useful to indigenous, ethnic and rural peoples? Why or why not?

5   The concept of the "concurrent majority" specifically seeks to protect minority rights by arguing that people have rights that the majority cannot deny. Do you feel this is a viable strategy for indigenous, ethnic, and peoples? Present any alternatives that you feel might be more effective.

References

Adams, John (1788). *A Defence of the Constitutions of Government of the United States of America*, Vol. 3 (London: Edmund Freeman).

Appell, G. N. (1977). "The Plight of Indigenous Peoples: Issues and Dilemmas." *Survival International Review*, 2(3), 11–16.

Boller, Paul F. and George, John H. (1989). *They Never Said It: A Book of False Quotes, Misquotes, and False Attributions.* New York, NY: Oxford University Press.

Calhoun, John C. (1851). *A Disquisition on Government* (Columbia S.C.: A. S. Johnston).

Durkheim, Émile (1984 [1893]). *The Division of Labour in Society*. Trans. E. D. Halls (New York: Free Press).

Harris, Marvin (1974). *Cows, Pigs, Wars, and Witches: The Riddles of Culture* (New York: Random House).

Hofstadter, Richard (1948). "The Marx of the Master Class." *The American Political Tradition and the Men Who Made It* (New York: A. A. Knopf).

Inglis, Judy (1957). "Cargo Cults: The Problem of Explanation." *Oceania*, xxvii(4), 249–263.

Kehoe, Alice Beck (1989). "Death or Renewal?," *The Ghost Dance: Ethnohistory and Revitalization*, pp. 32–33 (Washington, DC: Thompson Publishing).

Kroeber, Theodora (1964). *Ishi: The Last of His Tribe* (Berkeley CA: Parnassus).

Loomis, Ormund H. (1983). *Cultural Conservation: The Protection of Cultural Heritage in the United States* (Washington, DC: Library of Congress).

Maybury-Lewis, David (1977). "Societies on The Brink." *Harvard Magazine*, 56–61.

Merton, Robert K. (1957). *Social Theory and Social Structure*, revised edition (Glencoe IL: Free Press).

Mill, John Stuart (1859). *On Liberty* (London: John Parker).

Mooney, James. (1986). *The Ghost Dance Religion and Wounded Knee* (New York: Dover Publications).

Napoleon, Harold (1996). *Yuuyaraq: The Way of Being Human* (Fairbanks AK: Alaska Native Knowledge Network).

Romanov, K., Appelberg, K., Honkasalo, M. L. and Koskenvuo, M. (1996). "Recent Interpersonal Conflict at Work and Psychiatric Morbidity: A Prospective Study of 15,530 Employees Aged 24–64." *Journal of Psychosomatic Research*, 40(2), 169–176.

Salzman, Michael (2001). "Cultural Trauma and Recovery: Perspectives From Terror Management Theory." *Trauma, Violence and Abuse*, 2(2), 172–191.

de Tocqueville, Alexis (1835). *Democracy in America* (London: Saunders and Otley).

Wallace, Anthony (1970). *The Death and Rebirth of the Seneca* (New York: Knopf Doubleday).

Walle, Alf (2004). *The Path of Handsome Lake: A Model of Recovery for Native People* (Greenwich, Connecticut: IAP).

Worsley, Peter (1957). *The Trumpet Shall Sound: A Study of Cargo Cults in Melanesia* (London: MacGibbon & Kee).

Index

Page numbers in **bold** denote tables, those in *italics* denote figures.

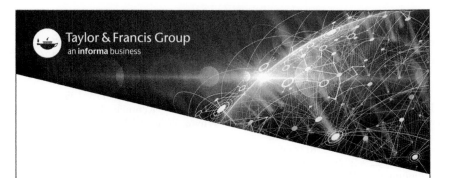

For Product Safety Concerns and Information please contact our EU
representative GPSR@taylorandfrancis.com Taylor & Francis Verlag GmbH,
Kaufingerstraße 24, 80331 München, Germany

Printed and bound by CPI Group (UK) Ltd, Croydon, CR0 4YY
01/05/2025
01858415-0001